WILLIAM WALLACE

ANDREW FISHER

JOHN DONALD

EDINBURGH

This edition published in 2002 by John Donald,
an imprint of
Birlinn Limited
West Newington House
10 Newington Road
Edinburgh
EH9 1QS

www.birlinn.co.uk

Reprinted 2003

First published in 1986 by John Donald Publishers Limited, Edinburgh

ISBN 0 85976 557 1

British Library Cataloguing-in-Publication Data
A catalogue record for this book is available from the British Library

Typeset by Initial Typesetting Services, Edinburgh
Printed and bound by Cox & Wyman Ltd, Reading

To the memory of my father,
who gave me my love of Scottish history

and

To my grandson, Josh, in the hope that
one day he will share in that love

Contents

Acknowledgements

I am grateful to my publishers for the opportunity once again to look at the enigma of William Wallace. My family, as always, has supported me through the days of doubt and sorrow with which I have been faced. In particular, I am indebted to my daughter, Claire, who has shown an unexpected talent for the deciphering of hieroglyphics – mine.

Preface to the Second Edition

In 1986 I wrote that William Wallace was 'at best a shadowy figure and likely to remain so'. The intervening years have not caused me radically to depart from that opinion. Valuable, and impressive, work on Wallace has, of course, been done in that period and I am happy to acknowledge my debt to it in the text. There has also been *Braveheart*. In essence Blind Harry writ large for the screen, the film was hugely popular. It undoubtedly made the name of Wallace more widely known than ever before. That, for many, was justification enough. But the Wallace it portrayed had neither depth nor character; he was, as in 'Harry', a one-man fighting machine, an automaton, programmed to kill on mention of the word 'English'. Nevertheless, *Braveheart* cannot be ignored; it has its place in the conclusion to this new edition. We do now have one significant piece of information on Wallace; his father was not Malcolm, but Alan, as we shall see. But even that change brings with it a question; was the family of the great Scottish hero quite the homogeneous unit devoted to the defeat of Edward I, as has been thought, or was it, rather, divided in its loyalties?

William Wallace continues to intrigue as well as to inspire.

Map 1. Scotland in the Early Years of the War with England, 1297–1305

Introduction

William Wallace was born into a Scotland long at peace with its southern neighbour and, since the celebrated if mistitled Battle of Largs and the subsequent Treaty of Perth in 1266, free from the fear of invasion from Norway. His family, though landed and established in Scotland for over a century, was not noble and was without influence. The education he received, perhaps in training for the priesthood, gave him a facility in languages but was distinguished above all by that love of liberty which he retained to the end of his life. It is possible that before his invasion of northern England in late 1297, he had never set foot outside of Scotland. His world, and much of his experience, was centred on the west of Scotland. We may reasonably suppose that his contacts were unexceptional, restricted and governed by the rigidly hierarchical nature of the society in which he was raised. His knowledge of great men and great events would be circumscribed by his immediate environment; the name of Stewart or Bruce would carry more weight with him than that of Alexander III. A younger son, he had few prospects and an uncertain future.

He was thus in no way prepared, by birth, education, or training, for a role of any consequence in the history of his native land. Yet when the ambition of Edward I combined with the weakness of John Balliol to usher in that conflict which we choose to call the Scottish War of Independence, Wallace was to rise within a year to an eminence and reputation, in Europe as in Scotland, which none could have foreseen. He led and directed the resistance to Edward, broke the sequence of English successes in the field, maintained the cause of John Balliol, restored his country to its rightful place in the councils of Europe, and where others, ostensibly his betters, yielded and collaborated, set an example of constancy and perseverance. Even his horrific death in London came to be seen as a victory. He became and remained an inspiration to both singer and poet.

Wallace was by any standards a remarkable man. But if undoubtedly heroic, he was not perfect. There is to Wallace not merely a dark but an unknown side. In an age of brutality, he was brutal. He was no less cruel than those against whom he fought. He repaid the sack of Berwick in 1296 with the ravaging of Northumberland the year after. To achieve his ends, he turned, often violently, on any, Scots or English, who stood in his way. The Church he supported in Scotland, its English representatives he treated less tolerantly. The crimes with which he would be charged by Edward's justices in 1305 were not wholly fabrications; Wallace himself at his trial, far from seeking to deny or excuse them, gloried in what he had done and regretted that he had not done more. Implacable to the end, he exuded defiance in the midst of his enemies.

Posterity, as in the case of his contemporary, Robert Bruce, has tended to look away from Wallace's flaws as if afraid of the truth. Wallace was, simply, a man of his time, with all that that means; our recognition of the fact does not detract from his stature. More significant, and more harmful to the memory of Wallace, is the manner in which our lamentable ignorance of his life before May 1297 and of the period between the defeat at Falkirk and his death seven years later has led us to neglect a number of crucial questions connected with him. The result is that we have made something of a one-dimensional figure of a man who cannot have been other than complicated. Of such questions three in particular present themselves for our consideration. First, how could a man untutored in the art of war – he had after all no Queen Eleanor to provide a translation of Vegetius for him – and without experience in its practice emerge with such authority and ability as a military leader in the summer of 1297? Second, on the basis of the admittedly meagre information available to us, what role can we allocate to Wallace after Falkirk which fits in with our knowledge of his character, temperament and talents? Third, given that the traditional link between Wallace's execution in August 1305 and Bruce's murder of Comyn in February 1306 and his rebellion is discredited, what was the relationship between Wallace and Bruce?

It is not to be expected that the answer to these questions is to be discovered in contemporary sources. Wallace is at best a shadowy figure and likely to remain so. But that has not prevented criticism of his decision to fight at Falkirk or general agreement that his defeat there inevitably brought in its train his resignation as Guardian. It has not prevented an unflattering comparison of him with Andrew Murray, or, more damaging, a view of him which is condescending and therefore unflattering. Wallace deserves better of us. It is too much to see in him one who, as it were, sprang forth ready-made in 1297, remained fixed and unalterable over a period of some eight years, learned and forgot nothing, was never tempted to despair, never profited from the study of the political manoeuvres of his Scottish associates, never deviated from a pre-ordained path. Wallace was not such a man. What we believe we know of him is more often interpretation than fact. That is understandable, given our ignorance. But if we accept that we do not know, and cannot know, the whole story of William Wallace, we can look at him again, and in offering an answer to our questions, come closer to an authentic picture of the first and most enduring hero of Scottish nationalism.

1

The Silent Years

'Bow and quiver'

When in 1124 David I succeeded his brother, Alexander I, as king of Scotland, he was already firmly committed to the introduction into his new kingdom of the Anglo-Norman system of government.[1] Raised at the English court from the age of eight,[2] he had studied the principles and the practice of that system at first hand, especially with the encouragement of his brother-in-law, Henry I. Through the administration of his own considerable estates in England[3] and, later, of those parts of Lothian ceded to him by Alexander, he had gained further and more personal experience. He thus brought with him as king not merely a philosophy of government but the first of those men from England who would help him rule Scotland on the Anglo-Norman model.[4] He began to surround himself with the acquaintances of his youth, ambitious, thrusting adventurers, men determined upon success and its corollary, the acquisition of land. To the reign of David I we may trace the appearance in Scotland of many of the great names of the country's history, among them Bruce, Balliol and Comyn. Of these particular families, the first two would in time themselves produce kings of Scotland, while the third, unlike them almost entirely forgotten today, may have been prevented from the achievement of monarchy by the precipitate and murderous action of the most famous of the Bruces.

In or about the year 1136, as part of the process of creating in Scotland what would become a new aristocracy, David took into his service as 'dapifer' or steward of the household a certain Walter, the third son of Alan Fitzalan and his wife Avelina.[5] It was a position of undoubted trust and responsibility that the king had offered Walter, although its holder did not at that time rank quite among the highest officers of state. Walter's family had been hereditary stewards to the lord of Dol in eastern Brittany since the middle of the eleventh century. Indeed, his eldest brother, Jordan, returned to Dol from England, where the family had settled in the early years of the reign of Henry I, to carry on the established tradition. We do not know the circumstances in which David the future king of Scotland and Walter his future steward first met. It may have been as early as 1114 when they, like Alexander I, campaigned in Wales under Henry I. Whatever the occasion of their meeting, David did not forget the other man. As a younger son, Walter had few prospects of advancement as long as he remained in England, and it is likely therefore that he accepted David's offer of employment with both alacrity and gratitude. The ability to recognise and, equally important, to act upon an opportunity was, after all, an inherited characteristic. Walter's father, Alan, had been a close associate of William the Conqueror's youngest son when the latter's route to the throne of England had seemed blocked. But when Henry took advantage of the unexpected death of his brother, William II, in August 1100, to make himself king, he did not neglect his old friend. Alan, it has been written, 'benefited substantially, not to say spectacularly, after Henry had acquired the English throne'.[6]

In keeping with his new dignity as steward, Walter Fitzalan was granted by David and his grandson and immediate heir, Malcolm IV, extensive holdings in Renfrew, Ayrshire, and Lothian.[7] In marriage he took Eschina de Londres, and their son, Alan, succeeded upon Walter's death in 1177 to what had by now become a hereditary office. Alan's son, Walter II, followed his father in office in 1204 with the more impressive-sounding title of 'seneschallus'. It was this Walter who was the first to be known as 'Steward of Scotland'. Yet another Walter, the sixth in the line introduced into Scotland by David I in 1136, married in 1316 Marjorie Bruce, daughter of Robert I. Through this union the Stewarts became the ruling house of Scotland in 1371 when the son of Walter and Marjorie became king as Robert II, and they were later, in the person of James VI and I, to ascend the throne of England.

The appointment of a steward by David I in 1136 was thus of immense significance for the history of Scotland. It resulted also in the arrival in the country of another family which, through the career of one man, was to become more celebrated in the popular imagination than the Stewarts themselves. We have seen that Walter Fitzalan decided to leave England at the invitation of David I because he was frustrated in his ambitions. His brother, William II Fitzalan, had been more fortunate. He had achieved a position of some standing in England, not least in Shropshire, where he was lord of Oswestry. Among those listed as owing him service in 1166 was one Richard Wallace.[8] At an unknown date Richard elected to follow Walter Fitzalan to Scotland, and as the other had profited from the move to the northern kingdom, so did Richard, although on a lesser scale. He thus formed part of a remarkable influx from the south into the Stewart honour of Renfrew under Walter I. Among those who, like Richard, appeared in this period, were Robert Croc, Henry of Nes, Gilbert fitzRicher, Robert of Montgomery and Simon Lockhart. Neither they nor any of the others drawn to join Walter Fitzalan bore a name comparable to that of Wallace.

Richard Wallace is found as a witness to a charter granted by Walter I Stewart to the abbey of Paisley in 1174. The name recurs in respect of more charters, by, for example, Richard de Lincoln and Richard de Nicholle.[9] Under the Stewarts Richard Wallace held land in Kyle, in Tarbolton, Mauchline, Auchincruive and, possibly, Riccarton.[10] The connection with the Stewarts was to continue, albeit in vastly different circumstances; towards the end of the next century, in the war against Edward I, the names of Stewart and Wallace would be linked.[11] At the time of Richard Wallace, no one could have foreseen that it would be the name of the vassal rather than of the lord which would be the more fondly remembered.

It is possible that Richard Wallace, having flourished under Walter I and his son Alan, survived as late as the time of Walter II (1204–1241). If so, Richard Wallace cannot have been unaware of the early manifestation of that rivalry between two families, Bruce and Comyn, which would in due course bedevil the attempts of William Wallace to lead a united Scotland to victory against Edward I. As early as 1174, the year in which Richard Wallace witnessed the Stewart charter to Paisley Abbey, the families were in opposite camps in Scottish politics. Richard Comyn, the justiciar of Lothian, accompanied

William I 'the Lion' on his invasion of northern England which ended with his capture at the siege of Alnwick, whereas Robert Bruce of Annandale threw his weight behind Henry II.[12] William I was, of course, no John Balliol, but the Comyn support for William perhaps now seems as ill-advised, if patriotic, as that which they gave to Balliol in 1296. The Bruces had picked the winning, if unpatriotic, side in 1174 and did so again in 1296. Richard Wallace, by the standards of his time, had a long life, but even if we allow for that, he cannot have seen an improvement in the relationship of Bruce with Comyn. As the thirteenth century wore on, the Comyns, relatively late starters in Scotland when measured against their rivals, were threatening to surpass them in terms of land and influence. By the middle of the century, during the minority of Alexander III, the situation between Comyns and Bruces was one which would have been depressingly familiar to William Wallace.[13]

It is from Richard Wallace or le Waleis, the 'Welshman',[14] vassal of the Stewarts, that the most famous bearer of the names of Wallace was for generations believed to be descended.[15] A genealogy was constructed, and widely accepted, for William, which appeared to stand the test of time and scrutiny. According to this, William was the son of Sir Malcolm Wallace of Elderslie near Paisley, the great-great-grandson of Richard Wallace, and his wife, variously Margaret or Jean, the daughter of Sir Reginald Crawford of Crosbie, hereditary sheriff of Ayr. The name of Crawford was at least as old as that of Wallace and another Reginald was, as sheriff of Ayr, a contemporary of Richard the 'Welshman'. William Wallace was neither an only child, nor the first born to his parents. The year of his birth has never been satisfactorily established. A great deal of effort has been spent, much of it on the basis of contradictory information supplied by his celebrated if unreliable biographer, to settle the question.[16] If it is futile to add to that effort, we shall not be far wrong if we content ourselves with the observation that William was still a young man when he first made his name in 1297. The nature of what might be termed his 'historical' life was such that only a man in his prime would be capable of living it. An outline of the details, sparse enough in themselves, serves to prove the point. Between 1297 and his death in 1305 William is known to have raised a rebellion against the English who occupied his country, defeated Surrey and killed Cressingham at Stirling, overcome the subsequent loss of the formidable and inspirational Murray, cleared Scotland of effective English troops, led an army on a destructive campaign in winter through the northern counties of England, returned to Scotland to carry on the government in the face of the doubts, not to say the opposition, of the native nobility, maintained an army in being and trained it, fought against and almost defeated the hitherto invincible Edward I at Falkirk, escaped that monarch, travelled to the Continent, certainly to France, where he survived a period of imprisonment, moved on to Rome and perhaps further still, made his way back to Scotland in hazardous conditions, and thereafter continued either openly or from hiding the struggle against the superior and relentless enemy into whose possession he was ultimately betrayed. We need none of the embroidery in which Blind Harry indulged to draw the obvious conclusion. It is difficult to see how the physical strength without which he could have done little of this, not to mention the robustness of mind necessary to sustain him in the face of adversity, could have been found in one who was not young.

A comparison with part of the career of Robert Bruce may help to underline the above argument. When in February 1306 Bruce murdered his enemy and rival, John Comyn of Badenoch, in Dumfries, he was forced not long afterwards to emulate William and go into hiding to escape the vengeance of Edward I.[17] Fortunately for Bruce, he was spared the years of pursuit suffered by William, for Edward was dead at Burgh-by-Sands in July of the following year and Edward II, although determined to retain Scotland, lacked his father's obsessive drive. Bruce's adventures are well enough recorded to make clear the strains under which he laboured while a fugitive from the first Edward's justice. At the time of the murder of Comyn, Bruce was five months short of his thirty-second birthday.

William's relationship with Andrew Murray[18] appears to support the view that in 1297 he was in his prime, perhaps of an age with Bruce. Murray was himself a young man when he and William joined forces, and he came of a family which was a major vassal of the Scottish Crown. He and William had, it would appear, nothing in common, the one the heir to a great and honourable inheritance, his new colleague at worst an outlaw. Yet, from the evidence available to us, we can see that each took at once to the other. Their alliance, however weighted,[19] was to prove of inestimable value to the Scottish cause. It could hardly have come about without trust. That trust, and their relationship as a whole, is more easily explained if we accept that they were of the some generation. The attributes which they shared and which united them were, too, those of the young. They did not hesitate or prevaricate where their elders had faltered with such disastrous consequences for Scotland. They did not respect, nor were they overawed by reputation. The slow but impressive parade of the English army before Stirling did not break their resolve. Given an opportunity by the incompetence of Surrey and Cressingham, they fought and were right to do so. The decision to attack the English army, despite the great power it had demonstrated in previous encounters with the Scots, surely belonged to young men, as did the victory which resulted.

We know that William had two brothers, John and Malcolm, both of whom we shall meet in intriguing circumstances. Blind Harry alone credits William with two sisters. William is said to have been educated by his uncle, a priest, and subsequently by a second uncle, also a priest, at Dundee. Quite why he should have been sent so far from home, and not nearby Paisley Abbey, with which the Wallaces had been associated at the latest since its inception, is not clear. But with such an educational background, wherever obtained, it is perhaps not surprising if, again according to Blind Harry, Wallace was considering a vocation in the Church as his life neared its close.

While a student at Dunipace Wallace, we are told, was taught by his uncle an abiding love of liberty, usually quoted in the Latin couplet:

> Dico te verum, libertas optima rerum:
> Nunquam servili sub nexu vivito, fili!
> I tell you truthfully, freedom is the best of all things:
> Never live under the yoke of slavery, my son.

If nothing else, this quotation rings true in the light of Wallace's career, dedicated as it was to the pursuit of liberty for his native land. During his sojourn at Dundee, he is said to have made the acquaintance of John Blair, a Benedictine monk. Blair, at this time or later, left the contemplative life, and became Wallace's personal chaplain, constantly at his side in the great struggle in which Wallace was embroiled. Typical of his day, Blair, according to Blind Harry, fought as well as preached and confessed. In his retirement at Dunfermline, where he died, Blair wrote a Latin prose life of Wallace, on which Harry, with due acknowledgement, drew. If we accept the traditional account, Wallace was for the time and given his origins, well educated. Thus he was familiar with Greek as well as Latin. His knowledge of the Bible was, it goes without saying, extensive. Since he was a younger son, with few prospects, he was, we are left to assume, intended for the priesthood, thus following in the steps of the uncles to whom he owed his education. What appears to have been an eventful and happy, perhaps even idyllic, life was interrupted by the machinations of the ruthless and evil Edward I of England, who saw in the death of Alexander III the opportunity to make himself master of Scotland.

This popular version of Wallace's life, with its combination of Blind Harry's narrative skills and a little fact, has exercised a considerable fascination for Scots. It has much, it would seem, to commend it: the virtue of continuity in a family established in Scotland for over a century; three brothers, all knighted, all of whom served with varying degrees of distinction in the war with England; a maternal grandfather who perished in the same cause,[20] and a villainous enemy. With this in mind, it is tempting not to dismiss it. We know little enough of Wallace before he made his explosive entrance on to the stage of history in 1297 to dare to discount entirely what has for many been not legend but truth. If Harry used the work of John Blair, now disappeared, who is to state categorically that he did not have access to other sources, also lost to us? Blair's account of Wallace would, if it had

13

come down to us, be invaluable, the sole contemporary authority. We might then be able the better to evaluate Harry's contribution to the story of the patriot.[21]

But we do not have Blair's account and if we return to the popular version for enlightenment, we find at once that it fails on two crucial counts. The first concerns Wallace's parentage. It is to Harry that we owe the name of Sir Malcolm Wallace of Elderslie as the father of the patriot. Harry does not identify the location of Elderslie, and this in itself has caused dispute.[22] Despite Harry, there was no unanimity on the name of Wallace's father. Both before and after Harry, sources offered Andrew rather than Malcolm.[23] We now know that Wallace's father was neither Malcolm nor Andrew but Alan. The evidence is indisputable. In 1297, after the battle of Stirling Bridge, the victorious Wallace and his wounded and dying colleague, Andrew Murray, sent a letter to the mayor and communes of the German towns of Lübeck and Hamburg. The purpose of the letter is discussed below,[24] but appended to it was a seal which resolves the question of Wallace's parentage. The inscription states '[Wilelm]vs Filius Alani Walais', that is, William, son of Alan Wallace.[25] For the most recent writer on Wallace, this fact will not change his (i.e. Wallace's) status as Scotland's foremost patriot since the fifteenth century, 'any more than would certainty on his date of birth or his marital status'.[26] Thus speaks modern man, acknowledging, a little wearily perhaps, the potency of the later accretions to the few facts we have about Wallace. It is not easy to disagree with this analysis.[27] But the revelation of Alan, not Malcolm, as Wallace's father provides, it can be argued, a new perspective on the patriot.

Who, then, was Alan Wallace? We have one possibility, and an intriguing one. On 28 August 1296, at Berwick, an Alan Wallace made his submission to Edward I. He is listed on the Ragman Roll[28] among 'tenantz le roi du counte de Are' or crown tenants, in Ayrshire. With him appear the names of John Crawford, Thomas Winchester, Robert Boyd, Alan fitz Grimbaud, Nicol Slanes and Patrick the Archer. If the Alan of the Ragman Roll was indeed the patriot's father, then the current argument in favour of an Ayrshire rather than a Renfrewshire origin for Wallace can be said to be settled.[29] We must also, as a consequence, reconsider the question of the relationship between the Wallace and Stewart families, which, as noted above, went back to the time of Richard Wallace and his lord, Walter FitzAlan. The relationship, if Alan, a crown tenant, was Wallace's father, can no longer be viewed as feudal. The contemporary English opinion that Wallace, in his rebellion, was the creature of James the Stewart,[30] is undermined.[31] Wallace in 1297 needed no such prompting.[32]

Another treasured belief that can now be challenged, assuming Alan to be Wallace's father, is the attitude to, and role in, the war with Edward I of Wallace's family as a whole. The contribution of Wallace's brothers, Malcolm and John, whose existence is proven, to the war with England has tended to persuade us that the family was united in its purpose. That comfortable assumption is not necessarily correct. Where, to begin with, did the loyalties of the Alan Wallace of the Ragman Roll lie? We may be confident that they were more complex than those of his putative son.[33] The name of William Wallace himself is, of course, absent from the Ragman Roll. Good reasons can be advanced for this.[34] But even if he had been a landowner, and thus required to swear fealty to Edward, we would no doubt prefer to think that the Wallace with whom we are familiar would not have been numbered among those who submitted to the English king in 1296. Alan Wallace, however, as a crown tenant, may simply have followed the lead of John Balliol,[35] a legalistic argument which Edward brought to bear on the patriot in 1305.[36] Alan may also have been a realist who, like so many others, saw survival as paramount. In this he was not unique. Nor did submission in 1296 preclude adherence to the patriotic cause at a later date. Robert Boyd, one of those listed with Alan Wallace in the Ragman Roll, was an early supporter of Bruce's rebellion and rose high in his favour, a fact reflected in the improvement in his family's fortunes.[37] No such change in status, as far as we are aware, awaited Alan Wallace, who may have been apolitical, devoid of any close interest in the evolving political situation in Scotland, his concerns local and personal rather than national.

Alan Wallace's apparent lack of involvement in the struggle against Edward I is not reflected in the careers of William Wallace's brothers, Malcolm and John. Both fought on the patriotic side and John paid with his life, suffering the same death as his brother. But as so often in the story of William Wallace, little is straightforward. In an incident at Peebles in 1299, to which we shall return,[38] Malcolm was involved in an unseemly brawl at a meeting of Scottish leaders. Malcolm had spoken out in defence of his younger brother, William, but was not, as one might expect, in the pro-Balliol camp, like William, but in the company of Bruce. This Bruce connection is also found in the case of John Wallace, who met his tragic fate in 1306 as a supporter of Bruce's rebellion, a victim of Edward I's retribution against any on the patriotic side unfortunate enough to fall into his hands. But can this conceivably be the same John Wallace who in

December 1304 was in English service? John Wallace and Robert Boyd were at this time accompanying two English clerks on their royal master's business in the west of Scotland.[39] The possibility that John Wallace was acting on behalf of that same king who was even then hunting down John's brother William is a disturbing one. It will be argued below[40] that before his capture William was outside the mainstream of Scottish political thinking. His brothers Malcolm and John were both at times associated with Bruce, and this tends to suggest that in the Wallace family itself, it was William whose views had become outdated. For Malcolm and John the future for Scotland lay with Bruce, not with John Balliol or his son, Edward. When they reached this conclusion we cannot tell, but in the case of Malcolm it was not later than the year after Falkirk. But it is a far step from support for Bruce to serving Edward I, as John Wallace would appear to have done. Can it be that John took his lead from Bruce? At the beginning of 1304, the year in which we find John collaborating with the English, Bruce himself was in pursuit of William Wallace;[41] perhaps by this time John had started on that association with Bruce which led to his death in London two years later.

Alongside Malcolm and John Wallace as allies of Bruce, we can place Reginald Crawford, not the maternal grandfather of the popular version of the patriot's life, but another of the same name, generally believed to be Wallace's uncle. In 1296, with Edward's defeat of John Balliol, Crawford was allowed to remain in office as sheriff of Ayr, an unusual decision in the circumstances. The date of Crawford's confirmation as sheriff is interesting; it follows on the battle of Dunbar but precedes Balliol's abdication. One modern writer sees this as a reward for service on the English side, along with the Bruces.[42]

Crawford continued for some time to enjoy Edward's trust, but then is lost to us for some ten years. In 1306 his lands were forfeited for his adherence to Bruce.[43] A year later, he was captured and executed by the English. In February 1307, Crawford, with two of Bruce's brothers, Thomas and Alexander, together with Malcolm MacQuillan of Kintyre, and an unidentified Irish kinglet, landed on the coast of Galloway with a considerable following.[44] They were at once set upon by hostile forces under Dungal Macdouall, a committed opponent of Bruce.[45] Macdouall defeated them comprehensively, beheaded MacQuillan and the Irish kinglet on the shore, and despatched their heads to Edward, then at Lanercost. The two Bruces and Crawford were carried to Carlisle, to suffer the death of traitors after Prince Edward had seen them. Crawford was hanged and beheaded; although the possibility has been advanced that he died elsewhere,[46] the record makes it clear that Crawford was executed at Carlisle.

The evidence that we have thus tells us that Wallace's family was not united behind him in the cause of John Balliol. Nor did it, if Alan was indeed Wallace's father, come from Elderslie in Renfrewshire. The link with Ayr has gained strength from the Lübeck seal, as has the connection, through his brothers and, perhaps his uncle, with Bruce. The picture of Wallace as one who earned his living or fought as an archer has also been confirmed by the seal. The reverse depicts a hand or hands pulling an arrow on a bow. That this is Wallace's seal, not that of his colleague, Andrew Murray, is borne out by an English account. This, while scorning Wallace's origins and upbringing, tells us that it was through 'bow and quiver' that he made his living. Can it be that the seal supports the contemporary English denigration of Wallace's social status? Alan Wallace, a crown tenant, would rank lower than Malcolm Wallace, a knighted landowner. Much also was made by English sources of William Wallace the outlaw. As we shall see, Wallace was undoubtedly outlawed at least once but the notion of Wallace as a Scottish Robin Hood has not been unpopular.[47] The 'bow and quiver' description would seem to add some potency to that belief.

It was stated above that the popular version of Wallace's life fails on two crucial counts. The first was the matter of his parentage. The second is the lack of conclusive evidence to answer the fundamental question of the transformation of the unknown younger son into the colossal figure of 1297. The standard account does have one advantage, it must be said; it leads quite naturally to what might be called the romantic and cataclysmic view of Wallace's first recorded assault upon the English. Wallace, we are to understand, could only have been forced out of the quiet and placid life he had known by some single violent act or by personal tragedy or, better still, by a combination of the two. In this context, the intervention of Edward I in the internal affairs of the kingdom of Scotland must, of course, provide the setting, the murder by the English sheriff of Lanark, the unspeakable William Heselrig, of Wallace's wife or mistress, Marion Braidfute, heiress of Lamington, the occasion. This explanation of the supposed conversion from the student of theology to the practitioner of warfare appears to contain a contradiction within itself. The relationship with Marion Braidfute, whether that of her husband or lover, is not what one would expect of a man bent, we have already been led to believe, on the life of a priest. The hot-blooded, savage murder of Heselrig, with no thought given to the consequences, is, on the other hand, exactly the reaction of the young man Wallace is generally perceived to have been in 1297.

The legend of Marion Braidfute, with its accompanying account of Wallace's life, persists. But even if based on truth, it is not enough. It does not address an absorbing question: the origins of Wallace's military skill. Nothing in the words of Blind Harry or in those who follow him prepares us for the genius of 1297–98. How, then, are we to explain that genius? There would appear to be three possible answers. The first is that, unknown to us, he had before 1297 served an apprenticeship as a soldier. It follows from this that he had left Scotland to fight, for no opportunity was to be found in his homeland. Whatever adventures he conjures up for Wallace, not even Blind Harry hints at such a passage in Wallace's life before 1297. Yet can we ignore this possibility? What better career existed for a younger, ladless son than that of a soldier, the more so if the young man was, as later events were to show, exceptionally equipped for the role? If Wallace did indeed seek employment as a soldier and therefore went abroad, both Wales and France suggest themselves as areas to which he might have directed his steps in, for example, 1293–94. In both countries Wallace's later enemy, Edward I, was engaged. It is an intriguing thought, but one incapable of proof, that Wallace might have already served in a campaign in which the English king was involved. It is even more intriguing to think, but just as incapable of proof, that he, like more than one of his fellow-countrymen, fought not against but with Edward.

If Wallace was a soldier, his involvement in the war with England prior to 1297 must be considered. While the possibility cannot be ignored, it seems unlikely that his involvement would have escaped the attention of later writers, whether Scottish or English. For the former, it would underline his total commitment to the Scottish cause; for the latter it would surely be used as an indication that his treason was of longer standing than is usually accepted. Each school of thought would be confirmed in its prejudice and not fail to give it expression.

The second answer, which, like the first, helps to fill part of the gap in our knowledge of his life, is that he learned something of the skill of a soldier while an outlaw. Wallace the outlaw is, of course, a familiar and appealing theme.[48] Blind Harry could not resist it. There is about Wallace's adventures, in the form they are transmitted to us by Harry, the mark of the outlaw: the bravado, the challenges given and taken, the impudence, the insults, the exceptional talent with the bow, the carelessness of death, the protection of and by the poor, above all, the heroic stature in the face of great odds. Thus, Wallace slays the son of Selby, the English constable of Dundee,[49] as, historically, he slew Heselrig, as an affront to a superior and detested enemy. The outlaw does not hide from the enemy but instead seeks him out. All this we can recognise as traditional outlaw lore. But it has a basic flaw. As will be seen, Wallace was a careful, even painstaking man. Far from seeking out the enemy, he prepared to meet him on Wallace's own terms. Neither at Stirling nor Falkirk did William seek battle.

We do not know whether Wallace was truly an outlaw before the murder of Heselrig. That same younger, landless son who might have become a soldier might, equally, have turned to a life of crime. The two indeed are not exclusive. The military catastrophe of 1296 must have forced many Scots into crime. If Wallace was an outlaw, his deeds may well have been far from heroic. There exists one tantalising piece of evidence from the year 1296. The records of the time tell us that on 8 August: 'Matthew of York, accused by Cristiana of

21

St John, of robbery, viz on Thursday next before St Botulph's Day, he came to her house at Perth in company of a thief, one William le Waleys, and there by force took her goods and chattels viz beer, to the value of 3s, replies that he is a clerk and not bound to answer. The jury finds the charge proved, and he is adjudged to penitence.'[50] At the time of this entry, Balliol had already been deposed and Scotland was an occupied country. Perhaps the William Wallace who robbed the unfortunate Cristiana in Perth, a favourite stamping-ground of the Guardian, had fought under Balliol and was now living as best he could. He was, at least, clever enough not to be caught, unlike his colleague, Matthew.

The outlaw depends for his survival not merely upon his wits and his skill but upon the sympathy and protection of those among whom he lives. Such sympathy and the protection it brings have to be earned, and it is common therefore to find the outlaw the friend and defender of the poor. The William Wallace of history has no such pedigree. His cause was a different one. Yet he could not have stayed out of the hands of the English without the goodwill of many. His murder of Heselrig made him an outlaw, whether or not he had been one under the law of Scotland. That murder was accomplished, as we shall see, with a band of followers. Where had he gathered this force? His personal magnetism would no doubt attract men to him, as it did to the end of his life. Deeds of which we are ignorant would add to his admirers. The disaffected, the disenchanted, those already feeling the weight of English oppression, would swell the ranks of those about him.

There was, however, another source on which Wallace could draw both before and during 1297: the Wallace family itself. The extent of the Wallace holdings before the death of Walter II Stewart has been shown by Barrow.[51] These, far from being limited to the west of Scotland, where Richard settled and where Wallace was born, stretched across the centre of the country, into the east and north into Moray.[52] They breach the barriers, that is, of region, language and culture. They guaranteed an inheritance of relationships and connections to the descendants of Richard Wallace. When Wallace came to his great endeavour, did he call upon that inheritance? Did he later, hunted by the English and their Scottish collaborators, use that inheritance in another and no less critical situation? Was he hidden from pursuers in the employ of the English king as once, perhaps, he had been helped while an outlaw before the war? It is evident that he could not have survived in the earlier as in the later part of his career had there not been an immense sympathy for him wherever he went. If, after 1297, he benefited from his exploits against the hated English, it is not unreasonable to argue that he could already rely upon the members of his own widely scattered family. His brother John, executed in London, his older brother Malcolm – they alone cannot represent the true contribution of the Wallace family to Wallace's work.[53]

The theory of Wallace the outlaw, however attractive, fails in one significant area to answer our question. It is not the way of the outlaw to fight pitched battles, least of all on the scale of Stirling and Falkirk. The outlaw is adept at the ambush, at the tactic of hit and run. Wallace, like Murray, began in this style and returned to it after Falkirk. By that time he had already demonstrated an ability to organise and use large armies for which the life of an outlaw is neither explanation nor preparation. We know of no one in his company either before or at the time of the murder of Heselrig from whom he could have learned the necessary skills. The Scottish leaders with whom he associated after the murder, even if we put aside their suspicion and distrust of him, had no record of proven success in the field and were, on the contrary, wholly discredited.

We are thus forced back on the third and most obvious explanation of Wallace's military genius: that he was born with it. The war with England provided an arena for a man possessed of such enormous talent, and not merely in the profession of arms, as would have guaranteed him success in whatever direction he cared to employ it. If the claim seems extravagant, one need only look at the challenge he faced as Guardian and the manner in which he dealt with it. The soldier became the governor and assumed the latter role with the same exceptional competence as he had the former. But in neither function could he have achieved what he did if he had been the one-dimensional figure with which we are accustomed to deal. If his talent as a soldier was innate, we have, in order to explain what he accomplished, to see him in a new light. In this connection it is instructive to turn to the work of an authority on the subject of war. Clausewitz writes: 'If we then ask what sort of mind is most likely to display the qualities of military genius, experience and observation will both tell us that it is the inquiring rather than the creative mind, the comprehensive rather than the specialised approach, the calm rather than the excitable head to which in war we would choose to entrust the fate of our brothers and children and the safety and honour of our country'.[54] Machiavelli is less ready than Clausewitz to speak of genius. He contents himself with listing general rules of military discipline.[55] In them and what follows we find that other characteristic which in Wallace balances the view of Clausewitz. Machiavelli states, firstly, that 'good commanders never come to an engagement unless they are compelled to by absolute necessity, or occasion calls for it'.[56] He then goes on to deal, in closing, with the qualifications which distinguish the general.[57] Whatever skill the general has, he will not prosper 'unless he has abilities to strike out something new of his own occasionally. For no man ever excelled in his profession who could not do that, and if a ready and quick invention is necessary and honourable in any profession, it must certainly be so in the art of war above all others. Thus we see how any invention, new, expedient, trifling though it may be, is celebrated by historians.'

We cannot be sure that the exploits of Wallace came to the attention of either Clausewitz or Machiavelli. He was perhaps too slight a figure on the scale on which they worked. Yet we cannot ignore the fact that in their writings we read of Wallace if not by name then through the attributes which they seek in the soldier and especially in the commander. Both were protagonists of the professional soldier, and their study of what was for them an art was exhaustive. While we can recognise in Machiavelli's words that particular feeling for improvisation which was so important in his career, it is in Clausewitz that we come closer to what Wallace was as a soldier. The qualities to which Clausewitz refers are not those with which tradition has endowed Wallace; they are too clinical, too cold even, for that Wallace. We are accustomed to thinking of him as a man of passion, driven forward against the English by his surpassing patriotism, the leader of an undisciplined army swept forward whatever the odds. There is, undeniably, something of that in the Wallace of history. It may have been there at Lanark. If it was, it disappeared in the new and more difficult circumstances in which he found himself. It is then that we see the Wallace who came so near to the ideal of which Clausewitz wrote. We need not dispense with the Wallace of tradition, burning with anger, brutal, unforgiving. He was all of that. But he had, too, a passion for success, for without that his country could not be free. He came to the war with England without the prejudices and preconceptions which his feudal superiors so frequently and wantonly manifested. He had to learn, and to learn he had to enquire. He was not bound by sectional interests, as were those superiors; his was the wider, if simpler, view. He approached battle in a rational, careful way and was not driven to it by the unmanageable bloodlust which had so inflamed Scottish leaders before him that they charged to defeat.

In William Wallace we are dealing with a man unique in his time and place. Scotland produced no one comparable in the War of Independence. Those who came before him taught him by default, those after learned from him the vital lessons which won the war. We can only wonder that, without formal training, lacking, as far as we are aware, reputation either inherited or earned, he emerged from obscurity so complete a soldier. It is a chastening thought that without war he would have remained unknown to history. That likelihood disappeared when the death of Alexander III of Scotland set in train the events which brought Wallace so memorably into the consciousness of his countrymen, from which he has never been displaced.

NOTES

1. For general reading on the reign of David I, see Ritchie: *The Normans in Scotland*, 1953; Barrow: *The Kingdom of the Scots*, 1973;

Barrow: *The Anglo-Norman Era in Scottish History*, 1980; Barrow: *Feudal Britain, the Completion of the Medieval Kingdoms, 1066–1314*, 1956; all passim. Dickinson: *Scotland from the Earliest Times to 1603*, 1962, esp. chaps 9, 11, 13, 15. On particular aspects of the reign, see Burleigh: *A Church History of Scotland*, 1960: Lawrie (ed.): *Early Scottish Charters prior to 1153*, 1905; Anderson (coll. & trans.): *Early Sources of Scottish History, 500–1286*, 1922; Barrow: *Scottish Rulers and the religious orders, RHS*, 5th series, iii, 1953, 77–100.

2. Of this period William of Malmesbury wrote: 'He [David] had rubbed off all tarnish of Scottish barbarity through being polished from his boyhood by intercourse and friendship with us.' (q. Cowan: 'Myth and Identity in Early Medieval Scotland', *SHR* lxiii, 2, no. 176, October 1984, 131)

3. Of these he gained through his marriage to Matilda, the daughter and heiress of Waltheof, executed for treason under William I, the earldom of Northampton and the Honour of Huntingdon, which proved fertile recruiting grounds for him.

4. Barrow: *Anglo-Norman Era,* and Ritchie: *The Normans in Scotland,* passim; Brown: 'The Origin of the House of Stewart', *SHR*, xxiv, 1927. J.G. Wilson: 'Walter Fitzalan, first hereditary high Steward of Scotland', *Scot Geneal.*, XXIIX, 1982, 84–85.

5. Barrow: *Anglo-Norman Era,* 14.

6. Barrow: *Anglo-Norman Era,* 13.

7. Brown: *Origin,* 265–279; Barrow: *Kingdom,* chap. 12.

8. Kightly: *Folk Heroes of Britain,* 1982, 157; Barrow: *Anglo-Norman Era,* 66.

9. Black: *The Surnames of Scotland,* 1993, 799.

10. Barrow: *Kingdom,* 347–49; Duncan: *Scotland: The Making of the Kingdom,* 1989, 139–40.

11. Chap. 3 below; Barrow: *Robert Bruce,* 81–82; Young: *Robert the Bruce's Enemies,* 1997, 165–66

12. Young, ibid., 18.

13. Ibid., 49, for the inability of the Comyns to ensure Bruce support in their problems with Alan Durward.

14. i.e., from the Welsh borderlands, and not necessarily of Welsh extraction. See, for views on this subject, Black, 799; Kightly: *Folk Heroes of Britain,* 1982, 153.

15. As, for example, in Kightly, 157

16. The article in *DNB* gives some idea of the problems posed by Blind Harry in this regard.

17. McNair Scott: *Robert the Bruce King of Scots,* 1982, chap. 8; Barrow: *Robert Bruce and the Community of the Reader of Scotland,* 1976, chaps 9 and 10. An interesting commentary on the view of Wallace found in Barrow can be seen in A.A.M. Duncan's review of the book in *SHR* vol. XLV, 2, Oct. 1966, 184–193. In particular Duncan states (193) that Barrow is 'extraordinary reluctant to see him [Wallace] as a free agent'. See also Barron: *The Scottish War of Independence,* 1934, chaps 21–24.

18. Barron: chaps 7 and 8 contains what is perhaps the most famous assessment of that relationship.

19. See Barron: chaps 7 and 8 for the weighting in favour of Murray. It reflects no doubt the need for a balance to the traditional view of Wallace but errs in the direction of according to Murray a pre-eminence which, in the light of his early death, cannot adequately be tested against events.

20. The Reginald Crawford who perished was William Wallace's uncle. See pp. 17–18, above.

21. See conclusion on Blair and Harry.

22. I have been fortunate enough here to draw on a paper by Dr Fiona Watson, *A Report into the Association of Sir William Wallace with Ayrshire* for East Ayrshire Council, 1999, 3–5. I have been equally fortunate in having the advantage of comments in correspondence on the subject from Professor Geoffrey Barrow. Interest in Wallace's birthplace is not, of course, limited to academics.

23. Fiona Watson, *A Report,* 3–5.

24. Chap. 5.

25. The document, thought to have been destroyed during the Second World War, survived, and in 1999 was brought on loan from Germany to the Museum of Scotland. See the *Herald* (Glasgow) article, 26 February 1999.

26. Morton: *William Wallace, Man and Myth,* 2001, 32.

27. Morton is careful to emphasise Wallace's 'status as Scotland's patriot since the *fifteenth* century'. See Conclusion, below, for a

discussion on the 'modern' Wallace as opposed to the Wallace of 1305. Blind Harry, of course, dates from the fifteenth century.

28. For the Ragman Roll, Barrow: *Robert Bruce*, 76–78; Nicholson: *Scotland the Later Middle Ages*, 1978, 51–52; Powicke: *The Thirteenth Century 1216–1307*, 1953, 615–16.

29. This view does not settle the question of Wallace's birthplace but places him in an Ayrshire 'context'.

30. The *Chronicle of Lanercost* has Stewart and the bishop of Glasgow, Robert Wishart, causing Wallace to rebel. The argument against such prompting is put below, chap. 4.

31. By his actions after Irvine. See chap. 4.

32. If the relationship between the Wallace family and Stewart was not feudal, what influence could Stewart bring to bear on Wallace?

33. Alan Wallace as a crown tenant owed a duty to John Balliol, but, it would seem, chose to interpret it in a different way from William.

34. Barrow, *Robert Bruce*, 77–78.

35. In 1296.

36. Bellamy: *The Law of Treason in England in the Later Middle Ages,* 1970, 37–38.

37. Barrow: *Robert Bruce*, 280–85.

38. Below, chap. 7.

39. Bain: *Calendar*, vol. II, 443.

40. See Conclusion, below.

41. Below, chap. 9; Barrow: *Robert Bruce*, 127; Reese: *Wallace, A Biography*, 1996, 98.

42. Watson: *Under the Hammer, Edward I and Scotland, 1286–1307*, 1998, 58 n. 27

43. Barrow: *Robert Bruce*, 325.

44. *Chronicle of Lanercost*, 179–80; McNamee: *The Wars of the Bruces*, 1997, 38; Barrow: *Robert Bruce*, 179–80.

45. On Macdouall's later career, McDonald: *The Kingdom of the Isles*, 1997, 197.

46. Perhaps the consequence of seeing Crawford as Wallace's grandfather.

47. Robin Hood has never been constrained by time or space. The Robin Hood of 'A Little Gest of Robin Hood' (printed in

one form in Barbour: *Myths and Legends of the British Isles*, 1999, p. 50ff) bears a marked resemblance to the Wallace of popular tradition.

48. Its appeal continues with *Braveheart*. The film ensures that it will remain a familiar theme.

49. A modern writer compares the means whereby Wallace escaped after the murder with those used by Bonnie Prince Charlie: Reese, *Wallace*, 42.

50. Bain: *Calendar*, ii, 191.

51. Barrow: *Kingdom of the Scots*, chap. 12.

52. Ibid.

53. *Dictionary of National Biography*, 563.

54. Clausewitz: *On War*, ed. Howard & Paret, 1984, 112.

55. Machiavelli: *The Art of War*, trans. Farneworth, 1965, 202–04.

56. Ibid., 203–04.

57. Ibid., 205–06.

2

The Time of Defeat, 1296–1297

'Alas for tomorrow, a day of
calamity and misery!'

The medieval mind was much obsessed by the concept of the Day of Judgement. All were agreed that there would come a time when an accounting would be called for; none would escape the consequences of their actions or even of their words for, as St Matthew put it, 'every idle word that men shall speak, they shall give account thereof'. Not surprisingly, prophecies abounded in such an atmosphere. One came from Thomas of Ercildoune or Earlston, Thomas the Rhymer, a semi-legendary Lowlands laird. In the presence of Patrick, earl of March, Thomas uttered these chilling words:

> alas for tomorrow, a day of calamity and misery! because before the stroke of twelve a strong wind will be heard in Scotland, the like of which has not been known since times long ago. Indeed its blast will dumbfound the nations and render somewhat those who hear it; it will humble what is lofty and raze what is unbounding to the ground.

Thomas was speaking on the eve of one day set aside in Scotland for what, according to the lives they had led on earth, some feared and others welcomed, 18 March 1286, in the thirty-sixth year of the reign of Alexander III, descendant of David I.[1] The earl, apprehensive on hearing Thomas's prophecy, relaxed somewhat as the hours passed without incident. Thomas, it was felt at the earl's castle of Dunbar, was a fool. Earl Patrick's peace of mind was, however, to be shattered, as he sat down to eat a little before noon. News reached him from a stranger, news which, we are told, would 'reduce the whole realm of Scotland to tears'.

From the beginning of this remarkable year, the weather, violent in the extreme, had removed any lingering doubt that the people of Alexander's kingdom were right to anticipate some dread event. Only a foolish or brave man would choose to disregard the omens. Such a man, as would become tragically clear, was Alexander. On the day in question he met with his council in Edinburgh Castle. Among the items which occupied the king and his council was one relating to John Balliol, lord of Galloway, himself to play an important part in the events which followed upon the aftermath of the meeting.[2]

The work of the meeting finished, the king fed his councillors and plied them with wine. Nor did he stint himself with food or drink. As night drew on, the king's thoughts turned from matters of state to the attractions of his young wife, Yolande, daughter of the count of Dreux, whom he had married in October of the previous year. Alexander was then forty-four years of age and in robust health. He resolved that he would no longer be separated from his French wife. Yolande was at Kinghorn, a distance from Edinburgh of some twenty-two miles.

Alexander was not deterred by the thought of a difficult journey made worse, not to say dangerous, by the darkness and the truly appalling weather. Perhaps the wine had affected his judgement. He referred with a joke to the universal despair which the year had engendered in his subjects. Dismissing the concerns voiced by the more timorous and superstitious among his councillors, he set out from Edinburgh that very evening for Kinghorn. Both at the ferry crossing at Dalmeny and, again, once over the Firth of Forth, he chose to disregard the urgent pleas of loyal servants and pressed on. With three esquires as companions and two local men acquired as guides, he rode impatiently along the coast road towards Kinghorn. Neither man nor nature could restrain him. The king had surely by this time forgotten what the humblest of his subjects could have told him: that this was the Day of Judgement. And so it was to be, not only for Alexander but for the country over which he ruled. The disaster which so many had foretold now came about. In the darkness Alexander disappeared from the sight of his companions. The king who had so rashly ignored all the omens and scorned the elements fell to his death from the cliffs. We can imagine the consternation of those who had ridden with him, but nothing could be done that night. His body was found the next morning, his neck broken, on the shore of the Forth.[3] His subjects mourned his death and feared for the future. The words attributed by Fordun to Walter Comyn, earl of Menteith, in 1249, when Alexander succeeded to the throne, would now appear prophetic. For him, 'a country without a king was, beyond doubt, like a ship amid the waves of the sea, without rower or steersman'.[4]

Thus perished Alexander III, king of Scots since the age of eight.[5] With him passed what in retrospect would be considered an age of peace, prosperity and stability. One commentator at least found that the dead king had shared similar characteristics to his father. Where the father had been 'compassionate to the unfortunate, generous to those in need, lenient to the just, but strict towards the arrogant, alarming to malefactors and merciful towards the defeated',[6] the son is described as 'gifted in wisdom, famed for his moderation, unshakeable in his inner strength . . . unwavering in the severity of his justice . . . and fair in all things'.[7] Both men had not hesitated to make an example of those who broke their peace. Where Alexander II mutilated the murderers of Bishop Adam of Caithness, his successor 'repressed the madness of rebels . . . with a rope round their necks and ready to be hanged'.[8] Whether or not we accept such reports, Alexander III was successful. Under him the nobles, many of them fractious, self-seeking and temperamentally violent, had become quiet, although, as became evident after his death, still alert to opportunity or perceived insult.[9] The country had been rendered safe from external pressures. The threat from Norway receded after the confrontation at Largs in October 1263 and the death in the Orkneys of the redoubtable Hakon IV.[10] Though neither a grand encounter nor the victory for Scottish arms that Fordun would later suggest,[11] Largs is noteworthy as the last battle on Scottish soil before the military disasters of 1296. The Norwegians, mourning the loss in December of their heroic king, were not long in seeking an accommodation with the Scots.[12] Despite an initial rebuff, the Norwegians persevered and the Treaty of Perth in 1266 gave Alexander possession of the Western Isles in return for an initial payment and an annual rent.[13] The marriage of his daughter, Margaret, to Hakon's successor, Eric II, in 1281, and the birth of their child, another Margaret, drew the former enemies closer together. Queen Margaret's influence on her Norwegian husband was reported to be a good one; she 'bore herself so graciously toward the king and people that she changed [sic] manners for the better; taught him the idiom of France, and of England; and raised him to a more honourable level in regard to food and clothes'.[14] Their union was a brief one, but after her death in 1283, he took as his second wife another Scot, Isabella Bruce, sister to the future Robert I. Eric's interest in Scotland was not to be limited to marriage; like another Bruce, Robert, lord of Annandale, he would become a competitor for the throne left vacant by the death of his daughter, Margaret.

At the same time, England was seen neither as a problem nor as the enemy it had once been. Here, again, in this happy state of affairs, marriage played a part. With Edward I, brother of his first wife, Margaret, Alexander enjoyed an agreeable relationship. Even after Margaret's death in 1275, cordial relations between the two royal houses were maintained. Ownership of the northern counties had ceased to be an issue likely to lead to conflict. The borderline between the two countries had been settled in the reign of Alexander's father by the Treaty of York.[15] The question of English suzerainty over Scotland, like the borderline so long a cause of friction, lay dormant if not forgotten by the English king. To the royal connection could be added the factor of Anglo-Scottish landholdings among the magnates. The Bruces and Balliols for example owned land on both sides of the border. The English Umfraville family had gained the earldom of Angus through marriage in 1243. The Quincys, first noted in Northamptonshire, later had substantial territory in Scotland, including part of Galloway.

Some Scots had a close relationship with the English king. Robert Bruce, lord of Annandale and grandfather of Robert I, had fought on the royalist side against Simon de Montfort in the 1260s and was with Edward's brother, Edmund, on the crusade of 1270. The lord of Annandale's son, Robert, likewise participated in the crusade, although not apparently in the elder Robert's company. More closely associated with Edward in this venture, and previously against Simon de Montfort, was Alexander Balliol, brother of John, later king of Scots.[16] These, and many others, helped to maintain the friendly relationship between Scotland and England which distinguished the reign of Alexander III.

Distance did not isolate Scotland from the rest of Europe. Where once the infiltration of Anglo-Norman families into Scotland under David I and Malcolm IV had ensured continued contact with the Continent, so, in the time of Alexander III, did trade, especially with those countries which lay on the North Sea.[17] Scotland in 1286 could therefore look to the future with confidence. It was, it has been written, 'a country which was being gradually welded together, a country under law and order, with a strong government ably served by an efficient local administration'.[18]

The belief that the death of Alexander III on the night of 18–19 March 1286 marked the end of an era, that it occurred on what might truthfully be called a Day of Judgement, had not faded in the fifteenth century. It found expression in the words of Andrew Wyntoun:

> Quhen Alysandyr our King was dede
> That Scotland led in lure and le
> Awaye was sons of ale and brede
> Of wyne and wax, of gamyn and gle

> Our gold was changed into lede
> Chryst born into vyrgynte
> Succour Scotland and remede
> That stad is in perplexite.[19]

The transformation of Scotland after Alexander's death was not by any means, however, as abrupt or as complete as the plaintive, familiar words of Andrew Wyntoun might lead us to believe. The country survived, despite the opportunity Alexander's death offered, in the first instance, to the forces of disorder and disintegration already present within its borders and, in the second, to an astute and patient monarch in the kingdom to the south.

It is a measure of the basic achievement of Alexander's reign that the survival of Scotland was possible at all, for he had failed in one of the primary tests of a ruler's value. Alexander had not provided Scotland with a legitimate male heir capable of outliving him. He had twice married. Through his first marriage, in 1251 at the age of ten, to Margaret, daughter of Henry III of England, herself a year older, he had three children. The younger son, David, died in 1281 at the age of eight. The other son, named for his father, died in January 1284, a little past his twentieth birthday. The daughter, Margaret, who had become the wife of Eric II of Norway, died in 1283, at or soon after the birth of her daughter, also called Margaret. For ten years after the death of his wife, Alexander remained a widower, if not celibate.[20] Whether he married Yolande of Dreux from love or through the need to produce an heir we do not know. Time, in any case, was not given him.

There was, however, an heir to the throne of Scotland in 1286. This was Margaret of Norway, Alexander's granddaughter. The king had acted quickly – it might be said, ruthlessly, given the circumstances in which he found himself – upon the death of his son and heir in January 1284. Whatever grief he must have felt at the loss of the third and last surviving child of his marriage to Margaret of England, Alexander had not neglected the duty forced upon him to guarantee the succession. At Scone, therefore, in the month after the death of his namesake, Margaret of Norway, it was stipulated, would be 'our lady and rightful heir of our said lord the King of Scotland, of all the kingdom . . .'[21] By this tailzie, Alexander had rendered an exceptional service to his people. Alexander caused his subjects, solemnly and in due form, to recognise his granddaughter as his heir, failing other children born to him.[22] If in March 1286, at the time of her grandfather's death, Margaret of Norway was no more than three years old, in poor health, and a stranger to her new subjects, her claim to the throne was nevertheless upheld. An oath of loyalty to her was sworn and an undertaking given that her inheritance should be protected and kept in peace for her.[23]

That Margaret's claim to the throne was upheld indicates the general determination within Scotland that continuity should be paramount. The funeral of Alexander III and the subsequent gathering of the foremost in the land at Scone towards the end of April permitted discussion of policy for the period up to the coronation of the young queen, whenever that should be. The government of Scotland was therefore placed in the hands of six men, chosen by common consent as being representative of the nation as a whole.[24] They were termed '*custodes*', which today is customarily rendered as 'guardians' rather than 'wardens'. In one account of the events of 1286,[25] they are referred specifically as '*custodes pacis*' or 'guardians of the peace', a more accurate description, at the beginning, of their primary and overriding function.

The peace of the kingdom was, indeed, soon under strain. Alexander III had hoped to ensure an undisturbed transfer of power by the oath of 1284, and that of 1286 had the same purpose. While there is no reason to doubt that those who gave their word on those occasions did so in sincerity, not all of them showed themselves capable of keeping it in the event. The centre of trouble was the south-west, inevitably, because of the relationship there of the Bruce and Balliol families. In what would today be called 'a pre-emptive strike', Robert Bruce the Competitor, lord of Annandale, and his son, Robert, earl of Carrick, seized the royal castles of Dumfries and Wigton as well as Buittle, which belonged to Balliol.[26] Further, at Turnberry, on 20 September 1286, the Bruces, father and son, joined with Angus Macdonald, lord of the Isles, the earl of March, the earl of Menteith, James the Stewart, himself one of the Guardians, and other interested parties, in a pact, the meaning of which has been the source of much discussion.[27] Whatever the precise intention of the agreement or 'Band' of Turnberry, it and the disturbances which accompanied it, foreshadowed the more crucial readiness of the magnates to act as their interests dictated.[28] The strife in the south-west faded as quickly as it had appeared without further complications. The action of the Bruces was a warning, a rehearsal, of the inevitability of another Day of Judgement for Scotland.

The concept of the Guardianship stood the test of the troubles in the south-west, as did the authority of the six men who held the office during the crisis. It was to this office that William Wallace would later succeed on his own merits, and if we consider the names and titles of the first six Guardians, appointed after the death of Alexander III, we may begin to understand something of his achievement. Two bishops, William Fraser of St Andrews and Robert Wishart of Glasgow, were named. With them served two of the earls of Scotland, Duncan of Fife and Alexander Comyn of Buchan, and two men drawn from the ranks of the barons, John Comyn of Badenoch and James the Stewart. Such men, unlike William, belonged to the class which was accustomed to playing a part in the governing of Scotland. The choice of the six reflected both the realism of the nation and its politics. In essence, the groupings within the Guardians balanced the forces most capable of defending Scotland but, conversely, most likely, if unrestrained, to destroy it. Bruce and Balliol were the two most powerful families in the country; each family had its supporters among the Guardians. Of the bishops, Fraser favoured Balliol, Wishart Bruce. If the Comyns held to the former, James the Stewart, as the Band of Turnberry showed, leaned towards Bruce. Nor was experience neglected. The bishops were well versed, by the nature of their profession, in administration, as was the Stewart. The Comyns for their part were not inferior in this regard: they had served in the minority of Alexander III. If Duncan of Fife was but a stripling by comparison, he was the senior earl of Scotland and therefore, for that if no other reason, not to be despised. The six carried on the government of Scotland for three hazardous years;[29] their success in that period tells us as much of their ability and their dedication to the task given them in 1286 as of the wisdom of them who chose them. It also tells us much of the true greatness of William Wallace that, in circumstances at least as difficult for Scotland, he was able to assume the office of Guardian with such unchallenged authority. If the choice

of the six in 1286 reflects the need for a corporate man-
agement, that of William twelve years later indicates how
far the situation had changed and the stature of the
unique individual who, alone, was judged fit for the office.

At this remove it is tempting to see the ultimate frustration of the work of the 'Guardians of the peace' as
inevitable; peace, that is, which was impossible to keep.
There was, after all, a villain to hand, ready in the wings,
awaiting the opportunity to intervene. There was a
kingdom beset by problems, lacking the guiding hand of
a mature ruler, with a native aristocracy willing to betray
the country for their own ends. There was a potential for
civil disturbance, fostered by events or interested parties.
But if all that appears to constitute a recipe for disaster,
that disaster – war with England – did not come until a
decade after the death of Alexander III. And when war with
England came, Scotland was united against Edward I,
however fragile that unity was to be. If Edward I had, as
Scottish tradition certainly tells it, been intent from the
beginning on bringing Scotland under his control, he
was restrained by a subtle patience and the demands of
his involvement in continental affairs from acting at once.
If he was relying on the Scottish capacity for self-
destruction to ease the accomplishment of a plan for the
seizure of Scotland, he was disappointed, for it took the
war itself to cause that self-destruction to assume the
necessary and desired proportions. The Scots were not
yet ready at the death of Alexander III to hand their
country over to war and to Edward I. Thus when at Scone
in April 1286 they gathered in parliament, they decided
to send a delegation to Gascony to seek out Edward, the
intention being to inform him of the dispositions made
for the government of Scotland in the absence of
Margaret of Norway and to ask for his approval. It was

not the intention of the Scots to invite his intervention in the affairs of their country. Nor when the delegation, composed of Sir Geoffrey de Mowbray, the bishop of Brechin, and the abbot of Jedburgh, finally came upon the English king at the town of Saintes in the modern department of Charente, in September, did he attempt to suggest any such intervention. He allowed the delegation to return to Scotland, happy in the optimistic belief that he was sympathetic to the work of the Guardians and the continued independence of Scotland.

When exactly Edward I determined upon the subjugation to his will of the Scots is a matter for speculation. While Alexander III lived, Edward appeared content with the vague definition of the relationship between the two kingdoms which had obtained for so long. The death of Alexander, as we have seen, did not result in immediate action on the part of the English king. How long he would have waited before taking some form of initiative, political or military, it is impossible to say. With his commitments in Wales and France, he needed to be certain that his northern frontier was secure. Alexander's death and the minority of Margaret of Norway threatened that security. Even then, Edward, who came back to England from France in the late summer of 1289, made no hostile move against Scotland. His proposal of marriage between his son, Edward of Carnarvon, and Margaret of Norway was, if not disinterested, statesmanlike;[30] it would have postponed, if it could not prevent, the collision with the Scots. The Guardians for their part saw the virtue in the proposed union, which was agreed in the Treaty of Birgham in 1290, although they were wary enough to sense a possible trap.[31] Edward, his patience, which Wallace was so sorely to test, still intact, confirmed the treaty at Northampton on 28 August. If he accepted that Scotland was to remain free and independent,[32] he had not failed, with his usual attention to detail, to restate in the course of the negotiations his view of his own role in the affairs of the northern kingdom.

At least one writer traces the increased likelihood of war between England and Scotland to the aftermath of the Treaty of Birgham.[33] It was, in his opinion, 'from that point onwards that the pressure was on the Scots, gentle at first but persistent'. It is natural, if fruitless, to offer a date as a suitable starting-point for the decline into war. This is especially understandable if based on the theory that Edward was himself planning to subjugate Scotland, by force if necessary, as early as Birgham. We may be nearer the truth if we consider the part played in that decline into war by unforeseen circumstances. The death of Alexander III, and more importantly perhaps, that of Margaret of Norway in September 1290, were events over which neither Edward nor the Guardians had any control. Each offered Edward an excuse for military intervention; he took neither. But each event made the involvement of Edward in Scotland likelier;[34] the Scots themselves would be forced to call upon him if the alternative was civil war. Once invited, Edward would know well how to profit from a situation which he welcomed, even if he had not himself created it. To say that is not to exonerate him from responsibility or blame for the tragedy of the war which began in 1296. He lived long enough to see the failure of the policy over which he had laboured before 1296 and, perhaps, to understand that he would leave behind him a legacy of bitterness and hatred greater than any which had previously affected relations between the two kingdoms.

The story of how Edward profited from the situation in Scotland and of the events leading to the outbreak of war has been told so often and at such length[35] as to make it unnecessary to repeat it here in any great detail. We need therefore to look at some of the more crucial events as a means of setting the background to the appearance of William Wallace. What he himself made of these events, if indeed he knew anything of them, it is impossible to say. We know only that from the time of his first fame he was, as he remained, Balliol's man.

The death of Margaret of Norway was known in Scotland in early October 1290. As he had in 1286, Robert Bruce, lord of Annandale, despite his advanced age – he was now eighty – moved quickly to protect his interests and to lay claim to the vacant throne. The strongest opposition to that claim lay in the hands of John Balliol, lord of Galloway; he had the advantage of the friendship of the bishop of Durham, Antony Bek, the bellicose friend of Edward I and one of the king's representatives at Birgham.[36] There were other claimants to the throne; they were not deterred by the weakness of their position. Civil war was closer than it had been in 1286. It did not come. The same common sense which had prevailed after the death of Alexander III worked again. All those involved in the events of 1290 reached the same conclusion: that recourse should be had to the wisdom of Edward I. If therefore Bishop Fraser of St Andrews, in asking for Edward's intervention, pressed the case of John Balliol, others, among them the earls of Angus, Atholl, and Mar, sought that intervention while arguing for Robert Bruce. Edward, recently bereaved by the loss of his beloved wife, Eleanor, did not neglect the opportunity. One account suggests that he was no longer disguising, at least from those about him, his warlike intentions; he would make Scotland his, as he had Wales.[37] Words were still to be employed, for Edward loved their use in the cause of his own interests, but he now intended a show of force. From Norham on Tweed, where he had taken up residence in the palace of the bishop of Durham, he invited the Scots to meet with him on 30 May 1291. His army he summoned for 3 June. When the Scots appeared before him, he was careful to treat them with respect, but struck at once. He would judge the various claims to the throne of Scotland, but only upon the acceptance of his paramountcy.[38] Not unnaturally disturbed by this attitude, the Scots were in time forced to agree to Edward's terms.

What Edward's motives were at this time we cannot tell. He had the opportunity to make himself master of Scotland in 1291. The Scots were divided, as they would be again, their morale damaged, their ability to raise an effective opposition gone. It is difficult to see how he could have been prevented from taking over the government of the country. Yet he preferred to enter into a prolonged and unnecessary selection process. If it could be argued that at the end of that process he had, through his choice of John Balliol, in any case made himself master of Scotland, we must still question his wisdom. Edward was renowned through Europe for mental powers, his experience and skill in diplomacy, his Solomon-like qualities.[39] The time for him to seize control of Scotland was in 1291. As he was to learn, even if he was not already conscious of the fact, some of the claimants to the throne of Scotland would be prepared to subordinate the independence of the country to their own interests. He could, had he wished, have used that attitude to ensure his own hold on Scotland; he could, that is, have bought off a number, if not all, of the claimants with land. They were realistic enough to settle for something rather than nothing. It is hard to believe that, of the claimants, only

John Hastings was ready to countenance partition if his own case failed. But Edward ignored the opportunity which such thinking presented to him. By doing so, by opting instead for what has been called the 'splendid façade'[40] of sitting in judgement on the claimants to the throne of Scotland, he showed, as he would do later, an inexplicable ineptitude. Ironically, it may be that Edward's failure to act in character in 1291 caused war. He gave disparate elements in Scotland the time to return to something of the unity of 1286, and by his actions, once he had appointed a king, guaranteed that that unity would not break in the face of war.

On 17 November 1292, at Berwick, Edward's decision was read by his justice, Roger le Brabazon. Edward had found the case for John Balliol proven. Once enthroned at Scone on St Andrew's Day, Balliol discovered what kingship meant. Later generations have tended to judge Balliol unsympathetically. We may wonder whether in the circumstances any other claimant would have been more worthy of our sympathy. There was no Scot strong enough to resist Edward. Balliol's opponent, Robert Bruce, known with reason as 'the Competitor', died in the year before the outbreak of war. The man who, as long before as 1238, in the reign of Alexander II, had first been seen as heir to the throne, may well have died with a bitter smile on his lips at the thought of Balliol acting at the dictate of Edward I. Bruce's son was ineffectual, his grandson an unknown factor. The time of William Wallace had not yet come. Balliol soon had cause to regret his elevation. If it was natural that Edward should require him, on 26 December, to repeat the oath of homage he had already given in the previous month, Balliol might more readily question the first of the humiliations to which Edward subjected him. A week after Balliol's enthronement, Roger Bartholomew, a burgess of Berwick, appealed to Edward against judgements entered against him in Scottish courts. Edward reversed one judgement. The reversal brought home to the Scots the fact that any promises made by Edward concerning the independence of Scotland were of doubtful value.

The inevitable reaction of the Scots to the reversal was dismissed by Edward. The English king aggravated the situation when, in the summer of 1293, his council insisted that the king of Scotland should appear personally to answer any appeals against judgements given in his courts. This was clearly insulting. Balliol continued for some time to conduct himself with dignity and authority in the face of Edward's pressure, but he could not do so indefinitely. If a later account is to be believed, he was in any case disillusioned with his role as king and suspicious of his subjects. On 1 April 1298, his kingdom long lost and himself in custody, although not uncomfortable in the London palace of his friend, Antony Bek, Balliol is reported to have said: 'When he possessed and ruled the realm of Scotland as king and lord of the realm, he found in the men of that realm such malice, deceit, treason, and treachery, arising from their malignity, wickedness, and stratagems, and various other execrable and detestable actions.'[41] Having thus attacked the Scots for certain characteristics – from not all of which he himself was free – Balliol went on to maintain that he had feared for an attempt by poison upon his life while he was still king. It is of course possible that Balliol, for good reasons, was saying what he thought his hosts would wish to hear. Moreover, it is unfortunate that at the time of his remarks, his former subjects were, under William Wallace, preparing to face the army of Edward I, and that many of them were, within three months, to perish in the defence of his right to the throne of Scotland. Nevertheless, he had been subject to pressure, perhaps verging on the violent, from his own people before the outbreak of war. His own increasing diffidence, not to say fear, when Edward grew more demanding, cannot have endeared him to those who remembered the strength of Scotland when put to the test in 1286.

If there was not in Scotland in early 1294 a war party as such, there was unquestionably a party ready to fight in the event of Edward's exceeding what was considered reasonable. He had come close to that. Clashing with Philip IV of France over Gascony, he now took the step which gave the Scots no further excuse to deceive themselves. Edward called upon his army for France to gather at Portsmouth. His absence from England might have given the Scots, as it gave the Welsh, the opportunity they needed. But they did not even have to wait for him to sail for France. Haughtily and mistakenly, Edward summoned Balliol and various of his subjects, among them James the Stewart, and Bruce the Competitor, then eighty-four years of age, to serve with him in France. Edward had turned the screw too far. The last Scottish king to serve abroad in the army of an English king had been Malcolm IV in 1159. Like Edward with Balliol, Henry II had established a sort of mental superiority over Malcolm.[42] But not even Balliol dared to go as far with Edward as Malcolm had gone with Henry, neither he nor the others summoned by Edward complied.

War with England could not now be prevented. The Scots began to seek allies and, understandably, turned to France. Philip IV was agreeable to discussions. In July 1295 four representatives were named to negotiate a treaty with the French king. They were William Fraser,

Matthew of Crambeth, John de Soules, and Ingram de Umfraville. They travelled to France and on 23 October concluded an offensive and defensive alliance with Philip.[43] The treaty was ratified in Scotland on 23 February 1296. What Balliol himself thought of these events is not recorded. Whether he wished it or not, he was at the head of a people ready for war. He was truly, as one chronicler aptly put it, 'a lamb among wolves'.[44]

Edward, meanwhile, had been diverted by rebellion in Wales. He postponed sailing to France and dealt with it. That done, he had decided that he could no longer defer action against Scotland. France would have to wait. It is impossible not to admire the energy with which the king, fifty-eight years old, faced with problems in France, wearied after the Welsh campaign, embittered by what he believed to be the treason of the Scots, flung himself against them. He ordered his army to assemble before him at Newcastle upon Tyne on 1 March 1296, arranged for a fleet of ships to sail from East Anglia round the coast to provision the army, and set out to punish those who had defied him. Those who were the target of his wrath had themselves issued their own call to arms to their fellow-countrymen. In the name of John Balliol, the Scottish feudal host was summoned to meet on 11 March four miles north of Selkirk, at Caddonlee. Not all the principal Scots chose to obey the summons. Among these were Patrick, earl of Dunbar and Gilbert, earl of Angus; both remained faithful to Edward and were to play a crucial role in the Falkirk campaign.[45] But more striking and disturbing was the attitude adopted by the Bruces. They stood apart. It may be true that their behaviour was 'clear and consistent', as one biographer of Robert I has put it.[46] They owed no loyalty to Balliol. They held to their oath given in 1292 to Edward. He had flattered their hope of, one day, replacing Balliol.[47] A precedent had been set. If William Wallace had known the reasoning of the Bruces, he would in all probability have thought it contemptible. Wherever he was, he was unlikely to have disregarded the summons to Caddonlee.

The war which followed was characterised in its early stages in two particular ways. First, it was an exceptionally brutal war, on both sides. On Easter Monday a Scottish army, under seven earls, crossed the Solway. The size of the army is unknown, but we can be in no doubt about their intentions. In the words of the *Lanercost Chronicle* the Scots began 'burning houses, slaughtering men and driving off cattle, and on the two following days they violently assaulted the city of Carlisle; but failing in their attempt, they retired on the third day'.[48] This is a sober and restrained account of what must have been horrifying. It was a rehearsal for worse still. In April the Scots raided into Northumberland. Again they burned houses, but now added sacrilege to their crimes. They burned churches and monasteries, and are reported to have burnt alive a group of schoolboys, perhaps as many as two hundred, at Corbridge.[49] What the purpose of these raids was we can only guess. They were futile, failed to break Edward's resolve, wasted energy, and diverted attention from what must be the main issue, the defeat of Edward.

He had not been idle. His response to the raid of the seven earls was the sack of Berwick. This was far in excess of anything the Scots had perpetrated and must cast doubt, again, on his stability. Whereas, at the time of the execution of Wallace, he had nine years behind him of frustrations and disappointments, he had no such excuse at Berwick. The failure of his first attack on the town, the jeers of the defenders, his own impatience and sense of betrayal, do not explain the slaughter which he condoned and even encouraged once the walls of the town were breached. For two days he allowed his army to kill and burn. Berwick, despite his own later efforts to rebuild and restore it, was never again to achieve its former status. If, strictly speaking, he had adhered to the rules of war in handing over to sack a town which had refused to surrender, Berwick was the first, and perhaps along with the execution of Wallace, the greatest stain on his reputation.

The second feature of the war at this time was the military ineptitude of the Scottish leaders. We have seen the futility of their raids into England. They were no more successful when put to a test for which, in theory at least, they ought to have been better prepared. From Berwick Edward moved slowly, confidently, north in the direction of Dunbar. He may have felt that Berwick was the true measure of the Scots' competence. Success may have bred a certain complacency. If this was the case, it was imperative that the Scots strike back effectively, in order to redress the balance. Although the earl of Dunbar, Patrick, was Edward's man, his castle had fallen into the hands of the Scots through the stratagem of his wife, who had embraced the Scottish cause.[50] Edward detached a cavalry force under John de Warenne, earl of Surrey, to recapture Dunbar. The Scots now scorned the opportunity for the ambush of Warenne or for any tactic other than the obvious one. There was no reason why they should meet Warenne in the open field, and pit cavalry against cavalry. Where the English, the Welsh campaigns behind them, were experienced and hardened, the Scots were untried. This did not deter them. With a sublime arrogance, they accepted what they took to be a challenge. There was no Wallace among them to dissuade them, to put the alternatives before them. They could have delayed any form of action at this time, for Dunbar was not worth the risk of defeat. They could have drawn the English on, as Wallace did before Falkirk – a tactic adopted by Robert I. They could have allowed the lengthening of the English lines of communication to work against the invaders.

That they did none of these things doomed them. Even then, patience and discipline in the ranks of the cavalry might still have won the day. Warenne, as Wallace would clearly demonstrate at Stirling, was not an exceptional soldier, but he knew enough to profit from the Scottish abandonment of a good position. He had divided his force; one section he left before Dunbar to contain the garrison, the other he led to face the Scottish army. That army, sensing an opening which did not in reality exist, broke ranks and rushed to the attack. No doubt it was a splendid sight. No doubt it was exhilarating. But it ended in disaster. From the safety of a hill, the Scots had charged into defeat. Warenne's troops had no difficulty in dealing with the Scots, whose own impetuosity had made the outcome certain. As quickly as they had attacked the Scots turned, intent on reaching Selkirk Forest, where not many months later a wiser man laid his own, different plans.

Warenne's victory at Dunbar effectively ended resistance to Edward. It was scarcely a battle; it is difficult to think of it even as an engagement but it was a rout. How many fought at Dunbar, how many were killed, we have no means of knowing. An English version which numbers the Scottish dead at over ten thousand is hardly credible.[51] The foot soldiers, left to their own devices by their leaders, suffered heavily. Many Scots of high position fell into English hands and were distributed in various prisons.[52] Of those who joined Sir William Douglas, Wallace's future ally, taken at Berwick, was the young Andrew Murray. Murray learned enough from the disaster at Berwick and the farce at Dunbar to recognise the need for change. It was unfortunate that those who did learn were to continue in the minority for some time.

After Dunbar, Edward undertook a leisurely progress through what was, in essence, his kingdom of Scotland. To emphasise his authority he caused the symbolic Stone of Destiny to be carried from Scone to Westminster Abbey. One after another the castles of Scotland were turned over to him. Balliol, meanwhile, bereft of ideas, slipped away before him. At length he begged for terms. He was forced to agree to a succession of public appearances in which he confessed to a variety of offences against Edward and, in the last act, he surrendered his kingdom to Edward on 10 July at Brechin. If humiliated, he kept his life, and was sent to the Tower of London, escorted by the earl of Lancaster. He remained a scapegoat for the failure of the nation as a whole and entered the Scottish consciousness as 'Toom Tabard', the pathetic, broken figure of Brechin of whom Wyntoun wrote:

> This Johun the Balliol dispoyilyeide he
> Off all his robis and ryalte.
> The pellour that tuk out of his tabart,
> Tuyme Tabart he was callit efftirwart;
> And all othir insignyis
> That fel to kynge on ony wise,
> Baythe septure, suerde, crowne and rynge,
> Fra this Johun, that he made kynge,
> Hallely fra hym he tuk thar,
> And mad hym of his kynrik bare.[53]

Edward returned to Berwick in late August. There he

produced his plan for the government of Scotland. He entrusted the functioning of it to Warenne, who was to be lieutenant or keeper. To assist Warenne, Edward named as treasurer Hugh Cressingham and as chancellor Walter of Amersham. His chief justice in the newly conquered kingdom was to be William Ormsby.[54] He placed his officials in other lesser posts, assured himself of the safety of the castles, and in all things was, as always, thorough. He had reason to be pleased with himself. There remained one other task before he left Scotland to the care of his subordinates. All substantial landholders were required to give, or renew, their oath of loyalty to Edward as lord of Scotland. Whatever the actual number of those who swore fealty to Edward at Berwick,[55] the name of William Wallace is not to be found among them. But, as has been noted, Alan Wallace is among those listed, with all that this might imply. Nothing however can alter the symbolic importance since attached to the absence from the 'Ragman Roll' of the name of William Wallace.[56]

NOTES

1. For genealogical tables relating to Alexander III and the subsequent disputed succession, see, for example, Dickinson, op. cit,. 53, 151; Barrow: *Robert Bruce*, 455; Duncan, op. cit., 628–29, 632; Nicholson, op. cit., 616.

2. Barrow: *Robert Bruce*, 9.

3. Bower, Book X

4. *Chron. Fordun.* II.

5. As an introduction to Alexander's reign: Dickinson, op. cit., passim; Powicke, op. cit., 589–98; Reid (ed.): *Scotland in the Reign of Alexander III*, 1990. Lanercost, 40, is one source for Alexander's addiction to the pleasures of the flesh during his widowhood.

6. Bower, Book IX.

7. Ibid., Book X.

8. Ibid., Book IX.

9. As, for example, in Bruce's activity in south-west Scotland in the winter of 1286–87.

10. Magnusson: *Hakon the Old,* 1982, offers an interesting and informative perspective on the period. Duncan, op. cit., 579–81, also warns us that the battle 'has been the subject of many misconceptions'. He seeks to reduce the numbers involved dramatically.

11. Bower, Book X, concurs, with 'thousands slain'.

12. Magnusson, op. cit., 22.

13. See 'The Treaty of Perth: A Re-examination', *SHR*, lviii, April 1979, 35–37. McDonald, op. cit., deals with Largs and the Treaty of Perth at some length.

14. McDonald: op. cit., 121–22.

15. Dickinson, chap. 8; Barrow: *Kingdom,* chap. 4; Powicke, 574, 588–89.

16. MacQuarrie: *Scotland and the Crusades 1095–1560,* 1997, chap.3 for Alexander Balliol and other Scots involved in the Crusade.

17. Barrow: *Robert Bruce,* 9.

18. Dickinson, 110.

19. Wyntoun, 266.

20. Lanercost, 40, is our sources for Alexander's addiction to the pleasures of the flesh during his widowhood.

21. *Foedera,* I, ii, 638.

22. Palgrave, *Documents and Records,* 42.

23. Ibid.

24. See Reid: 'The Kingless Kingdom: The Scottish Guardianships of 1286–1306', SHR, vol. LXI, Oct. 1982, 105–29.

25. Lanercost, 117.

26. Barrow: *Robert Bruce,* 17–18; McCulloch: *Galloway, A Land Apart,* 2000, 149–50.

27. Nicholson, op. cit., 28–29; Dickinson, op. cit., 144; Barron: *The Scottish War of Independence,* 1934, 112, and Barrow: *Robert Bruce,* 17–18, offer some of the opinions on the issue.

28. An attitude which persisted throughout the coming war, adding to the difficulties facing Wallace.

29. See Reid, n. 24 above.

30. Prestwich: *Edward I*, 1988, 360; Barrow: *Robert Bruce*, 27.

31. Barrow, op. cit., 28.

32. Ferguson: *Scotland's Relations with England*, 1977, 22–24.

33. Ibid., 23.

34. Ibid.

35. Prestwich: op. cit., chaps 14 and 18; Barrow: *Robert Bruce*, chaps 3 and 4; Barron, op. cit., chaps I & IX; Dickinson, chap. XVI; Powicke, op. cit., 598–607.

36. Despite intermittent, sometimes serious, disagreements, the two maintained a friendship. Bek it was who conducted Edward's funeral.

37. *Fordun*, 308.

38. *Rishanger*, 241.

39. He had been asked to use his good offices in the war between Castile and France in the early years of his reign. Prestwich, op. cit., 319ff; Salzman: *Edward I*, 1968, 49–50; Powicke, op. cit., 242–44.

40. Ferguson, op. cit., 24.

41. As an Englishman, Balliol now had little reason to love the Scots.

42. On Henry II and Malcolm IV see Warren: *Henry II*, 1983, passim.

43. *Chron. Lanercost*, 166.

44. *Rishanger*, 371.

45. See below, chap. 6.

46. McNair Scott, 34.

47. *Fordun*, 317.

48. Lanercost, 115.

49. Ibid., 174.

50. Barrow: *Robert Bruce*, 71.

51. As well as questioning such a figure, there is no unanimity on the scale of the battle, among modern commentators, c.f. Barrow: *Robert Bruce*, 101–02, and Preswich, op. cit., 473, for contrasting opinions.

52. Young, op. cit., 161 ff.

53. Wyntoun, 295.

54. See for an excellent account of Edward's government of 1296, Fiona Watson: *Edward I and Scotland 1286–1307*, 1998, passim.

55. Some, like William Douglas, submitted twice.

56. As has been suggested above, he may not have merited inclusion.

3

The Time of Victory, 1297

'A ripple of jubilation spread
through the oppressed'

Edward left Scotland on 17 September 1296. If pre-occupied with affairs across the Channel, he had reason to feel satisfied with the campaign he had just completed. The opposition, where it had not faded before him, had been futile, ill-conceived and badly led. Balliol had been ridiculed and exiled; no natural successor was available, even if Edward had been prepared to entertain the idea of a second puppet king. The war party in Scotland had been broken and many of its members were in English prisons. It is hardly surprising if Edward gave no apparent thought to a further rebellion against his authority. He knew of no source for rebellion; that there could be any potential leaders of opposition to be found outside the ranks of those he had so easily defeated never occurred to him. His blindness to the alternatives was shared by the Scots nobility. They, like Edward, had been raised to think of themselves as unique; failure, like success, opened no new avenues for them.

Something of Edward's contempt for Scotland and the Scots may be gleaned from a remark attributed to him at the time of his departure from Scotland.[1] It was directed to Warenne. As one old soldier to another, Edward is reported to have said: 'Bon besoiogne fait qy de merde se delivrer.'[2] He had been less coarse but equally dismissive when the son of the Competitor, Robert, lord of Annandale, reminded him, almost certainly timidly, of the promise of the throne of Scotland. Edward, with Balliol defeated, no longer needed to placate the likes of Bruce for whom he had the same contempt he had for other Scots. 'Have we nothing to do but win kingdoms for you?' he snarled at the unfortunate Bruce. Edward never lost that attitude to the Scots, although he was not always so forthright; to achieve his ends he would use whatever approach he thought appropriate.

His crossing of the Tweed back into England was not the signal for an immediate rising against the government for which he had made Warenne responsible. The nature of Edward's hold, in military and political terms, over the Scots ensured that for some months at least there would be a lull. Neither Warenne nor Cressingham, any more than Edward himself, can fairly be blamed for failing to realise that it would be no more than a lull. If Warenne and Cressingham can be charged with arrogance,[3] they had cause. They had seen and been a party to their king's achievements in Scotland. Warenne himself had, with little effort and few losses, chased from the field the best of the Scots. Only time would show how transient Edward's first success in Scotland was. The situation in the autumn of 1296 was in line with the pattern of Edward's relationship with Scotland for the rest of his life. While he himself was in the field or held the reins of government close, his supremacy was safe, certainly in military terms. It was as if he exercised some sort of mental hold upon the Scots, Wallace apart. His reputation, or their perception of it, appeared to negate the drive of the Scots. Against his ruthless practicality, their actions are seen as mere posturings. His preparations for a campaign were more thorough,[4] his assessment of the factors involved more realistic, his judgement of the commitment of the Scots more experienced. It may well be true that, in Barron's words, 'after Stirling Bridge the Scots under Wallace never won a victory in the open against any English force which could fairly be described as an army'.[5] Barron, of course, is pursuing in this context a comparison of his hero, Andrew Murray, with William Wallace, to the latter's detriment. Barron's passionate championship of Murray is a useful and important corrective to the lack of balance existing before. He does not, however, deal with one significant question: which of the Scots, while Edward was in charge of the English forces, achieved what he accuses Wallace of failing to do? Murray himself died before he could face the ultimate test of a Scottish commander: an engagement with an English army led by Edward in person.[6] Stirling, the credit for which Murray shares, was, in any case, a pitched battle: are we to assume that the decision to fight was Wallace's alone, that Murray allowed himself to be persuaded against his better judgement to fight? If that is so, it speaks badly for the powers of leadership which Barron so eloquently defends. Murray, after all, had been at Dunbar and there is no reason to suppose that he would have disagreed with the failed Scottish tactics there.

When we turn from Andrew Murray to Robert I, we find that his victory at Loudon Hill on or about 10 May 1307 may seem, at first sight, to contradict the argument of Edward's infallibility against the Scots. Bruce, however, never fought against Edward. At Loudoun Hill, he was opposed by Edward's lieutenant in Scotland, Aymer de Valence, earl of Pembroke, who had sent him scurrying away from Methven in the previous June.[7] Bruce at this period was an opportunist and a quick learner, creditable qualities in a general, no doubt, but perhaps not sufficient to bring victory against Edward I in his prime. When Edward left Scotland in September 1296, he *was*, as far as the Scots were concerned, in his prime, his superiority over them as yet unquestioned.

It was a superiority which, being personal, was not long to survive his departure. Edward's choice of subordinates to govern Scotland in his absence has been much criticized. Warenne in particular has been faulted both for his indolence and for his conduct of the Stirling Bridge campaign. Some eight years older than Edward, he was not enthusiastic about exercising in person the authority he had been given. The victor of Dunbar preferred to take his ease on his estates in Yorkshire; he feared for his health, we are told, in the unpleasant air of Scotland.[8] Edward's biographer[9] has fairly described the earl as 'a loyal, if unimaginative, supporter of the king'. Loyalty in his subordinates was a quality which Edward, not unnaturally, prized, and if Warenne was unimaginative, that would not distinguish him from the majority of his contemporaries, Edward himself not excepted.[10] Warenne's record as an associate of Edward over a period of fifty years was not to be despised. They were reconciled after a fall-out in 1262 and henceforth Warenne was Edward's man. He fought on the royalist side in the Barons' War and took the cross with Edward in 1268. He served with Edward in Wales and was one of those summoned to the Shrewsbury parliament of 1283, at which judgment was passed on the unfortunate Dafydd ap Gruffydd.[11] The

Scots had come to know Warenne well, even before the outbreak of war in 1296. He was in Scotland in 1285, was involved in the negotiations for the Treaty of Salisbury in 1289, and in 1290, with Antony Bek, was appointed by Edward to treat with the Guardians.[12]

Edward's reliance on Warenne after the defeat of Balliol in 1296 is thus perhaps more understandable. As reliable diplomat and subordinate, Warenne could not readily be overlooked in the allocation of responsibilities, and while Edward was prepared to appoint men of ability to leading posts in his armies, he did not always find it easy to ignore the claims of those, like Warenne, from the highest ranks in society.[13] Nor was Warenne's passivity in 1296 and 1297 necessarily a true reflection of his character. He had a fiery side to his nature and was prompt to defend his rights. He quarrelled violently with, among others, Henry de Lacy, earl of Lincoln, and Alan la Zouche, Henry III's justice in Chester.[14] One account, if it can be credited,[15] well illustrates Warenne's less passive side. In answer to a demand by Edward's lawyer that he prove his rights to land, Warenne held up a rusty sword, declaring, 'Look, my lords, here is my warrant. My ancestors came with William the Bastard, and conquered their lands with the sword, and I will defend them with the sword against anyone wishing to seize them.'

Warenne is remembered today for his failure at Stirling Bridge. But Edward had reason to trust him in 1296. Neither king nor earl could have foreseen the rise of Wallace, with a revolutionary approach to war, and Warenne's reputation and length of service would have seemed proof against any eventuality. In Cressingham, Edward had a servant of a different order, an administrator of no little experience. Of illegitimate birth and somewhat unprepossessing,[16] Cressingham, seconded by his colleague,

William Ormsby, the justiciar, effectively ran the government. The treasurer had learned his trade in the household of Queen Eleanor.[17] Her husband was devoted to her and she was by all accounts a cultured woman.[18] Her treatment of her tenants does not, however, bear close scrutiny, and on at least one of her estates, where Cressingham acted for her, her behaviour aroused great resentment. No less a figure than the archbishop of Canterbury, John Pecham, had occasion to write to her in unflattering terms about her methods, and both she and the king were taken to task in verse for their greed:

> The king he wants to get our gold
> The queen would like our lands to hold.[19]

As one of the queen's stewards and throughout his career, Cressingham was not noted for his probity. He was active on the king's behalf, as a commissioner of array in Norfolk, raising troops for service in Wales, and as a justice in the north of England. In Scotland, the treasurer was soon to be unpopular, both in himself and in his official capacity. His grasping nature prompted even an English commentator to state that he 'loved money'. The same source adds that the Scots referred to him not as 'treasurer but treacherer to the king', and they believed this to be the truth.[20] This, of course, may be a reflection of his ability to raise money for his king,[21] but he and Ormsby exercised their authority in an aggressive manner, certain to alienate those over whom they had been placed. Thus, Ormsby 'prosecuted all those who did not wish to swear fealty to the king of England without making distinction of person'. Even those who swore allegiance to Edward were subjected to a tax.

By May 1297 the English administration in Scotland was facing a series of insurrections throughout the country. Traditionally but inaccurately, the signal for rebellion was the murder by Wallace of the English sheriff of Lanark some time in May. The date reflects the dominance in popular thought of Wallace, but we know that there were disturbances over a wide area – whether spontaneous or organized is unclear – well before then. It is unlikely that all who participated in these disturbances were inspired by the highest motives. The activities of Edward's officials, as has been noted, must have been a considerable factor; however successful Cressingham and Ormsby were in implementing Edward's policies, it was inevitably at the cost of public resentment. Some of those who took to arms at this time would have hoped, for their own ends, to benefit from the lack of English garrisons in the more isolated areas. Itinerant outlaws, a perennial problem, would be attracted by news of what would soon threaten to lead to anarchy. A minor success against the occupying forces would breed confidence. But if there were squalid motives for involvement in the growing struggle, many who participated were, beyond dispute, genuinely patriotic, determined on ridding the land of a detested enemy, and on disproving the myth of English invincibility.

The effect of the disturbances which appear to have begun in the early months of 1297 was, whatever lay behind them, considerable. In the western Highlands, in Aberdeenshire, down in the south-west in Galloway, there were reports of violence and upheaval.[22] No one, let alone Cressingham, could have co-ordinated action against the insurgents over such an area. Had action been possible, the weather, like the distances involved, would have militated against the necessary response. The time was well chosen, the tactics of the insurgents realistic; a lesson had been learned from the campaign of 1296.

What prompted the timing and the change in approach we do not know. If there was a single guiding hand behind the disturbances, it was surely that of a genius.

That there was subsequently such a guiding hand became the firm opinion of the English. It is interesting that the names advanced were not those of the two men most closely identified in the popular imagination with the destruction of English power in 1297, William Wallace and Andrew Murray. Rather, the English saw in Robert Wishart, bishop of Glasgow, and James the Stewart the instigators of rebellion. This belief was not perhaps without foundation. If Edward attempted to appoint English rather than Scottish priests to Scottish benefices, he was bound to arouse resentment. The Church in Scotland already possessed the framework for the dissemination of rebellious ideas and the integration of one uprising with another. To the English, therefore, it was peopled with subversives. The *Chronicle of Lanercost* was emphatic on this point:

> In like manner, as we know that it is truly written, that evil priests are the cause of the people's ruin, so the ruin of the realm of Scotland had its source within the bosom of her own Church; because whereas they who ought to have led them, misled them, they became a snare and a stumbling block of iniquity towards them, and brought them all to ruin. For with one accord both those who discharged the office of prelate and those who were preachers, corrupted the ears and minds of nobles and commons, by advice and exhortation, both publicly and secretly, stirring them to enmity against that king and nation who had so effectively delivered them; declaring falsely that it was far more justifiable to attack them than the Saracens.[23]

Wishart, who lived until 1316 and thus saw the triumph of Robert I, was without doubt a persistent supporter of the Scottish cause and therefore deserved the abuse of the English.[24] As for the noble James the Stewart, he belonged to that category about which another English chronicler was no less scathing than Lanercost, if somewhat more restrained in his language. It was Cressingham's opinion that the Scottish lords were not to be trusted in this year of 1297, and Guisborough shares the treasurer's suspicions. He tells us that wherever their bodies might be, 'even when . . . present with the king . . . at heart they were on the opposite side'.[25] It is, however, when we turn again to Lanercost that we find the bishop and the Stewart linked in what is seen as a common culpability:

> Hardly had a period of six months passed since the Scots had bound themselves by the above-mentioned solemn oath of fidelity and subjection to the King of the English, when the reviving malice of that perfidious race excited their minds to fresh sedition. For the bishop of the Church in Glasgow, whose personal name was Robert Wishart, ever foremost in treason, conspired with the Steward of the realm named James, for a new piece of insolence, yea, for a new chapter of ruin. Not daring openly to break their pledged faith to the king, they caused a certain bloody man, William Wallace, who had been chief of brigands in Scotland, to revolt against the king and assemble the people in his support.[26]

Here we have Wishart and the Stewart not merely guilty of breaking their oath to Edward and indulging in a conspiracy against him, but in league with the most notorious outlaw and rebel of them all. Just as we cannot place Wallace's first action against the English with any certainty before May 1297, so we are ignorant of the role of Wishart and the Stewart in events before then. It is reasonable to suppose that, perhaps like Wallace, they profited from a situation not of their making. If that is the case, we are left with the fact that the earlier disturbances were spontaneous and haphazard, not the work of any one person or group. This does not reduce the value to the Scottish cause of Wishart and the Stewart any more than it lessens the impact of Wallace.

What is to be made of Lanercost's statement that Wishart and the Stewart persuaded Wallace to rebel? Failing reliable evidence to the contrary, we are free to believe that Wallace was a faithful son of the Church in Scotland. His later violence against English priests suggests an almost pathological hatred of those who had, as he understood it, persecuted the Scottish Church.[27] It is a big step from accepting that loyalty to the Church, from accepting also that Wallace was an ally of Wishart and the Stewart in 1297, sharing their views, to agreeing that they had led him into rebellion against Edward I. However little we know of Wallace, it can be said with some assurance that he was, if nothing else, his own man. He can be pictured listening to the other two, giving them the respect due to them by reason of their station, sympathising with their distress at the English occupation of Scotland. Perhaps they were better able to articulate the emotions which all felt. It is far less easy to visualise his being led by these two representatives of that class which had so dismally failed to uphold the honour and freedom of Scotland in 1296. It is quite conceivable that as a preliminary he asked Wishart's blessing – no doubt speedily given – for the undertaking upon which he was entering. A pledge of support from James the Stewart would be no less welcome. All of this would be in keeping with his dedication to due procedure, which manifested itself in its most extreme, and fatal, form in his allegiance to Balliol.

Such formalities apart, Wallace required no prodding, no permission. He was, then as always, fully capable of making up his own mind. We have only to compare the fierce, even explosive, nature of his conduct in May 1297 with the dithering of Wishart and the Stewart in June and July to see the truth.[28] The English determination to denigrate Wallace at all costs may help us to understand why he is portrayed as subordinate to Wishart and the Stewart. Only be relegating him to a supporting role – all that his social origins entitled him to – could his achievement be explained. Those who wrote of him in this way could not see that, with Wallace, a new age was beginning. He rose to prominence through his own ability. What is true of Wallace – that he was essentially his own inspiration – was true of the friend and colleague he was about to make, Andrew Murray.[29]

The threads of the resistance to Edward I came together in the persons of Andrew Murray and William Wallace in the late summer of 1297. It is appropriate to rank Murray first for the reason that we know more of him at this time than we do of Wallace. The son of Sir Andrew Murray of Petty, he was present at the débâcle of Dunbar and there, with his father and uncle, made prisoner.[30] During his incarceration at Chester he had occasion to reflect upon the futility of the Scottish tactics at Dunbar. Escaping from Chester,[31] he made his way to the family lands in Moray and there, secure from English interference, planned rebellion. It does no disservice to Murray, 'one of the chivalric figures of Scottish history' as he has been called,[32] to stress that, unlike Wallace, his prominence in the early days of his fame depended upon his position in society. He had, after all, gained no reputation as a soldier; Dunbar was no recommendation. That intriguing figure, Alexander Pilche, burgess of Inverness,[33] may well have been a more potent factor in the north than Murray. But there is no question that, once he chose to exercise it, leadership of this part of the rebellion lay with Murray as of right. With Pilche and those others who had already made their mark on events added to his own following, Murray had a formidable force at his disposal. Mobile, urgent, impassioned, they struck at the English with such effect as can best be measured from the pleas for help sent from the north to Edward.[34] If the writers of these pleas, 'diligent and faithful friends' of the English king as they were careful to describe themselves, were prone to hide behind the excuse of superior enemy numbers – Murray, they said, led 'a very large body of rogues'[35] – we cannot doubt that the pressure upon them was intense.

It must be a matter of regret that we do not know the source of the new Scottish tactics, for such they were. It is quite understandable that the likes of Pilche should rely upon hit-and-run. But what of Murray himself? He had been raised in a tradition which, as Dunbar demonstrated, was both outmoded and self-destructive. Yet it does appear that, once returned to his homeland from Chester, he had no difficulty in adapting to the situation. Did he come to realise, once involved, that the tactics of the Pilche and the others with him were the only ones suitable in the circumstances? Or had he reached the obvious conclusion while a prisoner of the English? If we had the answer to this problem we might be closer to a realistic assessment of the respective merits of Murray and Wallace. All that can be said with any pretensions to accuracy is that Murray was swift to learn and a charismatic leader of the rebellion in the north. Throughout the summer, from May to August, he continued to pose an insuperable problem for the English and their supporters. Arrogantly he laid siege to Castle Urquhart, and although foiled in that attempt, he was not diverted from his purpose. He took from the English other castles, Inverness, Elgin, and Banff among them.

Edward had not been slow to react to news of the events in the north. Not all Scots were sympathetic to Murray; on them Edward had relied to keep the country quiet. Murray had not taken long to prove that the administration, in which Henry Cheyne, bishop of Aberdeen, and Effie, countess of Ross ranked high, could not cope with him. To stiffen their resolve, Edward released from his retinue of the Scottish lords whom he had summoned to join him on his continental expedition, John of Badenoch and John, earl of Buchan, both of them Comyns.[36] They, like a number of other Scottish lords, were perhaps less dedicated to the English cause than Edward would have wished. That at least was the opinion of Cressingham who was driven to report to Edward in the following terms:

> The peace on the other side of the Scottish Sea is still in obscurity, as it is said, as to the doings of the earls who are there. But at all events we hope that if our business succeeds well on the day of Saint Laurence as to the bishop of Glasgow and the others, as far as the people on the other side of the Scottish Sea are concerned, we hope soon to have them at our pleasure by God's grace. Sir Andrew de Rait[37] is going to you with a credence, which he has shown to me, and which is false in many points and obscure, as will be shown hereafter, as I fear; and, therefore, sire, if it be your pleasure, you will give little weight to it.[38]

Thus Cressingham relayed both his suspicions and his concern.[39] Indeed, Cressingham had seen his suspicions confirmed. By the time he was writing to Edward,[40] the volatile nature of the Scottish lords had already declared itself.[41] But both they and Cressingham had been overtaken by one far greater than they. In May, William Wallace, in the words of Fordun, had 'raised his head'. It is a curiously effective and telling phrase. Wallace, we learn from it, had suddenly erupted upon the scene, no longer obscure, to embody henceforth the spirit of Scottish nationalism. With the murder of the sheriff of Lanark, he sprang full-blown, as it were, into the national conscience and has remained there since. It was an act which was accorded a significance which it has not lost.

As is so often the case with Wallace, the events of May 1297 are unclear. The reason for the murder of William Heselrig, Edward's sheriff of Lanark, escapes us even now. The traditional account has not lost its potency:

Wallace had become a magnet for the discontented. He had recently married a young woman who lived in Lanark. Visiting her by stealth, as a marked man, he clashed with an English patrol. Fighting his way clear, he retreated to her house and as his pursuers hammered on the front door he escaped by the back to the rocky Cartland Crags. Enraged by the failure to capture him, Sir William Heselrig,[42] Sheriff of Lanark, ordered the house to be burned and all within it, wife and servants, to be put to the sword. From that day Wallace vowed an undying vengeance against the English.

Gathering together a band of desperate men, he fell by night on the sheriff and his armed guard, hewed the sheriff into small pieces with his own sword and burned the buildings and those within them.

> For the first time one of the high officials of the hated
> conquerors had been slain and a ripple of jubilation spread
> through the oppressed.

What we are offered here is the account by Blind Harry,[43]
rendered into today's English. Wallace thus gains his
revenge for the murder of his beloved in that bloody
fashion which so characterises him in the work of Blind
Harry. Heselrig, in this scenario, cannot simply be killed;
his body must be dismembered.[44] Those who made up
the sheriff's suite, whether they had played a part in the
murder of Marion Braidfute or not, cannot escape retribution and must be made to suffer, and with appropriate
horror.[45] Measured against certain of Wallace's later
recorded actions, this version of events at Lanark, open
to question though it may be, has the ring of authenticity.
The fate of Heselrig compares with that of Cressingham
after Stirling. The burning of buildings in Lanark differs
only in scale from what Wallace did in the north of
England. The burning alive of English soldiers was
something of which he was capable, especially if the story
of the Barns of Ayr is based on fact.[46] That Wallace
behaved violently at Lanark is indisputable. He was a
ferocious man; however motivated, he employed no half-
measures when faced with the enemy. Something of the
horror of Lanark can be gauged from the words of
Thomas Grey of Heton, whose father, also Thomas,
survived the event. Wallace

> came by night upon the said sheriff and surprised him,
> when Thomas Grey, who was at that time in the suite of
> the said sheriff, was left stripped for dead in the mêlée
> when the English were defending themselves. The said
> Thomas lay all night naked between the two burning
> houses which the Scots had set on fire, whereof the heat

kept life in him, until he was recognised at daybreak and carried off by William Lundy who caused him to be restored to good health.[47]

The origins of Wallace's ferociousness at Lanark need not lie in the death of Marion Braidfute. She, like another and far more celebrated Marion in an earlier age, belongs to the outlaw tradition rather than to history. Revenge may, of course, have taken Wallace to Lanark, revenge for an unknown friend or for other actions on the part of the English. A less romantic era, such as our own, might look for the reason for the murder of Heslerig in more reliable if pedestrian sources. Perhaps the most important clue to the circumstances it to be discovered in the indictment laid against Wallace at his trial in 1305.[48] There he was charged with having slain Heselrig on a day when the latter was holding a county court in Lanark. If this is the case, two explanations may be offered for Wallace's actions. The first is that he had personal reasons for murdering Heselrig. Heselrig in his official capacity may have entered some judgement against Wallace which led to a quarrel, then to murder. It will be remembered that neither Wallace's own name nor that of his brother Malcolm appeared on the Ragman Roll. Should that omission indicate that one or both of the brothers had been outlawed or found guilty of some offence against Edward, Heselrig's assize at Lanark may have been connected to the previous event. Wallace's descent on Lanark may therefore have been prompted by a desire to right a wrong; a refusal or threat on the part of the unfortunate sheriff may have brought about his death. The second explanation, more perhaps in keeping with Wallace's reputation, is that the assize at Lanark offered the chance to strike a blow at the representative of the English king as he was dispensing justice to an oppressed people. Wallace, therefore, would have no personal reason for acting. This second explanation, at least in retrospect, would seem symbolic, as was the absence of the Wallace name from the Ragman Roll.

It is debatable whether Wallace's motives at Lanark mattered at all. Premeditated or not, the timing of the murder was remarkable. Much of Scotland was already in a ferment; news of the disturbances could not entirely be suppressed by the authorities. The murder of Heselrig, dramatic, barbarous, had an immediate impact. Heselrig's death had several consequences. Of these, one perhaps has not always been given sufficient emphasis. Whatever his status before Lanark, Wallace was now an outlaw, one whom Edward was unlikely to pardon.[49] Like Bruce after Dumfries, Wallace after Lanark could not go back to what he had been. He was no longer anonymous; he was now identified as an enemy, soon no doubt to be the prey, of the English king. At Lanark Wallace had posed a challenge and offered an insult; Edward was not the man to ignore either. Strangely, however, in the light of the later significance attached to the murder of Heselrig, we can find no evidence of Edward's own reaction. This contrasts vividly with his behaviour in 1306, when he was informed of the incident at Dumfries. At first apparently loath to believe in Bruce's guilt, he did at length order action of the most extreme kind. Aymer de Valence was instructed, as Barbour tells us, 'to burn and slay and raise dragon',[50] and Edward without doubt planned for Bruce the same punishment he had inflicted on Wallace. If in 1297 he was as angered by the murder of Heselrig, we have no proof of it. His later viciousness is usually explained by the events of the intervening years and his own instability. Despite this, one cannot but wonder why, as far as we are aware, Wallace did not in 1297 seem to affect him personally.

Nonetheless, Wallace, in May 1297, may be said to have had no alternative to full-scale rebellion. In this he could not have succeeded, unless he is acknowledged to be of the stuff of heroes. After Lanark he did not run into hiding; he was available, visible, potent. For once English and Scottish chroniclers agree; Wallace's original band of some thirty men grew at once. It is to be expected that in the English accounts those who joined him would be characterised as scum and criminals. Thus we read: 'He [Wallace] . . . convoked all who were outlawed to himself, and acted as if he were the chief of them, and they increased to many people.'[51] Guisborough's description of Wallace's followers, who in his eyes are nothing but 'vagrants, fugitives, and outlaws', is balanced on the Scottish side by Fordun.[52] Here more honourable motives are ascribed to the Scots: 'From that time there were gathered to him all who were of bitter heart and were weighed down beneath the burden of bondage under the intolerable rule of English domination, and he became their leader.' For these unfortunates, rebellion was preferable to slavery. The calibre of person drawn to Wallace, whether we accept the one or the other version of events, cannot have been high. It tells us much of his ability that he was able to weld them into a coherent and successful force; no mere rabble could have defeated the English at Stirling.

In the increase in his force we may find a second consequence of the murder of Heselrig. It has been argued above that the assertion of the Lanercost chronicler that the bishop of Glasgow and James the Stewart inspired Wallace to rebellion is erroneous. His success at Lanark in killing the representative of the English king, and its effect upon recruitment, cannot have been unknown to the other two. It is at this point, rather than earlier, that they are likelier to have become involved with Wallace. Here was the opening for these rather timid men to stand with the new hero, to give him advice, above all perhaps, to provide men, horses, equipment. This is a less important role than Lanercost allocates to them. It is not to be disparaged, however. The support of Wishart and the Stewart, given their standing in Scotland, must have guaranteed Wallace a certain legitimacy and, with it, power.

With Heselrig dead, Wallace acted with great energy. That he was able to move, apparently, with total freedom cannot wholly have been the consequence of Lanark. A riposte on the part of the English was called for in these circumstances; no such is recorded. The English admini-stration was either paralysed by the speed of events both in the west and elsewhere or unable for some reason to put troops in the field. It is possible that attention was, after Lanark, concentrated on the border; the fear of a Scottish incursion was ever-present and Wallace's murder of Heselrig may have been seen as a preliminary to a raid south. Certainly, the atmosphere on the English side of the border was already tense; 'all the knights and free tenants (of Westmorland) are in Cumberland to defend the march between England and Scotland against the coming of the Scots.'[53] The propaganda value of Lanark was no doubt considerable, but English inertia gave Wallace space and time in which to plan and carry out his next endeavour.

Heselrig had been an important official but Wallace now aimed for a more senior figure. He raced to Scone where William Ormsby, like Heselrig the dispenser of Edward's law, was in residence. At Wallace's side was a

new colleague, Sir William Douglas, who had surrendered the castle of Berwick to Edward in the year before.
Douglas, know as 'Le Hardi', the Bold or the Rash,
shared a propensity for violence with Wallace; it did not
require the sack of Berwick, where the inhabitants 'fell
like autumn leaves',[54] to turn Douglas to extreme conduct. In his early years, he had survived an attack on the
family home at Fawdon in Northumberland. According
to his father, the assailants wounded William so badly
that they all but severed his head from his body.[55] Well
before the outbreak of war, Douglas had fallen foul of
Edward I, by whom he was imprisoned, because of 'certain transgressions imputed to him'. One such trans-
gression concerned the circumstances of his marriage to
his second wife, Eleanor of Lovain or Ferrers. While
Eleanor, the widow of the lord of Groby in Leicestershire,
was staying at Tranent with friends, Douglas abducted
her and forced her into marriage.[56] Because Eleanor had
given her word not to remarry without permission from
the English king, Edward reacted angrily, had Douglas'
lands in Northumberland seized, and ordered his arrest.
Douglas' imprisonment was brief enough, and where he
had defied Edward with his marriage to Eleanor, he also
treated the Guardians of Scotland with as much contempt.[57] He found himself in prison once again, for
imprisoning three of their men unlawfully; one escaped,
one Douglas had beheaded, and the third died in prison.
Under King John, he manifested the same disregard for
authority, when he kept royal officials locked in his castle
against their will.

Douglas' word could not be trusted. This Edward
knew well and when the garrison of Berwick surrendered
in 1296, Douglas was exempted from the terms granted
to the two hundred members of the garrison. In his case,

Edward insisted that Douglas remain with him until the end of the campaign. Douglas was still with Edward in June 1296, when he swore allegiance to him in Edinburgh. Two months later, he again swore allegiance to Edward, this time at Berwick.[58] What his motives were in subsequently joining Wallace is unclear. At least one authority on the Douglases sees him as a patriot[59] and his death as an English prisoner, by some attributed to murder,[60] may help to portray him as such. But he was a restless, brutal man, drawn by the prospect of action, not merely against the English. Wallace, at this time possibly an outlaw and of an inferior class, was not a natural ally for Douglas, who not long after the attack on Scone returned to his normal environment, association with with his peers. Even there, some doubts exist as to that relationship. As unreliable to the English as Douglas himself was Robert Bruce, the future king. Because of this, Guisborough reports,[61] Bruce was required to swear allegiance by the bishop of Carlisle, John de Halton. He did so, and to prove his loyalty raided Douglas Castle and carried off Douglas' wife and children. Bruce's biographer describes this venture as 'a mock attack . . . to deceive the English',[62] an opinion also found elsewhere. [63] He is then said to have attempted, fruitlessly, to persuade the men of Annandale to join him against Edward; his words, if reported accurately, are indeed stirring.[64] But we cannot be certain that the raid on Douglasdale did not have some other motive, perhaps personal; Douglas was, as we have seen, an erratic man, like Bruce himself, and it is not inconceivable that at this time there was bad blood between them.

Whatever Douglas' motives, he proved valuable to Wallace after Lanark. The raid on Scone, some eighty miles from Lanark, was carried out on horseback. The

mounts may have been Douglas' contribution to Wallace's
force. Wallace almost succeeded in his intention. Ormsby,
however, learned of his approach and fled, but, like
Edward II after Byland, was forced to leave valuables
behind.[65] He was back in England in August, still
retaining the confidence of his king; it was to Ormsby
that Edward entrusted the investigation into the affairs
of the see of Durham, when Bishop Bek had fallen foul
of Edward.[66] If Wallace had failed in his primary
intention, of freeing Scotland from another English
official, the raid encouraged further action against the
forces of the occupation. The rebellion flared between
the Forth and the Tay, with the support of Macduff, the
son of the earl of Fife. The English were forced behind
the walls of their castles, against which the Scots could
do little, although Wallace himself would later return to
besiege Dundee.

At his trial in 1305, Wallace would be charged with
atrocities committed during the war. These included the
murder of English clerics. This was not a charge he dig-
nified with an answer, perhaps because it was true. If the
worst atrocities were committed either at his order or in
defiance of him during the raid into England after Stirling,
it seems that as early as the summer of 1297, attacks
were being made upon English clergy. If we are to believe
Guisborough,[67] the Scots, foiled perhaps by the retreat
of the English soldiers into their castles, vented their
spleen on such unfortunate clergy as they could lay their
hands on. Neither age nor sex saved lives: 'They [the
Scots] took old men, priests and women of the English
nation (whom they had specially kept alive for the
purpose) to bridges over the rivers; and when they had
tied their hands or feet together so that they could not
swim, they threw them or pushed them into the water,

laughing and jeering as they struggled and went under.'
For sport, others were brought to trial before Wallace
himself, 'that bandit' as Guisborough calls him. Still
others were seized from sanctuary and butchered.

If Guisborough was not concerned, any more than
other chroniclers, with strict accuracy as regards Wallace,
it is to be expected that the Scots would not distinguish
between any of the hated English who fell into their
hands. Berwick was too recent a memory and the Scottish
clergy themselves were not moved by Christian charity
towards their English brethren. We should not be surpised
if English clergy in Scotland were viewed with hostility.
Before the outbreak of war, the expulsion of foreign
nationals had become the practice on both sides of the
border. Matters deteriorated with the murder in Berwick
of some English merchants, an event which moved the
English king, himself not free of the charge of xenophobia,
to an indignant outburst.[68] English clergy who remained
in Scotland would in all probability be viewed as a
potential fifth column, to be dealt with as harshly as circumstances might suggest. The Church in Scotland itself
cannot be cleared of complicity in the maltreatment of
the English. One authority has argued that the Church
'preached the sacred duty of war against the English yoke
and in the persons of her bishops and her priests often
led the way on the field of battle itself'.[69] Bishop Wishart
was no warrior, unlike William Sinclair, bishop of
Dunkeld under Robert I, but Wishart, from what we
know of him, could inspire by words rather than deeds.
In all likelihood, the lesser clergy were as bellicose as
their betters; the case of Thomas of Edinburgh, who
dared to excommunicate Edward I publicly, cannot have
been unique.[70] With the Church so militant, the laymen
of Scotland had an example to follow in the matter of

captured English clergy. A precedent and a tradition of violence had been set from the beginning of the war and Wallace would not restrain his men even if he had wanted to. As he had shown at Lanark, he was fully alive to the use to which atrocity could be put. It had brought him recruits then and stultified the English response; he had no cause to change his approach afterwards.

Whether inspired by the example of Wallace or not, those Scots who had failed against Edward in 1296 were ready to try again. Wishart and James the Stewart had plucked up their courage and with Robert Bruce, grandson of the Competitor and the future king, were in rebellion independently of Wallace. Douglas, from the vicinity of Perth where he had been with Wallace, joined with them, as did others. This aristocratic uprising did not endure. The participants were not sustained by a single-mindedness similar to Wallace's. If it is unnecessary to disparage their motives, we may question their dedication. Wishart and James the Stewart were not without courage but were not in military terms heroic figures. Their strength was in political manoeuvring. Bruce, although Barrow's defence of him is, as always, authoritative,[71] cannot easily be cleared of the charge that his cause was always Bruce. Unlike his father, who remained faithful to the English king who so despised him, Bruce was not unworthy of the English suspicions to which the bishop of Carlisle gave expression.[72]

The English had no difficulty in dealing with the Scots. Already in June, Henry Percy, grandson of Edward's viceroy Warenne, and Robert Clifford, a member of the great Westmorland family, had received their instructions from Edward.[73] The two were to 'arrest, imprison, and "justify" all disturbers of the peace in Scotland'. Cressingham was 'to give his personal aid and counsel' to the northerners. Percy and Clifford did not delay. Perhaps in part motivated by the knowledge that any success by the Scots might lead to an invasion of the north of England with consequent effects upon their own lands, they gathered levies in the Border counties and by the end of June were at Ayr.[74] In choosing to move against Bruce, the Stewart, and Wishart, Percy and Clifford achieved much at little expense. They had no difficulty in facing down the Scots lords who surrendered to them at Irvine (*see* Chapter 4) without striking a blow.

NOTES

1. *Scalacronica*, 17.

2. 'A man does well to rid himself of shit.'

3. It is Cressingham who is generally considered the more arrogant of the two. Certainly he was not spared in the chronicles, e.g. Guisborough, 294, 302, 303. His birth may have counted against him. Surrey had no such excuse for his arrogance towards the Scots.

4. Prestwich, *The Three Edwards, War and State in England, 1272–1377*, 50: 'Edward's successes were achieved as a result of well-organised logistics, not by tactical or strategic skill.' For Edward's wars consult principally J.E. Morris, e.g. *The Welsh Wars of Edward I*, 1901; *Bannockburn*, 1914, chap. 3 entitled 'Tactics before Bannockburn'. For a more specialised aspect of the war with Scotland see his article, 'Mounted Infantry in Medieval Warfare', *Trans. Cumb. & West. Ant. & Arch. Soc.* 23 April 1914.

5. Barron, 77.

6. We are in any case left to guess what Barron meant by the term 'an army'.

7. Barrow: *Robert Bruce*, 216, writes of Methven as 'a rout rather than a battle'.

8. Guisborough, 294.

9. Prestwich; *Edward I*, 27–28.

10. A characteristic more evident in his campaigning than in his politics.

11. On the trial see Bellamy, op. cit., 24 ff. Prestwich; *Edward I*, 202, comments that 'a judgement of blood' was expected from the parliament.

12. *Dictionary of National Biography*.

13. His own brother, Edmund of Lancaster, may be cited as an example.

14. *Dictionary of National Biography*.

15. Guisborough, 216; Clanchy: *From Memory to Written Record*, 1979, 21–28.

16. Guisborough, 303.

17. Prestwich: *Edward I*, 124.

18. Ibid., 123.

19. Ibid., 124.

20. Guisborough, 303.

21. Watson: *Under the Hammer*, 38.

22. Barron, op. cit., chaps 3–6, has the fullest account of these uprisings.

23. *Lanercost*, 122.

24. Barrow: *Robert Bruce*, 114. For the role of the Scottish Church in the war, see Barron, op. cit., 24–25, and Barrow: *Kingdom*, chap. 8.

25. Guisborough, 299.

26. Lanercost, 163.

27. But see below, chap. 5, for the famous incident at Hexham.

28. See below, chap. 4.

29. As Wallace is linked with Wishart, so is Murray with his uncle, David of Moravia, who became bishop of Moray in 1289; Barrow: *Kingdom*, 238–39.

30. Barron, op. cit., 32–57, is the major, if partial source, on Murray.

31. *Cal. Docs Scot.*, ii 742.

32. Barron, op. cit., 33.

33. *Cal. Docs Scot.*, ii 922.

34. Ibid., 922, 931.

35. Stevenson (ed.): *Docs Illustrative of the History of Scotland, 1288–1306*, ii, 212.

36. Guisborough, 297.

37. Of Rait Castle, near Nairn. He was a neighbour of Andrew Murray.

38. Barron, op. cit., 56.

39. Similar suspicions are to be found in Guisborough, 297.

40. 5 August 1297.

41. See below, chap. 4.

42. Barrow: *Robert Bruce*, 117 n, argues the case most convincingly for this spelling in preference to any other. Kightly, op. cit., 158, has 'Haselrig'.

43. Sixth Book. The modern version is to be found in McNair Scott: *Robert Bruce*, 1982, 39.

44. *Harry*, Sixth Book.

45. Ibid.

46. We may take leave to doubt the episode, although Randall Wallace in the script for *Braveheart*, cannot resist it. It is in an English atrocity, recounted by Harry, that we find Sir Reginald Crawford hanged, not at, as is historically correct, Carlisle but at the Barns of Ayr. The same inaccuracy occurs in Barbour: *The Bruce,* ed. Duncan 1997, 152. Wallace, according to Harry, exacted a fearful revenge at the same place. The poet dwells with relish on the burning alive of English soldiers here.

47. The *Scalacronica*, from which this excerpt is taken, was written when the author was a prisoner of the Scots a generation after Lanark. He has surely captured the horror of the event.

48. See below, chap. 10. Also Bellamy, op. cit., 36 ff.

49. Although in the indictment, mention is made of the offer of a pardon, which, presumably, included the murder.

50. Barbour, op. cit., 90.

51. Guisborough, 295.

52. See also Bower, Book XI.

53. Watson: *Under the Hammer*, 58.

54. *Rishanger*, 373.

55. Fraser: *The Douglas Book*, vol. I, 1885, 60.

56. Ibid., 75 ff; Barrow: *Robert Bruce*, 83; *Cal. Docs Scot.*, ii, 357, 358, 365, 429, 431, 466.

57. Interestingly, however, the Guardians, anxious to preserve

the integrity of the Kingdom of Scotland, were loath to hand over Douglas and his new wife when Edward I demanded that they be handed over to him after the marriage: Fraser, op. cit., 76–77.

58. 28 August 1296.

59. Fraser, op. cit., 102. Barbour, op. cit., 60, refer to him as 'a martyr'.

60. *Scalacronica*, 124.

61. Guisborough, 295.

62. Barrow: *Robert Bruce*, 84.

63. McNair Scott, op. cit., 40–41, tells us that Edward I had ordered Bruce through his father to attack and seize Douglas Castle.

64. Guisborough, 297–98.

65. Guisborough, 295.

66. Prestwich: *Edward I*, 544.

67. Guisborough, 295.

68. Edward's attitude was not always consistent, he had no trouble in enlisting felons, including murderers, to campaign against the Scots. His opinion of the Scots was made clear in his comment to Warenne, which see above.

69. See Barrow: *Kingdom*, chap. 8. Sinclair, who repulsed an English invasion in 1317, was called 'my bishop' by Bruce. On Sinclair's subsequent career, note Conclusion, below.

70. Barrow: *Robert Bruce*, 154.

71. Barrow, op. cit., 119ff.

72. John de Halton became a staunch opponent of Bruce after the latter's rebellion.

73. *Cal. Docs Scots*, 887.

74. Guisborough, 297–8.

–4–

The Time of Revenge, 1297–1298

'We shall prove this in their very beards'

Wallace shared with the great commanders of history the ability to recognise and take advantage of an opportunity.[1] Lanark and Scone had brought him to prominence. It was not merely those of his own station who rallied to him, for according to Guisborough, while he was at Perth, he was approached by representatives, who came to him 'in great haste on behalf of certain magnates of the kingdom of Scotland'. This has been taken to mean that these messengers were acting for the Stewart, Bishop Wishart, and Bruce.[2] Such an opinion concurs with the belief that they were behind Wallace's uprising at Lanark in May; they were now seeking, that is, more directly to involve him in their endeavours. Whether or not that is the case, in July 1297, they were now to present Wallace, albeit inadvertently, with a crucial opening. Irvine marked a significant stage in his public career, perhaps more so even than Lanark. He was, as so often, swift to profit from it.

Wallace and Andrew Murray, alone of the Scottish principals in the events of that summer, were untainted by the fiasco of Irvine. It is not clear whether, like Douglas, Wallace had ridden south to join with Bruce and the others. If present at all during the preliminary manoeuvrings,[3] he had left, it may be guessed in disgust, before the capitulation to Percy and Clifford on 7 July.[4] The failure of the nerve of the Scots leaders had one interesting consequence which may help us to understand Wallace's own attitude to his colleagues. So distressed was he by the behaviour of Bruce, Wishart and the Stewart, that Sir Richard Lundie switched to the English side.[5] He was a useful acquisition.[6] That contemporary criticism of the Scots leadership cannot be discounted. It is impossible to believe that others did not share his despair, even if they did not at this point defect with him. His action has, however, been balanced by a more sympathetic view of those he had criticised, and a different role suggested for them. Thus a connection has been drawn between the undoubtedly protracted negotiations with the English at Irvine and the freedom these same negotiations offered to Wallace.[7] That the Scots had a definite purpose in prolonging the talks with Percy and Clifford appears to be the opinion of at least one English chronicler. For him the link with Wallace is evident: 'And there [i.e. at Irvine], day after day slipped by in time-wasting bickerings and arguments, while that bandit Wallace gathered the people to him . . . By now, indeed, he had raised an immense army.'[8]

Wallace was extremely active in the month after the surrender at Irvine.[9] To see in him one who was in any part of a plot hatched before Irvine stretches the imagination. He is more likely to have gone ahead with his own plans in contempt of the other leaders in the west. His vigour contrasts starkly with their hesitation. One factor must not be overlooked in the light of their future attitude to him. They were intent upon protecting their position and their lands, something denied to Wallace who because of the murder of Heselrig, was an outlaw. They were, at Irvine as ever, both more realistic and self-seeking than he was or became.[10] By seeking terms on 7 July, they must have enraged if not yet alienated Wallace. His reaction to the disgrace at Irvine was a sharp raid on Wishart's palace at Ancrum.[11] From there he carried away not only a number of the bishop's possessions but also his sons who are, perhaps for reasons of delicacy, referred to as his nephews. But the grudge which the raid suggests he bore against Wishart did not last.

Percy and Clifford, surprisingly, did not immediately trade upon their defeat of the Scots. Wallace can only have been encouraged by this. Percy and Clifford do not appear to have been averse to the period of relaxation which the negotiations allowed them. Having defeated the Scots in the simplest of ways, they were, understandably but mistakenly, somewhat smug. The martial determination of the Irvine campaign had lapsed, as Cressingham indicates in a letter of 23 July to Edward.[12] He was himself not without military pretensions, and his account of recent developments is informative. He represents himself as bent upon action against the Scots while the victors of Irvine will not move, he tells his king, until the arrival of the dilatory Warenne at Berwick. It is from this letter that we learn that Wallace, 'with a large company', was in the Forest of Selkirk.[13] Cressingham was already describing Wallace to Edward as 'like one who holds himself against your peace'. It is a revealing and accurate phrase. For Cressingham, rather more perceptive than his English colleagues, not to mention certain of the Scots, Wallace was not waiting upon events or orders.

Such was not, of course, Wallace's nature. Once his mind was made up, and he was far from rash in making it up, he acted forcefully and with dispatch. Thus, there is no evidence that in July 1297, or indeed at any time until after he had resigned the Guardianship in the next year, he allowed his conduct to be dictated by his ostensible superiors. If he had ever been subservient, other than in the purely formal sense, to the likes of Wishart and the Stewart, that had passed with the murder of Heselrig. It is therefore possible that it is from the summer of 1297 that we may trace the animosity of the Scots lords to him. Wallace's inherent aggressiveness, in the personal and military senses, cut across preconceptions of what was fitting. He acted on his own judgement. This cannot have endeared him to Bruce or later to Comyn, any more than it did to Edward. These three, even when enemies, shared a common heritage from which Wallace was excluded. A later comment may help us to understand his relations with the Scots nobility.[14] Having being regaled with a list of Wallace's virtues, we are told:

> Gaining strength daily, he in a short time, by force, and by dint of his prowess, brought all the magnates of Scotland under his sway, whether they would or not. Some of the magnates, moreover, as did not thankfully obey his commands, he took and browbeat, and handed over to custody, until they should utterly submit to his good pleasure. And when all had thus been subdued, he manfully betook himself to the storming of castles and fortified towns in which the English ruled; for he aimed at quickly and thoroughly freeing his country and overthrowing the enemy.

It is easy to detect in this passage the prejudice of the writer. We are required to believe that not until he had mastered the forces within Scotland itself which hindered independence was Wallace able to turn his attention to the English. A potential opposition to his strategy had to be eliminated. The existence of this hostile element is a matter for debate, of course. It is also true that what we read relates to the period of Wallace's ascendancy, when because of the Guardianship he had absolute authority. Yet we can recognise here the Wallace of the summer of 1297. He was already distinguished by his single-mindedness. It led him into that kind of ruthlessness of which we have read.[15] He did not scruple to force fellow-Scots, of whatever station, to obey him in the war against England.

An interesting example of Wallace's attitude is to be found in the case of Michael de Miggel.[16] In September 1305, a month after Wallace's execution, Michael was called to explain his conduct at Perth before, among others, Malise, earl of Strathearn, and Sir Malcolm de Inverpefray. To them he related his treatment at Wallace's hands. He claimed that he had twice escaped from Wallace and that, recaptured, he had survived only through the intervention of some of Wallace's men. Wallace relented but warned him that a third attempt at escape would mean death. Aware no doubt of the danger in which his unwilling association with Wallace placed him, Michael pleaded that 'he remained with William through fear of death and not of his own will'. Fortunately for him, his story was believed. Edward, who with the death of Wallace seemed to have become more reasonable, ordered that Michael's goods and chattels were to be restored to him.[17] There is no reason to suppose that Michael de Miggel was in any way unusual in having been dragooned into service by Wallace.[18]

If this is indeed so, two questions pose themselves. Firstly, who in Wallace's eyes was the enemy? The answer must be that he regarded as such not merely the English who occupied his country but also any who did not identify themselves, to his satisfaction, as actively hostile to the English. It was a simplistic and dangerous stance to take. It demonstrated an ignorance of, or perhaps an indifference to, the realities of political life and, finally, it undid him. There can be no doubt, however, that in the circumstances of the summer of 1297, it was the only position for one with his intentions and temperament.

That brings us to the second question: what was Wallace trying to do at this time? If the answer is obvious – to rid Scotland of English rule and to restore Balliol – it is not complete. Wallace was intelligent enough to realise that to expel the English from Scotland would not of itself restore Balliol to the throne. Such a restoration, being essentially a political matter, was not something of which Wallace was capable in the summer of 1297, although he remained dedicated to the idea. He was, however, able to inflict on the English enemy such blows as they had not yet suffered. In this connection a consideration of his actions after Irvine is instructive.

As has been seen from Cressingham's letter of 23 July, Wallace was based on the Forest of Selkirk. At the same time, Cressingham was telling Edward how desperate the situation, from the English standpoint, had become: 'By far the greater part of your counties in the Scottish kingdom are still not provided with helpers, because they have been killed, besieged, or imprisoned, or have abandoned their bailiwicks and dare not go back. And in some shire the Scots have appointed and established bailiffs and officials. Thus no shire is properly kept save for Berwick and Roxburghshire, and they only recently.'[19]

It has been argued that Wallace alone could not be responsible for the conditions which Cressingham was describing.[20] In that he had certainly not taken into his hands the reins of government, the argument is correct. The authority he enjoyed was still military rather than political; there was no question of his being endowed with the Guardianship at this period. But who other than he on the Scottish side had the name, backed by success, to inspire the reversal portrayed by Cressingham? The Scottish officials who are referred to by the treasurer were not and could not be Wallace's creation. We are therefore speaking of their resuming a role with which they had been familiar under Balliol. Nevertheless, they could not have resumed that role unaided. Wallace, by his actions and his example, made that possible.

He had with him in the Forest of Selkirk a large following. He made no effort, to our knowledge, to move with it against the English who, as Cressingham's letter of 23 July makes clear, were waiting for their commander, Warenne, to arrive.[21] That Wallace did not do so is important. Given the use he made of intelligence, he might well have thought that an attack on the English, leaderless and gathering as they were, was worthwhile. If he considered that possibility, he did not act upon it. Instead, as we know, he turned north and east from Selkirk. Blind Harry has him reach Aberdeen,[22] where he burned a hundred English ships. Time and distance combine to make this, as is true of so much of what Harry tells us, impossible. Wallace, however, did move rapidly. He swept across Perthshire and Fife, clearing them of the English, and in early August began the siege of Dundee castle.[23]

Cressingham refers to the size of Wallace's army. As the speed of Wallace's progress proves, it can have been an army in name only; he would have been hindered rather than helped in what he did by large numbers.

There is another factor to be considered. A strong rumour current in the summer of 1297 must have contributed both to the numbers and the dubious quality of many who came to him in the Forest of Selkirk. It was the intention of the English king, according to the rumour, 'to seize all the middle folk of Scotland and send them overseas in his war [i.e. with France], to their great damage and destruction'.[24] We cannot confirm the truth of this rumour. But the Scots had reason perhaps to be afraid. With the conquest of Scotland, as he imagined, complete, Edward had already taken with him a number of Scots lords as he prepared for his campaign against Philip IV. The exactions of his officials under Cressingham supported the argument that he looked upon Scotland as a fief, to be used as he thought suitable, its people therefore at his disposal.[25] However, anxious to serve under Wallace in the light of this threat to their freedom, not all who believed the rumour can have been skilled soldiers. They required training and discipline, qualities which he had succeeded in instilling in them by the time of Falkirk.

Bower offers a fanciful version of how Wallace achieved his aim:

And as he regards the whole multitude of his followers he decreed on pain of death that once the lesser men among the middling people (or in practice those who were less robust) had been assembled before him, one man was always chosen out of five from all the groups of five to be over the other four and called a quaternion; his commands were to be obeyed by them in all matters, and whoever did not obey was to be killed. In a similar manner also on moving up to the men who were more robust and effective there was always to be a tenth man, called a decurion over each nine, and a twentieth over each nineteen, and so on moving up to each thousand, (called a chiliarch), and beyond to the top. At length he himself as pre-eminent over everyone else was regarded as commander or general, whom all were bound to obey to the death. With everyone harmoniously approving the law (or substitute for law), they chose him as their captain, and promised to keep the said statute until the succession of a legitimate king.[26]

We may question whether Wallace would describe his officers in classical terms. Equally, Wallace is seen here as emulating Moses, who in Exodus, 'chose able men out of all Israel, and made them heads over the people, rulers of thousands, rulers of hundreds, rulers of fifties, and rulers of ten'. But, Greek, Roman and Biblical references aside, Bower does emphasise those methods through which he sought to mould those under him into a cohesive fighting force: iron discipline, promotion on merit rather than social class, general agreement, and himself as supreme and sole commander. By the time of Falkirk he had come near to his ideal; at Stirling, the forces which he then used had a different role, one which depended on an ability to improvise, as well as on the other characteristics on which he laid stress.

The force which he led out of the Forest of Selkirk must have been only part of the 'immense army' of which Cressingham wrote. Wallace, interestingly, was returning across the Forth to an area with which, both in fact and in fiction, he was familiar. It was here that he had struck in that raid which had almost resulted in the capture of Ormsby. That exploit, it has been noted, required horses, and it is possible that, two months later, he was again at the head of a force largely if not entirely mounted.

Mobility was essential if he was to carry out his plan of harassment of the English. He would be unwilling to be hampered, in this undertaking, by any great mass of infantry. The nature of any occupation of a country is that it can never be complete. Key centres are used for the purpose of local government, castles held, the network of roads dominated. Wallace, like Murray, knew this, hence his strategy. Part of his force must have been professional, composed of soldiers owing their first loyalty to the great feudal figures, such as the Stewart and Robert Bruce. Their presence with Wallace may be proof of the most valuable contribution that the magnates themselves, found wanting first at Dunbar then at Irvine, could make at this time to the cause which Wallace now personified.

If Wallace had detached part of the army of the Forest of Selkirk with the intention of harassing the English north of the Forth, another consequence followed. It drew the English army at Berwick, with Warenne at last at its head, away from the secure base which that town offered. Warenne was at first no more willing than before to stir himself.[27] He was no longer young, less than enthusiastic about the war in Scotland, and would therefore be far from disappointed when, on 18 August, he was recalled. He was to join Edward on the Continent. To take his place as keeper of Scotland, Brian Fitzalan of Bedale was nominated. Warenne's replacement was a man of considerable experience of Scottish affairs, having been made a Guardian by Edward I as early as June of 1291.[28] Fitzalan was, however, very conscious that he was not a wealthy man. Unless that unfortunate situation was remedied, he reasoned, he felt unable to accept the honour which Edward held out to him. The king, with heavy commitments, sensed an opportunity to use the change of command to reduce both Fitzalan's salary and the forces available to him. He rejected Fitzalan's argument. The lethargic and indifferent Warenne was to remain in command in Scotland.[29]

The contrast between Warenne and Cressingham, the one less than eager, the other, if we can rely on his own words, pressing for an early engagement with the Scots, did not augur well for the English army as it advanced from Berwick. It is doubtful if either understood the threat which Wallace, the new man, posed. Warenne had learned his trade as a soldier in the baronial wars of the reign of Henry III, some thirty years previously. His success at Dunbar in 1296, if important, did not prepare him for what faced him now. Cressingham, lacking the advantages which his nominal superior enjoyed from birth, was both impatient for and intent on advancement through solving the problem of Scotland.[30] It was a fateful liaison. They did, however, share a contempt for the enemy. Warenne, for so long absent if not in hiding in England, did not have the advantage of direct involvement in the rapidly changing situation of the country for which he held responsibility. Cressingham, who did have that advantage, was as conservative as the other when it came to the means of dealing with the resurgent Scots. Neither appears to have been in the slightest doubt that the Scots, lately humiliated at Irvine, would once again be readily trounced by the traditional use of the English army.

The size of that army eludes us. As always, we turn in vain to the contemporary chronicles if we hope for accuracy. Guisborough, even if able to draw on the experience of a participant, Sir Marmaduke de Tweng, cannot be cleared of exaggeration. Tweng was a veteran soldier who later fell into Wallace's hands but survived to fight and be captured at Bannockburn; he would hardly be the source, as has been suggested,[31] of the figure which Guisborough gives.[32] One thousand horse and fifty thousand foot are nicely rounded numbers, but debatable. Wiser perhaps, Lanercost, eschewing the need to be precise, is content with a reference to 'a great army'.[33] This vague but suitably impressive description was to be echoed by Fordun. We may come nearer to the truth if we revert to the letters of Cressingham in the search for some approximation of accuracy. The treasurer, whose industry in reporting to his king is quite remarkable, had no cause to distort the numbers of those at his disposal when he wrote to Edward on 23 July. He stated that he had mustered at Roxburgh three hundred horse and ten thousand foot.[34] This was for the time, after all, a not inconsiderable force, one which bears comparison with those on either side at the majority of battles with which we are most familiar.[35] To Cressingham and Warenne, both assuming the outcome guaranteed, it would have seemed more than adequate for the purpose.

When we turn to the numbers of the Scottish army which would face them at Stirling we are no better informed. That army was the joint responsibility of Wallace and Andrew Murray, each of whom had brought contingents. The exact numbers with each of the two are not recorded, nor is there any way of measuring the proportion of foot to horse soldiers. If, like Wallace, Murray had relied on cavalry to give him success against the English, he, again like Wallace, would have recourse to infantry in the forthcoming battle. Cressingham and Warenne had reached Stirling by the first week in September. At some date before this Wallace and Murray, whose respective campaigns were so similar, had met and at once had discovered an affinity which caused them to realise the advantages of a single opposition to the English. We cannot suppose that their meeting was accidental. Each would have known of the other; their successes were based on the same strategy, and that strategy depended upon good intelligence. It is possible that they met at Dundee, which Wallace was besieging. If so, the date may have been on or about 8 September. Lanercost informs us that it was at this date, the Nativity of the Glorious Virgin, that 'they [i.e. the Scots] began to show themselves in rebellion'. It is a strange remark in the light of what had gone before; it may reflect a later view that the decision to fight the army led by Warenne and Cressingham, was taken then. Since Wallace and Murray were at the head of the Scots at Stirling, the chronicle may be referring to them. In any case Wallace and Murray would have been in no doubt as to the destination of the English. The strategic importance of the castle of Stirling, overlooking the crossing of the Forth, was as clear to them as to the English.

Fordun casts an interesting light on the actions of Wallace as he moved from Dundee to Stirling. Wallace, he tells us, learned of the advance of the English and at once got ready to march to Stirling. Before setting out, however, he 'entrusted the care and charge of the castle to the burgesses of that town [Dundee] on pain of loss of life and limb'. Here again we have, if the evidence is correct, an example of Wallace's ruthlessness. He appears to have had no hesitation in employing threats in pursuit of his aims. We know him to have been a harsh man, but why was it necessary, once again, to browbeat those who ought to have been his allies? The incident tells us perhaps more about the attitude of adherents to the Scottish cause than about Wallace himself. The good folk of Dundee were alive to the possibility of retribution if Wallace, the hero of the moment, failed at Stirling. They cannot have been unique in their uncertainty.

The battle of Stirling was fought on 11 September. It was preceded by an intriguing intervention on the part of certain Scots nobles. The English reached the Forth in the first week of the month. On 9 September James the Stewart and Malcolm, earl of Lennox at the head of other nobles approached Warenne with the offer of arbitrating with the Scots who were stationed on the Abbey Craig. If Cressingham, as seems possible, demurred, Warenne was more agreeable. We can only guess at the motives of the nobles and whether they made a genuine attempt to carry out their promise. According to Lanercost, the Stewart at least was guilty of treachery. A more modern view suggests that the Stewart and his companions hoped to avert a slaughter of the Scots.[36] If they approached Wallace, he would not be of a mood to put faith in them; Irvine was too close. The lords, in any case, returned to Warenne the next day to confess failure. Perhaps as a sop, they undertook to join him on the eleventh with forty knights.

As the lords left the English camp, an incident occurred which demonstrated the volatile nature of the situation. Guisborough tells what happened in these terms:

> As they [i.e. the Scots] were leaving our camp that evening, they met a band of our returning foragers and began abusing them, and Lennox wounded a foot-soldier in the neck with his sword. When this was known to our army, everyone hurried to arm themselves, and they brought the wounded and bleeding man before the Earl of Surrey, crying out that vengeance should be taken that very night. But the earl replied, 'Let us wait tonight, and see whether they keep their promise in the morning; then we shall better be able to demand satisfaction for this insult.

Warenne's quaint belief in the knightly right to reply is

faintly ridiculous to us. It is as incomprehensible as the exact role of the Scots lords. Wallace, as has been suggested, can have had no faith in them. They may, despite this, have acted after a discussion with him and Murray; the two commanders would not be unwilling to benefit from any delay which the lords could gain for them. It is difficult to believe that Lennox and the Stewart could hope to assume command of the Scots army, even if they had the courage. This was the time of Wallace and Murray. The lords did in the event have a further part to play in the battle of Stirling, but it was a minor one and far from heroic. Their force of cavalry was allocated no function in the plan which Wallace and Murray employed on 11 September. That plan appears to have been largely improvised, and was the work of men of a different mentality from the lords'. It is noteworthy, nevertheless, that the contemporary accounts of the battle lay such emphasis on the involvement of the lords. If noteworthy, it is not surprising; we sense that the chroniclers are no more able to give credit to Wallace than they were in describing what had happened at Lanark.

On the evening of 10 September, having allowed the Scots lords to depart, Warenne had informed his officers that the army would cross the bridge the following morning. Amazingly, he slept in. Before he rose, the army began the crossing. In the account in Guisborough, from which so much of our information comes, some five thousand infantry had reached the other side of the bridge. As it was capable of taking only two men abreast, this manoeuvre could not have been speedy. Wallace and Murray, with a coolness remarkable in the circumstances, held fast on the Abbey Craig. The temptation to attack the English must have been great, but it was resisted. In their restraint it is possible to see the implementation of a scheme, which was at length put into effect. This, of course, is the accepted view. In this, Wallace and Murray intended from the beginning to throw their army down on the English as they crossed the bridge. If that is so, one wonders why they did not take this first opportunity. That they did not then launch the onslaught makes it likely that they had not yet decided to fight at all. Thus, they watched and waited. That part of the English army which had crossed did not remain over the bridge; it was recalled because Warenne had not yet risen. This failure of the English to consolidate their hold on the river-bank was a piece of good fortune for Wallace and Murray. If it is indeed true that five thousand infantry had made the crossing, that was a formidable force; it would have given the two commanders pause. The outcome of the battle might have been different, if indeed an engagement had taken place at all.

What was already, from the English point of view, farcical, grew worse. In keeping with his somewhat inappropriate code of honour, Warenne insisted on creating several new knights. Of these, Guisborough dolefully tells us, 'many were to fall that day'. Warenne then ordered the crossing to begin. Once more those who had gone forward were called back, for it was seen that the Stewart and Lennox, set on a place in history, were returning. They had not brought with them the forty horsemen they had promised. This was interpreted as a good sign; the Scots, Warenne thought, were come to surrender. On the contrary, the lords had come to confess failure. As Guisborough relates, 'they only made excuses, saying they could neither persuade their followers to submit nor even obtain horses or weapons from them'. Quite who these followers were we can only guess. If it is a reference to

Wallace and Murray, it is ludicrous, since they were in no sense followers. If a mention of the retinue of the lords, their numbers were hardly sufficient to be of consequence in the battle to come.

Warenne was not yet done with talking. Despite the threat which Wallace and Murray posed from the height of the Abbey Craig, despite the admitted futility of the endeavours of the Scots lords and their brief but vicious treachery of the night before, he was not ready to fight. To Wallace and Murray he sent two Dominican friars. In Guisborough it is, noticeably, Wallace not Murray who is credited with a terse but famous rejoinder to Warenne's demand for surrender: 'Tell your commander that we are not here to make peace but to do battle to defend ourselves and liberate our kingdom. Let them come on, and we shall prove this in their very beards.'[37]

Wallace's words before the battle of Stirling Bridge must surely rate with any in similar circumstances which have come down to us. Courage in battle, and at the moment of death, was much valued, and where evidence was lacking writers did not hesitate to invent the appropriate speech. This was particularly true of Greek and Roman historians; they saw nothing wrong in creating a set-piece address for the great figures with whom they were concerned. Polybius and Livy may be quoted as examples of this practice. It persisted much later. The *Song of Roland*, said to have been performed before Hastings by Taillefer, is illuminated by the words and deeds of Roland and Oliver and the twelve peers of France, who died at Roncesvalles. We may reasonably compare Wallace's words to the Dominicans sent by Warenne with those, for example, put by Arrian into the mouth of Alexander the Great before the Granichus or with those attributed to Vercingetorix by Julius Caesar.

The ability to choose the appropriate phrases was not given to all. King Stephen, at the battle of Lincoln in 1141, realising his limitations, allocated the task of inspiring his forces to Baldwin FitzGilbert.[38] But Wallace, it appears, had no such inhibitions, and rightly so. Although, according to Guisborough, Wallace's defiance was addressed to Warenne's representatives, we may assume that is was delivered in a manner intended to carry to the Scots who would fight with him.

These splendid remarks do not, given the time at which they were uttered, invalidate the argument that Wallace and Murray had not at first necessarily been intent upon giving battle. They had seen the various actions of Warenne's army, they knew of the approaches made by the Scots lords even if they did not necessarily approve of them; they knew now that they had nothing to fear. Their confidence was well placed. Below them the English, having failed to achieve a second Irvine, were at odds. That same Sir Richard Lundie who, angry and disgusted, had left the Scots camp at Irvine, put the cause for caution: 'My lords, if we cross that bridge now, we are all dead men. For we can only go over two abreast, and the enemy are already formed up: they can charge down on us whenever they wish'.

Lundie foresaw what was to happen. Wallace and Murray were stationed on the southward-looking slope of the Abbey Craig at a distance to the north of one mile from the bridge over which the English, some of them for the third time, were preparing to cross. Between the foot of the Abbey Craig and the northern end of the bridge was a causeway which ran over soft ground unsuitable for the heavy cavalry on which Warenne's army relied for impact, both physical and psychological. Once the English had crossed, not only would it be difficult if not impossible to deploy the cavalry, but the infantry would be surrounded on three sides by the river as it formed a horseshoe loop. Lundie understood the double danger offered by Wallace and Murray; even if the crossing were unimpeded by the Scots – an unlikely eventuality – the chances of Warenne's being able so to order his deployment in the face of an attack which would then, if not before, occur, were slight. Lundie, therefore, proposed that a detachment under his command move along the river and set upon Wallace and Murray from the rear. 'There is', he told Warenne, 'a ford not far from here, where sixty men can cross at a time. Give me five hundred cavalrymen, then, and a small body of infantry, and we will outflank the enemy and attack them from behind: while we are doing that, the earl and the rest of the army will be able to cross the bridge in perfect safety.'

If Lundie's advice had been heeded, the outcome of the battle of Stirling must have been different. Wallace and Murray would have been forced to divide their army and would have lost the opportunity to attack the English, as they crossed the bridge, with sufficient strength. But if Warenne had lost the first and perhaps the best opening by calling back those troops who had established themselves over the river before he had risen from his bed, he now made another gross mistake. He allowed Cressingham, who had not so far been prominent, to intervene. The treasurer urged an immediate crossing and an attack upon the Scots. It was natural that Cressingham should be concerned about the cost of keeping an army in the field; he it was who had sent men home to England on the grounds of expense. He now used the same argument in support of the crossing. He rounded on Warenne who seemed about to agree with Lundie: 'It will do us no good, my lord earl, either to go bickering like this or to waste the king's money by vain manoeuvres. So let us cross over right away, and do our duty as we are bound to do.' If Cressingham was a fool, his superior, Warenne, was even worthier of the title. He overruled Lundie and ordered the advance. For Lundie it is impossible not to feel sympathy. If the Scots at Irvine had lacked courage, the English at Stirling lacked intelligence. The words of Guisborough might well be his own:

> Thus (amazing though it is to relate, and terrible as was to be its outcome) all these experienced men, though they knew the enemy was at hand, began to pass over a bridge so narrow that even two horsemen could scarcely and with much difficulty ride side by side – and so they did all the morning, without let or hindrance, until the vanguard was on one side of the river and the remainder of the army on the other. There was, indeed, no better place in all the land to deliver the English into the hands of the Scots, and so many into the power of the few.

What happened appears to us, with the benefit of hindsight, inevitable. Wallace and Murray watched the parade of the English on to the bridge. With that fine judgement which marks the exceptional commander, they released their infantry down the slope of Abbey Craig when the vanguard of the English army had almost made the crossing. The Scots, their patience rewarded, fell upon the vanguard as it attempted to debouch from the bridge. The vanguard was now cut off from the rest of the English army which was forced to watch from the far bank. The narrowness of the bridge made any move to reinforce those unfortunates already over the bridge impossible. Wallace and Murray had, with part of their force, blocked the northern end of the bridge. What the larger part of the English army saw was horrifying.

The Scots in their advance from the Abbey Craig would have gathered an immense momentum. This must have driven many of the English off the bank and into the river. Such as escaped this fate cannot have had time to offer any kind of concerted opposition. Their superior weapons could not be brought to bear in the crush. Retreat was impossible. One English version of events has Wallace break the bridge down at this point. Whether this is so, or whether Warenne, who had not crossed the bridge, had it destroyed to save himself and the larger part of the army, we do not know, but it did not matter. The Scots made great slaughter of the vanguard. A hundred knights and many infantry, perhaps as many as five thousand, died, either killed or drowned.

Among those who perished was Cressingham. If Warenne had not crossed the bridge, the treasurer had been less prudent. He had charged at the head of the vanguard, his mind no doubt filled with the dreams of that glory which the office of treasurer had denied him. Misguided, pompous, less than popular with his own army, he nevertheless met the sort of end which was more appropriate to such as Warenne. He was dragged down from his horse and died under the spears of the Scots infantry. In telling of his death, Guisborough does not spare him: 'Of all the many who were deceived that day, he was deceived most of all.' After the battle, the Scots, in a gruesome ceremony, flayed his obese body. Strips of his skin were sent throughout Scotland to proclaim the victory of Stirling. Other strips were used to make saddle girths. Tradition tells us that Wallace himself had a belt made for his sword from what was left of Cressingham's skin.

Of those who escaped from the massacre, some swam the river. These were the Welshmen who fought, as always, without armour. The most famous of those who did survive was Sir Marmaduke de Tweng, the Yorkshire-man. He refused to join the Welshmen as they swam the river and rode his horse through the Scots and over the bridge to safety. He, clearly, had seen the hopelessness of the situation very early, for the bridge was still intact. His courage and his continued devotion to the English Crown, first in the person of Edward I and then in that of the king's son, ensured that his reputation did not suffer. The same could not be said of Warenne. He gave Stirling Castle into Tweng's keeping and fled for Berwick with unseemly haste.

There was a postscript to the battle. We left the Stewart and the earl of Lennox after their report to Warenne on the refusal of Wallace and Murray to surrender. Now with the battle over and Warenne in flight, they re-appeared on the scene. They had been spectators of the slaughter at the river, and it is not certain what use, if any, they had made of their men. Their target was the English baggage-train, the camp-followers, and other refugees from the battle. These were moving in the direction of Falkirk when the lords emerged from the shelter of the woods alongside the Pows and fell upon them. Many of the English were killed and large amounts of booty seized. It was the sole contribution of the Stewart and Lennox to the Scottish achievement of Stirling.

NOTES

1. For Machiavelli (op. cit., 202) this attribute ranked highest in the rules of military discipline. Clausewitz deals with the question, op. cit., book 1, chap. 3

2. Watson: *Under the Hammer*, 45.

3. If Wallace was present, it is difficult to see in what role. He could only have been there as the leader of an independent force gathered since Lanark or in the following of one of the magnates. The second of these possibilities is unlikely; in his own right, Wallace may well have had with him a considerable number of rebels, attracted by his success at Lanark and Scone. There is in any case no mention of him at Irvine. Had he been present, his departure would surely have been noted, especially if there had been a quarrel prior to that departure.

4. *Cal. Docs Scot.,* ii, 908.

5. Lundie fought for the English at Stirling. See pp. 100–01 for the part he played.

6. Trivet, 357, describes him as 'miles strenuus'.

7. Barrow: *Robert Bruce,* 120–21. Mackay: *Robert Bruce King of Scots*, 1974, 62, sees the Stewart as particularly responsible for this tactic. Barron, op. cit., 46, states categorically that the Scots 'had been compelled to make peace'.

8. Guisborough, 299. See note 3 above for the suggestion that he already had a large force with him *before* as well as after Irvine.

9. This is in contrast to the leaders at Irvine. As late as 5 August, Wishart, Bruce, and the Stewart were still, for whatever reasons, haggling over terms with the English: Barrow, *Robert Bruce*, 120 n. Douglas, in some respects a man of Wallace's own temperament, having failed to provide hostages, was a prisoner, first at Berwick, where he continued to be 'very savage and abusive', then in the Tower of London, where he died. The Scots believed that he had been murdered.

10. It is fair to state that Bruce, at least, was in a difficult position in the negotiations. he was required to give his daughter, Marjorie, as a hostage. He was understandably reluctant and Wishart, with certain others, stood as a guarantor until he should produce Marjorie: *Cal. Docs Scots*, ii, 910.

11. Guisborough, 299.

12. *Cal. Docs Scots*, ii, 453. Cressingham had been instructed on 24 June to hold a colloquy with Percy and Clifford on the situation. *Cal. Pat. Rolls*, 1292–1301, 251.

13. On the significance of the forest or 'Greenwood' in outlaw legend, see Keen: *The Outlaws of Medieval Legend*, London, 1961, 1–8.

14. Fordun, 98

15. A different interpretation is placed on this aspect of Wallace's methods by *DNB*. There, on p. 564, we read that Wallace 'showed wisdom by associating with himself, when possible, representatives of those barons who encouraged by his success, supported him for at least a time'. Even here, however, we are left to draw the conclusion that the arrangement on Wallace's side did not exclude harsh means, while the nobles, for their part, were ready to withdraw the support which he forced from some of them.

16. Michael de Miggel was captured by the English at Dunbar and imprisoned in Nottingham Castle. *Cal. Docs Scot.*, ii, 742. He was still there on 23 September 1299, when arrangements were being made for him to be exchanged with James de Lindsey, then in Bothwell Castle. *Cal. Docs Scot.*, ii, 1093. None of this – his endeavours on behalf of the Scottish cause in the early part of the war, the suffering which he underwent in an English prison – seemed, if Michael is to be believed, to weigh with Wallace.

17. *Cal. Docs Scot.*, ii, 1689

18. If the case of Michael de Miggel is not unique, it is interesting that there is no record that the execution of Wallace was followed by a rush of people anxious to dissociate themselves from him. The nobles, of course, had already made their peace with Edward and were collaborating with the English.

19. *Cal. Docs Scot.*, ii, 455.

20. Barrow: *Robert Bruce*, 121.

21. It was not until 1 August that Surrey reached Berwick.

22. Seventh Book. Barron, op. cit., 60–62, argues that Harry confuses Wallace with Murray and it was the latter who was at Aberdeen, joining with Henry de Lathom, the English sheriff of Aberdeen, who had gone over to the Scots.

23. Bower, ii, 171.

24. *Docs Illus. Hist. Scot*, ii, 198.

25. Edward neglected no source for the levying of troops. On

11 April 1298, for example, he invited 'criminals and vagrants' to serve with him. *Cal. Docs Scot.*, ii, 38. Geoffrey Entredens, pardoned because of his service in the Scottish war, was but one of many guilty of 'homicides, robberies, and outlawry' and other assorted crimes before Edward offered them a kind of respectability. *Cal. Pat. Rolls*, 199. The effects of such a policy of recruitment may be seen both at Stirling and Falkirk. In the latter case, it came close to bringing defeat for the English king when he found he could not rely on the Welsh contingent in his army.

26. Book XI.

27. He had, in fact, been ordered to resume his appointment in Scotland on 14 June. Edward's continued confidence in this unwilling warrior is not easy to explain. It was disastrous at Stirling, yet Edward did not dismiss Warenne. For a man of such reputation as a soldier, Edward did not show himself more astute than his son and successor. Edward II, at least, was capable of wise military appointments, most notably in the case of Andrew de Harcla who, however, made the fatal mistake of recognising his monarch's futility. It was Harcla who inflicted the most serious reverse suffered by Robert I, at Carlisle in 1315. Lanercost, 230.

28. On the role of Brian Fitzalan in Scotland there are references in Powicke, 597 and n., 604, 686 and n., & 13n.; Barrow: *Robert Bruce*, 49, 50, 108.

29. *Docs Illustr. Hist. Scot.*, ii, 230.

30. He was, however, astute enough not to embark on any adventures against the Scots on his own initiative.

31. Kightly, 164.

32. Guisborough, 301.

33. Maxwell trans. 163.

34. Stevenson, ii, 202.

35. See Prestwich: *Armies and Warfare in the Middle Ages*, 1996, passim.

36. McNair Scott, 45.

37. Guisborough, 300.

38. Prestwich, *Armies and Warfare*, 313.

5

The Time of Power, 1298

'William the Conqueror'

᭒᭒᭒

Posterity has found that the battle of Stirling was not decisive.[1] In that it did not end the war with England, that was certainly true. But in this it was no different from other great battles of the Scottish struggle for independence, however bloody they were. After Dunbar and Falkirk, the former a victory of the professional over the amateur, the other accomplished with a great slaughter of Wallace's army, the Scots, seemingly crushed, did not succumb. After Bannockburn, with Edward II revealed at a terrible cost to his men as the incompetent he was, militarily as well as politically, it took a further fourteen years to bring peace. The bitter momentum of the war which began in 1296 was not to be so readily halted, the legacy of hatred not so easily forgotten. The personalities and motives of the leading figures – Wallace, Edward I, Bruce, Edward II – were such as to ensure a continuation of the war whatever the current situation. Suffering intensified determination. A reverse led to revival.

But if Stirling was not decisive, its impact on the war and on the psychology of both sides cannot be denied. It was revolutionary in its concept and in its effects, more so even than Bannockburn. The leadership on the Scottish side was of a kind not seen before. Wallace and Murray had broken the canons of warfare as they were then understood; theirs was a challenge to the military establishment both in England and in Scotland itself. Whatever their quarrel, the natural leaders on both sides of the Border shared the same creed. It was no longer possible, after Stirling, to pretend that that creed had survived in its entirety. It is Wallace and Murray who, to modern eyes, appear the professionals. The characteristics which the two commanders exhibited before and during the battle – an appreciation of terrain, selection of position, patience, an iron discipline, improvisation, realistic appraisal and recognition of the moment – were those one would expect to find in their opponents, with the experience of war in Wales and France on which to draw. Wallace and Murray were, after all, in a situation unknown to them: the handling of a large, potentially undisciplined army. Their experience had been of the leadership of small, mobile groups for which success was measured in minor gains. Their confidence verged on brashness; it was justified by events. No one, whether Scots or English, could be ignorant either of their ability or of what the future held in military terms.

Which of the two was the more responsible for the victory at Stirling has exercised historians.[2] Underlying the discussion there has been a preference to see in Murray rather than in Wallace the genius which won the battle. The origin of this preference resides in the simple but understandable equation that Murray's presence on the Scots side meant victory, his absence, at Falkirk,

defeat. In the debate on the relative positions of Murray
and Wallace, little note has been taken of two aspects of
Murray's career which are to his credit. The first is his
ability to adapt his methods to circumstances. It is too
easily forgotten that his background and military experience predisposed him to just that sort of mentality which
brought disaster to the Scots at Dunbar; that he was able
to see the need for different methods upon his return to
the north after his escape from Chester speaks well for
his adaptability. The second is that, despite his origins,
he recognised the talents of Wallace, a man who was his
social inferior. Murray's achievement at Stirling, like
Wallace's, was shared. The similarities in their campaigns
before the battle are enough to suggest that their
relationship was the unique one of two men of contrasting
backgrounds who, in military matters if nothing else,
thought alike. We cannot know what if any influence each
would have had on the other if Murray had lived after
Stirling, although it is tempting to speculate. Would
Murray, by virtue of his social position, appear a more
attractive leader than Wallace to the magnates? Could
the dual leadership which functioned so well at Stirling
survive a new set of circumstances? If we have no answers
to such questions, we can aver that Wallace continued,
after Stirling, to demonstrate the same qualities of leadership which he, like his colleague, possessed before their
historic meeting. Murray's achievement was great, but it
is idle to attempt to extend it beyond the obvious point.
Wallace had much to do without Murray; that he did it
shows him for the man he was.

The wound which Murray had received at Stirling was
ultimately fatal.[3] It was not until November, however,
that he died, and until that time his name is associated,
as will be seen, with that of Wallace. Whether he was

able to play an active role must be doubted. The established assumption[4] is that he played such a role, but that assumption may owe more to sentiment than to reality. The colossal impact of Stirling required immediate action if it was not to be lost. It is perhaps significant that it is Wallace who is portrayed as the man who undertook, as it were, the necessary physical labour of benefiting from the victory. We would not expect the seriously wounded Murray to carry out the sweep across the south of Scotland which occurred after Stirling. This obvious fact has not always been sufficiently acknowledged. Murray did not lose his authority because he was incapacitated, but he must have had not merely a different but a less demanding part than his colleague and friend. Warenne, it will be recalled, had fled the field at Stirling. Tweng, whom he had left with Sir William FitzWarin, in charge of the castle,[5] could not long hope to hold it. When they surrendered it to Wallace because of a lack of provisions, he showed himself as chivalrous as Bruce, who has always been considered a paragon in this regard. He recognised the courage of Tweng and allowed him to live, as he did FitzWarin. A third man bore the name of Ros. He too Wallace spared, for this was the brother of that Robert de Ros whose defection to the Scots at the beginning of the war had endeared him to the Scots as it endeared him to historians. Wallace was not, then, ignorant of that code by which others laid such store. It was a revealing incident.

Wallace had made no attempt to pursue Warenne, who was so desperate that his horse was allowed no time to eat between Stirling and Berwick and foundered on arrival there. Warenne had reserved his energies for escape rather than for battle. Wallace did, however, strike out for Berwick shortly afterwards, but turned away when faced by the English.[6] Berwick, unwalled because of the economies ordered by Edward, which Cressingham had carried out so enthusiastically, now had little strategic value, but perhaps because of its fate under Edward, it exercised a continuing fascination for both sides. Its inhabitants expected the worst from the victorious Scots, whose bloodlust had not been sated by the carnage of Stirling; such as had not fled into England offered no resistance. The numbers of the force Wallace led to Berwick are not recorded, but it would not be, nor needed to be, large. His intention was in part to underscore his triumph and that of Murray, in part to clear the area of English. Berwick in all likelihood had fallen to the Scots within the month after Stirling[7] but whether or not to Wallace himself is unclear.[8] He did not at this time follow his appearance outside Berwick with a raid across the Border, although his reputation was now such that the inhabitants of Northumberland sought the safety of Newcastle.

The effects of Stirling were felt throughout Scotland. Dundee castle, from which Wallace had moved to Stirling, surrendered and was placed in the care of Alexander Scrymgeour, one of the many minor figures devoted to the end to the Scottish cause.[9] Edinburgh and Roxburgh fell to the Scots but, as was true of Berwick, their castles remained in the hands of the English.[10] But the capture of these towns and the burning of others south of the Forth[11] was not the main preoccupation of Wallace at this time, however enthusiastically he may have participated in or encouraged these gestures of retribution. His mind was filled with a great ambition.

Wallace and, as far as known, the ailing Murray, had not lost sight of a primary and dominating concern: the restoration of Balliol. To encompass this it was necessary not only to destroy if possible the military power of the English, but to retain, in political terms, the name of Balliol as king of Scots. Stirling had gone some way towards achieving the first; it may be that such was the euphoria in Scotland that it was thought the battle was decisive. Wallace did not share that opinion but, if he worked towards the day when there would be a decisive battle, he turned his attention at the same time to the second aim. This called for other and more demanding qualities than those which had brought success in the recent great battle. At Stirling both Wallace and Murray profited from the innate attributes necessary in war. Now they (and after the death of Murray, Wallace alone) proved they possessed a genius in the political and diplomatic fields.

If Scotland was seized after Stirling with a renewed patriotism and a drive towards unity, it lacked the cohesion which a central government gave. Wallace, in the most revolutionary of his acts, supplied this. It is of him alone now that we must speak. To include Murray, even if, as we shall see, his name was associated with Wallace's is quite wrong. Murray was in decline; within two months of Stirling he was dead, leaving behind a pregnant wife. She in time gave birth to a son, also Andrew, destined to be as devoted to the patriotic cause as his father. In the son, guardian of Scotland and victor at Culblean against the pro-English forces of David of Strathbogie in 1335, Barron purports to find evidence of 'hereditary military genius' in the Murray family.[12] The strategy adopted by the son in the period 1332 to 1339 was, in Barron's words, 'of a nature very similar to that exhibited by his father in 1297, and was just as successful'.[13] It follows, therefore, that for Barron Wallace was a 'guerilla leader', clearly a lower status, although Barron

describes him as 'great'.[14] But Murray, Barron's hero, was spared the test of time and circumstance, unlike Wallace. We cannot know what the elder Murray might have achieved, but with his removal from the scene, Wallace was unquestionably the governor of Scotland. To be such required skill and, let it not be forgotten, nerve. He stepped beyond the constraints imposed by his origins. In doing so he saved Scotland from the possibility, in time, of civil war, even in the face of a renewed threat from England. At the same time, however, he condemned himself to the hostility of the most influential of his fellow-countrymen as well as, of course, the hatred of Edward I.

One of the effects of Stirling had been the rediscovery by certain of the Scots lords of their patriotism. We saw that once Wallace and Murray had massacred the English vanguard, the Stewart and Lennox emerged both from the woods and their own hesitation to strike a blow for the Scottish cause. They were not alone of their kind. To the north the earl of Buchan, the Comyns, the earl of Strathearn and others were happy to be identified with the Scottish cause. More significant for the future was the reappearance of Robert Bruce, a somewhat mysterious figure after the capitulation of Irvine.[15] He was again active in the south-west. Bruce prompted a retaliatory attack into Annandale of his former opponent, Robert Clifford, some time before Christmas. Clifford killed such Scots as he could lay hands on, burned ten townships, then retreated back into England.[16] Warenne too found the courage which deserted him at Stirling, and took Berwick. The English were unwilling to undertake anything of more consequence before their king returned from Flanders. Indeed, Warenne would receive in the following February clear instructions that no major campaign against the Scots was to begin until Edward had returned to take personal command. The slight successes which the Scots lords were achieving in the face of moderate English opposition could lead to over-confidence and with it a renewed determination to take the government upon themselves.

Wallace's seizure of the government therefore ensured unity. If it is difficult now to see an alternative to him,[17] there were undoubtedly others among his contemporaries who thought themselves more suited to the role he henceforth had. The taking into his own hands of the reins of government is evidence, if any were needed, of his courage. It is evidence also of his selflessness. Intelligent as he was, he must have been aware of the chance to make himself more than governor. The suggestion must have been put to him. He resisted it. If by resisting the temptation he showed himself to be, as has been argued, 'more conservative than the greater magnates',[18] history has not judged him a failure for that, but rather a man of honour. To have made himself king would have torn Scotland apart and left it the easiest of preys to Edward. Wallace knew this, fortunately for Scotland.

He was not yet given the obvious title, that of Guardian, by those he had led to victory over the English. Whether he sought it or was offered it and refused it, we do not know. He was careful, first with Murray and then alone, to employ in the documents he issued a formal, accurate description of his station as he saw it. From Haddington on 11 October the two wrote to the mayors and communes of Lübeck and Hamburg. The letter had a double intention. It informed the readers that Scotland, an independent kingdom again, had been won back by battle from the English. It was at the same time in the nature of the reopening of those Scottish trading connections with Germany which had been such a feature of the reign of Alexander III. In this important letter, almost certainly one of many on similar themes, the two commanders referred to themselves as 'Andrew Murray and William Wallace, commanders of the army of the kingdom of Scotland, and the community of that realm'.[19] When in November they issued a letter of protection to the abbey of Hexham, the formula was no different from that used earlier: 'Andrew Murray and William Wallace, commanders of the army of the kingdom of Scotland, in the name of the famous prince the lord John by God's grace illustrious king of Scotland, by consent of the community of that realm.'[20] With Murray dead, Wallace saw no need to alter the style of greeting, save that he now described himself as knight and Guardian, both titles which he had been given by the time of the grant of a charter to Alexander Scrymgeour. As well as being entrusted with the responsibility for Dundee, Scrymgeour was given land, in return for which he was required to pay homage to Balliol and to act as standard bearer to the king. Even at this stage, March of 1298, Wallace, despite a later claim, had no intention to make himself ruler of Scotland. We can therefore see that he retained, beyond any question, his loyalty to Balliol and held himself to be acting with the agreement of the people of Scotland. That he actively sought both advice and consent is evident from one of the charges brought against him in 1305, that he called 'parliaments and assemblies'. These conferred authority on the actions which he took. No less true, they emphasised his superiority over any pretenders to the position which he had earned since Lanark.

It was as the representative of the Scottish nation that he took an army on an extended raid into the northern counties of England. That nation demanded retribution from the English. It was not a desire from which he dissented. Under him there was in October and November 1297, a return to that savage and indiscriminate kind of warfare with which the Scots had opened the struggle against England. It was, indeed, a long-standing feature of relations between the two countries – and continued to be so for centuries after Wallace – that each side should indulge in destruction and killing for their own sake. Wallace needed neither excuse nor reason for the raid. It was an end in itself. The conduct of his troops, as will be seen, was such as to suggest that Wallace was bent on punishment. It was an emotion which the Scots understood. The need to lead out of a famine-stricken Scotland what must have been a considerable force in the search for sustenance may also have carried some weight.[21] Equally important, however, would be the problem posed by the inactivity of the army of Stirling, successful, enthusiastic, perhaps over-confident. The north of England offered an easy target. The name of Wallace guaranteed a lack of opposition.

The fear of Scottish attack after Stirling was already present in the north of England before Wallace moved over the Border. At Carlisle, always a target, action had been taken in October to prepare for the expected assault. Command of the castle was entrusted to the redoubtable bishop of Carlisle, John de Halton. He replaced Robert Bruce, lord of Annandale, a victim perhaps of the questionable loyalty of his son, the earl of Carrick. Henry Percy brought a not inconsiderable force of fourteen crossbowmen and ninety-five foot soldiers to stiffen the garrison[22] and it is probable that ditches were dug outside the city walls as a further defensive measure.[23] But it was upon Northumberland that the Scots descended in that same month. Guisborough dates the start of Scottish attacks from the Feast of St Luke, 18 October. It has been argued that this early phase of the cross-Border operation was a series of raids which, if tolerated by Wallace, were not controlled by him.[24] The argument is a strong one. There is some evidence that he turned his attention after Berwick to the reduction of Dundee.[25] The argument may well gain greater potency from the possibility that, inevitably, the euphoria generated by Stirling would lead the Scots into uncoordinated but damaging attacks into enemy territory. There was the opportunity for revenge and with the English in disarray, for plunder. The Scots established their base on Rothbury Forest and raided the surrounding countryside with impunity.[26]

These first uncoordinated Scottish assaults on Northumberland, if in themselves ferocious and destructive were but a prelude to a period in which, we are told by the chronicler, 'the service of God totally ceased in all the monasteries and churches between Newcastle and Carlisle, for all the canons, monks and priests fled before the force of the Scots, as did nearly all the people'.[27] The words are familiar, for the burning and killings were reminiscent to the people of Northumberland of times as distant as those of Malcolm III and David I and as recent as 1296. Against indiscriminate and widespread raids such as occurred in late October 1297 only walled towns and castles offered protection. Newcastle itself was seemingly under threat; as with Carlisle, the garrison was strengthened, with six men-at-arms and a total of over a hundred and sixty archers and crossbowmen.

In November the Scots began to act in a more systematic manner. This change has been attributed, with some reason, to Wallace himself.[28] He took control of what became an invasion of the north of England. He made no attempt on Newcastle, but instead turned west, into Tynedale. Corbridge, the scene in the previous year of the murder of two hundred schoolboys, if an English account is to be believed, was put to the torch. Wallace moved on to Hexham, where he arrived on 7 November. It was there that a strange incident is recorded. The priory had not been wholly abandoned. Three canons had come back and were found by a party of Scots, who called upon them to produce the priory's treasures. The canons answered that everything of value had been stolen by other Scots. At this point Wallace arrived. He felt the need for the services of the canons and asked them to celebrate mass. In keeping with pious practice, he went from the abbey to lay down his arms after the Host had been elevated. In his absence some Scots entered and removed holy articles without which the service could not continue.

When Wallace learned of this, he ordered the capture and hanging of the thieves. A half-hearted attempt was made by the Scots to carry out his instructions. At this Wallace admitted to the canons that the thieves could not really be brought to justice and gave the canons a letter of protection. Barrow compares this incident with a similar one in the reign of David I.[29] That king had hanged men guilty of attempted robbery from the same priory. It is Barrow's view that Wallace's failure to bring thieves to justice proves that, despite his success at Stirling, he had none of the royal authority which David enjoyed. It is no less likely he was wise enough to realise that the volatile Scots would not see the justice in the execution of a number of their comrades for that violence against the English clergy in which they had been encouraged, not merely by Wallace but by their own priests. Wallace was not without a sense of what was possible. The propaganda value of his pretence to capture the thieves and, still more to the point, his letter of protection to the canons would not escape him.

Cumberland and Durham felt the anger of the Scots. Wallace's men ranged as far as Cockermouth. At Carlisle, always a challenge and a hurdle to the Scots, he essayed a brief assault, despite his lack of siege equipment. The citizens, as so often in the face of Scottish pretensions to the capture of Carlisle, were not impressed. They themselves were well prepared with defensive weapons. Wallace called upon them to surrender. His intermediary was a priest whose words are transmitted to us through the *Chronicle of Lanercost*, a fact which must cast some doubt on their accuracy. The priest, 'shameless' that he was, cried: 'William the Conqueror, whom I serve, commands you to give up this town and castle without bloodshed; then you may leave unharmed with all your goods. But if you do not instantly obey him, he will attack and kill you all.' Wallace's summons cannot have been serious; he was too hard-headed to believe that surrender would follow. It was a formality, as was his presence, intended to parade before the citizens the army he led as a means of ensuring that no counter-attack would be mounted against him. If for his part he could not take this or other fortified places, he guaranteed that there would be no attempt on the part of their garrisons to interfere with his progress through the north of England. Wallace sought no battles on this raid.

The reply of the citizens of Carlisle would not have surprised him. As it is reported to us, it contained no hint of compromise.[30] They dared him to do his worst; they remained faithful to the king who had put the town and castle into their keeping. They were in any case under no illusion as to the temper of Wallace and the Scots;

surrender to these men who had slaughtered and burned would not mean safety. They followed up their defiance with a show of the engines of war which stood on the walls of the town. Wallace did not delay at Carlisle; there were other, easier pickings. The Scots vented their spleen on the villages and hamlets which lay within the great forest of Inglewood. It was reported that at this time they were guilty of 'devastating everything by way of the forest of Inglewood, Cumberland and Allerdale to the Derwent at Cockermouth'.[31]

If Wallace was defeated in Cumberland by the walls and castle of Carlisle, he met a far more formidable obstacle when he planned to ravage the county of Durham, which enjoyed the protection of St Cuthbert. Wallace's route into Durham was the traditional one, over Stainmoor. At Bowes on or about 11 November, the Scots were turned back by the intervention of God and Saint Cuthbert. Supernatural events took place: 'Such a storm of snow and ice rose up that many of them died of cold and hunger.' Where before there had been no opposition to them, St Cuthbert had inspired the people of his county to rise against the invaders. An unspecified but large number of Durham men was reported by Scottish scouts to be marching against them, while the Scots themselves had fewer than one hundred horsemen and under three thousand infantry. This was nevertheless a powerful force; its size may explain the desertion of many Englishmen which even the English chronicler cannot disguise. Despite these defections the Scots were dismayed: 'If men were lacking, the power of Saint Cuthbert was in no way diminished [and] the enemy's plan to enter his land was foiled.'

By now the momentum of the Scots was halted. The weather was increasingly severe, they were weighed down by their booty, and their rebuff by St Cuthbert would have convinced them that they could expect no more. Wallace himself could not remain absent from Scotland indefinitely. In his absence those elements in the country over which he had to maintain the control which Stirling had brought him could not be relied on to adhere to the cause of Balliol. The invasion of the northern counties of England, if it had failed to capture a single town, had been successful in inflicting a memorable punishment on the English. The name of Wallace would not be readily forgotten. The Scots were bringing back a considerable booty with them as evidence of their weeks over the Border. As they returned home, the Scots still had time for a last orgy of destruction in the lower valley of the Tyne.

Wallace was back in Scotland towards the end of November. Guisborough relates that before the return over the Border, he gave to the contingent from Galloway their entitlement from the booty. The Gallovidians were not the easiest of allies for any Scottish leader, for they looked upon themselves as a separate entity. They had long enjoyed a reputation for cruelty, and it is certain that in 1297, as before, they were well to the forefront in the perpetration of the atrocities which occurred in the raid. For Wallace they would have been useful shock troops, brave if undisciplined, fearful to behold, utterly ruthless. It would be natural to see in them the thieves of the incident at Hexham priory. Wallace would not be unhappy to be rid of them once he had decided to return to Scotland.

The enterprise had achieved nothing in terms of practical or strategic value and may therefore be thought a luxury, an indulgence. Wallace himself would not, however, have seen it as such, for his aims were more immediate and limited. We cannot doubt that the enterprise was a popular move. Indeed, it was necessary to strengthen still further his hold over affairs. To those who, for him, counted – the people – it had brought retribution upon the English and plunder. Although a longer absence from Scotland would have been dangerous for him, the name he had earned at Stirling was sufficient to allow of no opposition from within the country. When, therefore, he came back to Scotland he was able to assume the reins of government with no apparent difficulty.[32]

By now, of course, he was deprived of the presence of Murray. If it made any difference to him, there is no record of it. His principal concern was to prepare for the onslaught which would come from Edward I. That and the continued government of Scotland would have taxed any man, of whatever origins. Wallace's relatively humble birth was an obstacle to the co-operation of those who considered themselves his superiors. That obstacle, at least in theory, was removed by his knighting. That symbolic act took place at some time before 29 March 1298.[33] On that date he was at Torphichen in West Lothian, where he issued the charter to Alexander Scrymgeour to which reference has already been made. In it we find him referring to himself both as Knight and Guardian. Who bestowed the knighthood is not known; from a remark in an English chronicle it must, almost certainly, have been one of the premier earls. A case has been made for Bruce,[34] but definite proof is lacking. The knighthood moved Wallace several rungs up, as it were, on the social ladder. It afforded him of itself a certain authority, not least in his relationships with others.

More significant, although associated with the bestowing of knighthood, was Wallace's election to the Guardianship. The two may, indeed, have occurred in the course of the same ceremony; there is no record of the date of either. Wallace was sole Guardian, the choice of a special council of nobles and churchmen. His was a massive achievement. The English, in one of their political songs, poured scorn and hatred on what he had done:

> After this [Stirling] the leader of the plot calls together his part, knowing that our king would be gone over the sea; he made an order to ravage Northumberland . . . William Wallace is the leader of these savages . . . To increase the wickedness which they had hitherto perpetrated, these wicked men deliver Alnwick to the flames . . . Now the malignant people returns to Scotland; and the honour of knighthood is given to William; from a robber he becomes a knight, just as swan is made out of a raven; an unworthy man takes the seat, when a worthy man is not by.[35]

If we may wonder whether Wallace did not need to wait upon Edward's departure for France to strike at the English, we may also readily believe that what he had been given, he had earned by his own merit. The abuse of this and other songs is the clearest proof of his accomplishment. The fear in which the English held him was well deserved. To their credit, the Scots, with the knighthood and the election as Guardian, had seen in him something more than the scourge of the English. They had seen in him a man possessed of unique talents: a soldier and a statesman. If it was an uncommon combination, the task ahead was daunting.

It is likely that in the aftermath of his knighting Wallace was forced to leave the fine detail of government in the hands of those more experienced in this work than himself: the clerks, the bishops, those officials who had returned to their posts as Cressingham wrote of the disintegration of the English hold over Scotland. Wallace's strong hand was, however, seen in one crucial matter at least. On 20 August 1297, William Fraser, bishop of St Andrews and a former Guardian, died at Auteuil, near Paris. Fraser had played a leading role in the negotiations with France in 1295 and never saw Scotland again.[36] Wallace, devoted to the Church in Scotland and well aware of its role in the struggle against England, saw the necessity of replacing the patriot, Fraser, with a man of like persuasion. How the English saw the election of a successor to Fraser is obvious from their later charge that Wallace had compelled the installation of William Lamberton.[37] When the day came, as they hoped, that the English domination of Scotland was to be re-established, they would need reliable prelates sympathetic to the English cause to help maintain that domination. Lamberton was not one such, as his later career was to prove.[38] He was to suffer greatly, on the orders of Edward I, for his part in the rising of Bruce. Threatened, abused, imprisoned with his fellow bishop Wishart, always with the knowledge that the paranoic English king was capable of having him executed, he was not deflected from his determination to see Scotland independent. This he lived to see, for it was not until 1328, the year of the Treaty of Edinburgh and its ratification at Northampton, that he died. It was on the instructions of Wallace, given while he was in England, that Lamberton was elected to the see of St Andrews. It was not the least of his bequests to the future of Scotland.

For the foremost authority on the period, 'the three main achievements of Wallace's régime were the invasion of Northumbria, the filling of the vacant see of St Andrews, and the successful revival of the idea of guardianship'.[39] The first may be seen as the natural expression of the drive of an outstanding soldier bent on revenge against an enemy as implacable and violent as himself. The second, if it reflects a political wisdom, no less demonstrates a grasp of reality; he saw, and acted upon, the necessity of keeping the Church in the hands of those whose dedication to the Scottish cause was unquestioned. The third required of him outstanding, even unique qualities. He had to achieve and hold on to what was by no means open to him. If he had the support of the people, if the Church, practical as ever, recognised in him the saviour of its independence from English claims to superiority, the magnates would be sceptical if not cynical. They were as practical as the prelates. For the English, the magnates' loyalty to Edward I was liable to melt away 'as frost in May'.[40] With Edward they had at least the rapport of nobility, the common experience of upbringing and aspirations. With Wallace they could not pretend to that. For later generations their loyalty to him was as dubious as that to Edward. That may be too simple an explanation. Wallace would, however, be unable to take their support for granted. When he was brought to trial in 1305, he faced the charge, among others, that he had persuaded and urged the magnates and prelates to fight with Philip IV of France against the English. His methods of convincing the recalcitrant were often, as has been seen, based more on fear than on reason. There is more than one kind of patriotism; Wallace's was not necessarily that of the magnates. For them, more than for him, the ends, in the phrase, justified the means. Had he understood that, he might have survived. But he did not; it is unlikely that he could have done. He must have been conscious of the possibility of defection, even if he did not anticipate treachery. The problem of the magnates must have occupied a large part of his thinking as, in the first half of 1298, he looked to the south. Edward I had returned to England from Flanders on 14 March. The king, no less single-minded than Wallace himself, now devoted all his energies on the problem of Scotland and the defeat of Wallace. He was an angry man, one who considered himself betrayed. Nothing was to be allowed to interfere with his obsession.

NOTES

1. See, for example, Barrow: *Robert Bruce,*126; Prestwich: *The Three Edwards, War and State in England, 1272–1377*, 48.

2. Most notably, of course, Barron.

3. The nature of the wound or the circumstances in which he received it are not recorded. Barron, chap. 7, deals with the former belief that he had, in fact, been killed in the battle.

4. It is surely based on nothing other than the appearance of his name, with that of Wallace, on such documents as have survived.

5. *Cal. Docs Scot.*, iv, 1835.

6. McNamee: 'William Wallace's Invasion of Northern England in 1297', *Northern History*, vol. 26 (1990), 43. There is no better and more stimulating account available than this.

7. Ibid.

8. Ibid.

9. See Guisborough, 273–2, for Robert de Ros. Scrymgeour was executed at Newcastle on the orders of Edward I on 4 August 1306 as an adherent of Robert I.

10. It is impossible to say how much energy Wallace devoted to the capture of such castles. He does not appear, as far as we know, to have undertaken the building of the necessary engines or to have enlisted in his service engineers who might be capable of educating him. It was not, of course, an art in which the Scots in general seem to have been interested at this period.

11. The English were as enthusiastic as the Scots in this regard, e.g. Guisborough, 307–08.

12. Barron, op. cit., 78.

13. Ibid.

14. Ibid. Traquair: *Freedom's Sword, Scotland's Wars of Independence*, 1998, 76, questions Barron's belief in Murray's primacy.

15. There are certain periods of Bruce's career which pose difficulties even for the most dedicated of his biographers. If Falkirk is perhaps the most obvious of these, his actions after Irvine remain unclear also. At what stage he became, as McNair Scott says (53), once more the 'leader of the resistance in the south west' is open to question. Not even Barrow, who describes Bruce (*Robert Bruce*, p. 119) as 'inept' at Irvine explains how he might have achieved the necessary ability, after Irvine, to rank high in the Scottish leadership. It is, of course, true that as a major contender for the throne he could never be ignored.

16. McNamee, op. cit., 43.

17. The comparison between Irvine and Stirling must, equally, have been obvious to contemporaries.

18. Barrow: *Robert Bruce*, 127.

19. Dickinson, Donaldson, Milne (eds): *A Source Book of Scottish History*, I, 1985, 136–37.

20. Guisborough, 306.

21. Kightly: *Folk Heroes of Britain*, 168; McNamee, op. cit., 56–57.

22. Summerson: *Medieval Carlisle, the City and the Borders from the Late Eleventh to the Mid-Sixteenth Century*, 1993, vol. I, 194.

23. Ibid.

24. McNamee, op. cit., 44. Wallace's reputation after Stirling Bridge was such, however, that present or not, his was the name heard.

25. Bower, Book XI, tells that the castle was surrendered by the garrison, terrified by news of Stirling Bridge.

26. Guisborough, 304.

27. This also we learn from Guisborough, while the *Lanercost Chronicle*, for good measure, has the Scots 'committing arson, pillage and murder'.

28. McNamee, op. cit., 47. That Wallace could come late upon the scene and take control of marauding bands, already heady with success and laden with plunder, accustomed to ranging over a wide area, and weld them into a coherent force, is evidence of his personality and character.

29. Barrow: *Robert Bruce*, 131.

30. In 1315, the citizens of Carlisle defied Robert Bruce with as much determination and, considering the circumstances, greater success.

31. Guisborough, 305. McNamee, op. cit., 49ff, argues that, contrary to recent wisdom, it was here rather than in Northumberland that the greater damage was inflicted.

32. For a stern judgement on Wallace's leadership during the invasion of northern England, the reader is recommended to turn again to McNamee, op. cit., 56ff.

33. The earliest use of the title.

34. McNair Scott, 241.

35. Wright: *Political Songs*, 172–73.

36. On the career of Fraser, see Barrow: *Robert Bruce*, passim, and the same author's *Kingdom of the Scots*, 236–38 and 246.

37. Wright: *Political Songs*, 172–73.

38. His relationship with Wallace, like that of Wishart with Wallace, was a strange one. Although he did not cease while in France to exhort Wallace to continue the fight against Edward, he did not himself find it a problem to collaborate with the English king in 1305.

39. Barrow: *Robert Bruce*, 130.

40. Wright: *Political Songs*, 214.

6

The Time of Despair, 1298

'Let them perish entirely, both fathers and sons'

It took just over two weeks for reports of the catastrophe at Stirling Bridge to reach London. Defeat, as no one could have anticipated, eased Edward's position at home. The slaughter of an English army, the undignified escape by Warenne, the treatment of the body of the dead Cressingham, Edward's treasurer, these were insults not to be borne. There is no evidence that the English as a whole had formed a more favourable opinion of the military prowess of the Scots because of Stirling. Undoubtedly, however, there was a spirit of revenge in the air and immediate action was called for. A muster was ordered for Newcastle on 6 December, with thirty thousand infantry summoned.[1] With Edward still on the Continent, his son now aged fourteen was the intended leader of the punitive expedition. Warenne, summoned to London to explain his failure against Wallace and Murray, must have been persuasive, for in the event it was he to whom command was entrusted. The earls of Gloucester, Hereford, Norfolk and Warwick were to participate as, was Henry Percy.[2] Scottish magnates were not exempted, Dunbar and Angus, always pro-English, Comyn of Badenoch, Menteith, and Buchan, were among those named in writs.[3] Inevitably, with the approach of winter, the response to the Newcastle muster proved disappointing and Warenne, nor surprisingly, was late.[4]

The English managed one foray into Scotland before the end of 1297. Robert Clifford, captain of the Carlisle garrison, who with Henry Percy had faced down the Scots at Irvine,[5] led a force into Annandale, burning and killing in the traditional manner.[6] With this done, Clifford left behind him a hundred soldiers. This precautionary measure was undertaken because of a rumour that the Scots were advancing; no one could be sure that Wallace was not once more intent on action south of the Border. In early 1298 Warenne's army moved at last. He was able to relieve both Roxburgh and Berwick but made no further progress. Supplies, a perennial problem, were short and desertions numerous, and by the middle of March Warenne's army had shrunk to a fifth of its original size. What the earl, a few months after his disgrace at Stirling Bridge and now becalmed in a hostile land, would have made of the situation, we can but guess. He was spared embarrassment by an instruction from Edward to delay a campaign against the Scots until he returned from Flanders; the king meant to lead his army in person.

Whatever problems Edward had faced before his departure for the Continent, he returned to a country united against the Scots in general and against Wallace in particular as it had never been. The threat of civil war had been lifted.[7] The discontent of the nobles, led by Norfolk and Hereford, had already been alleviated in the king's absence when Prince Edward, acting as regent, had become reconciled with them in the previous

October.[8] From Ghent Edward had accepted his son's action, and he declared himself ready to give his assent to undertakings given in his name by the prince. These he would confirm at a parliament called for Whitsuntide. The clergy, no less by the need for reconciliation, produced subsidies for the forthcoming campaign from the provinces of York and Canterbury. Mindful as the clergy were of the opportunities which the subjugation of Scotland offered, such subsidies, involving as they did the protection of England, were to be distinguished from others intended for use in foreign adventures. The chronicle and songs of the period sustained the vilification of Wallace which was essential if Edward was to be certain of the goodwill of his subjects.

Edward was back in England from Flanders on 14 March 1298. He was not slow to act in the matter of Scotland. On 8 April he called Warenne, together with Norfolk, Gloucester, Hereford and Warwick, all of whom had remained at Berwick after Warenne's army had disbanded, to a council at York later that month. Secrecy was essential, the earls were warned, lest the Scots learned of Edward's intentions. On the same day, summonses were issued for the army to muster at Roxburgh on Wednesday 25 June.[9] York became the seat of government for the next six years, with the transfer there of the exchequer and the common law courts. With his usual care Edward summoned the Scottish lords to attend him in council there. Their failure to come to York allowed him to pass a sentence of forfeiture on them. He thus had at his disposal lands in Scotland with which he could reward those of his subjects who joined him in his great endeavour against Wallace.

In his determination to avenge Stirling, Edward was at pains not to neglect any potential sources of support.

Before going to York for the parliament summoned for Whitsuntide, he toured a number of shrines in the south of the kingdom, notably that at Walsingham in Norfolk, to seek inspiration and guidance. Walsingham, with its shrine to the Virgin Mary, held a special place in Edward's affections.[10] But in 1298 it was upon the northern saints, over whose jurisdiction Wallace had ranged the previous winter, that he concentrated his attention. He first went as a supplicant to the shrine of St John of Beverley and bore away the saint's banner as insurance against defeat in the campaign.[11]

It was an action sure to win favour with his army, for Edward was aware of the propaganda value of what he did. John, bishop of Hexham from 687 and of York from 705, enjoyed great and deserved popularity with the English. His power was well attested. Even after the translation of his remains from their original resting-place to the grander location of York on 25 October 1037, his shrine at Beverley continued to be a centre of pilgrimage. It was assured of his protection against enemies of whatever kind. In 1069, while William I was crushing the last of rebellion in the north of England, Beverley was saved from destruction by the intervention of the saint. John was especially potent in battle; his name had been on the lips of the English in the savage wars of the Scottish border for centuries. The passage of time did not detract from his authority or his fame. Henry V, the equal of Edward I as a soldier, ascribed the victory of Agincourt to John.

Edward's visit to Beverley has been seen[12] as a deliberate imitation of that undertaken by Athelstan, king of the English, who at Brunanburh in 937 defeated the alliance of Constantine, king of Alba, Owan, king of Strathclyde and Guthfrithson, leader of the Danes of

Dublin. Constantine lost his eldest son in the battle, and no fewer than five minor kings and five earls are said to have died with him. Athelstan, in traditional fashion, went on to ravage Scotland. Edward, a propagandist of no little skill if no exceptional honesty, would be content to let the parallel between himself and his successful predecessor be remarked among those he commanded.

To the banner of one saint he next took the precaution of adding another, that of Cuthbert of Durham, whose reputation as a defender of the English, miracle worker, and inveterate foe of the Scots outstripped even that of John of Beverley. Less than a year before Edward's appeal to him, Cuthbert had given evidence of his awesome power over the affairs of men. It was then that he turned back to Wallace and his army from the borders of Durham. Not only had the saint aroused in the men of the country the will to challenge the hitherto invincible Scots, he had called up a winter storm of such ferocity that Scots died where they stood and Wallace was forced to abandon his plans.[13]

Far from being the routine behaviour of a superstitious man, Edward's public veneration of the northern saints and his enlisting of their raid was part of the policy, initiated upon his return from Flanders, of maintaining that feverish hatred of Wallace which sprang from the latter's achievements. Not until the murder of Comyn in February 1306 would Edward again be able to rouse his people to such a pitch of patriotic fervour. Under his direction the campaign of 1298 was assuming the nature of a holy war. Wallace had challenged the king's supremacy and must be made to pay. The English might continue to grumble at the increasingly heavy taxes they were made to pay to subsidise the war in Scotland,[14] the nobility might still regard their king with some suspicion, but Edward rode to battle in the well-founded belief that the country was with him. For Wallace there was no such certainty. In a song of the period,[15] written shortly after Falkirk, the mood of the English is unequivocal. The English, as might be expected, are conquerors, compared to angels, provoked into righteous retaliation by the perfidy of their enemies. Edward's wrath, great though it is, is just. He is the chosen of God, from whom he derives the strength to chastise the Scots, as he had already chastised the Welsh and the French. Wallace is not spared. He is 'a robber', 'unworthy', 'scarcely better than a mouse'. His cruelty and viciousness in the north of England are recorded. Those he leads are 'filthy', 'swine', 'malignant', 'savages', 'murderers'. They cannot expect to escape punishment for that treachery which alone explains the success they have had. 'Let them perish utterly both fathers and sons', the song calls. This, although common some thirty years later'[16] is far beyond the ritual exchange of insults in which both sides had always indulged. Now, with the absolute certainty that the saints watched over his venture, knowing that his people, however much they might complain, were united behind him in his mission to deal with Wallace, Edward made his way into Scotland by way of Newcastle and Alnwick, where he rested briefly before proceeding to Roxburgh. There he arrived in early July.

Edward's army in 1298 has been described as 'formidable'[17] and 'impressive'.[18] It is difficult to argue with these judgements. The foot alone reached a massive total. One authoritative assessment of the numbers of foot gives a total of almost twenty-six thousand immediately before Falkirk.[19] That figure had been exceeded in 1294–95, albeit not for long,[20] but after Falkirk Edward was never again able to raise foot in numbers comparable to that campaign.[21] Certainly, in his attempts to deal with Robert Bruce in 1306–07 he could find no more than three thousand foot.[22] In preparation for the 1298 campaign 12, six hundred Welsh, together with a thousand foot from Lancashire, were summoned to appear at Carlisle by 17 June.[23] Contributions from Ireland, and from Shropshire and Staffordshire and elsewhere in England, added to the total. Over a thousand foot were brought from the garrison of Berwick. It appears that the most significant factor in the foot recruited, in terms of numbers and of potential impact, was provided by archers. The Welsh had a high reputation in this element, but, as will be seen, they proved unreliable at Falkirk, and Derbyshire, Lancashire and Cheshire proved to be the areas whose archers did the greatest damage to the Scots.[24] Figures for the cavalry, the elite, on whom Edward would rely heavily and against whom the Scots were prone to be vulnerable before Wallace, suggest a total of between fifteen hundred and two thousand.[25] The army marched in four brigades or 'battles'.

That part of the Falkirk campaign which began with the departure of the English army from Roxburgh has, perhaps not surprisingly in view of the importance attached to the battle itself, received less attention than it deserves. This neglect of a significant phase of the campaign has damaged Wallace's reputation, unjustly. Once Edward set out from Roxburgh a pattern developed, soon to become familiar and destructive of the morale of successive English armies in Scotland. As a matter of policy, Edward devastated the land over which he passed. The consequences of such a policy appear to have escaped as seasoned a soldier as he was. It is, of course, possible that he was relying for the provisioning of his troops on the grain ships which were then making

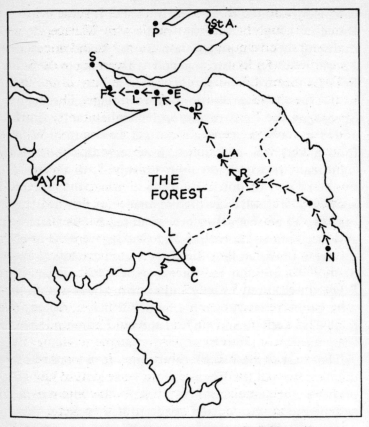

C: Carlisle L: Lochmaben N: Newcastle R: Roxburgh
E: Edinburgh L: Linlithgow F: Falkirk S: Stirling P: Perth
StA: St Andrews LA: Lauder D: Dalhousie T: Temple Liston

Map 2. The Falkirk Campaign, 1298. The arrows indicate Edward's advance: at Falkirk 22 July. The solid line indicates Edward's withdrawal at Carlisle 9 September.

their way up the east coast. But there is some evidence that, although he meant to settle with Wallace, he was also intent on a punitive expedition;[26] he did not eschew destruction for its own sake and as a warning to the Scots. They, meanwhile, had retired before him, in the belief that the situation was to their advantage. The country south of the Forth was empty of inhabitants; Edward was short of intelligence, his men of sustenance.[27] Wallace knew very well the value of such a withdrawal, which formed an integral part of his strategy. Such a technique was not the creation of Robert I, although his successful employment of it against the armies of Edward II has somewhat obscured the fact. There is a parallel here with Edward II's invasion of 1322; so lacking were the English then in food that they are reported to have found in the whole of Lothian only one cow. At that, the earl of Warenne, son of Wallace's old enemy, commented that he had never seen dearer beef.[28] His father, riding with Edward I and in similar straits, would have understood the sentiment. How close Wallace came to victory over Edward without a fight will emerge. It is too often forgotten that only with hindsight do the events of July 1298 assume their familiar shape. Wallace was content to draw the English on, and the wisdom of that tactic was to become apparent.

Although we lack precise evidence as to his movements at the time of the English advance, we may reasonably make certain basic assumptions. There must have been a strong temptation to meet the English early rather than later; there always was. Wallace cannot have taken the decision to avoid confrontation with the English in the south-east without great thought. Edward had chosen to lead his army through an area which was, and would remain, a fighting-ground, where the Scots, although

141

often unsuccessful, had engaged the enemy on numerous occasions. Dunbar had been but one of a series of defeats suffered by the Scots in this part of the country. Pinkie, and again, Dunbar, lay in the future. The route which Edward followed, through Lauderdale and thus to the outskirts of Edinburgh, which he reached on 11 July, was that favoured by English armies invading from the east. It was therefore a natural focal point for an assault upon the invader. News of his ravaging of the land would reach Wallace. It would rouse the anger of his men. It is not unlikely that Edward intended this.

Yet Wallace was not tempted. He did not deviate from his plan. He waited, as Robert I would wait in other campaigns. Wallace's decision to stand on the defensive, to allow for the wasting of the English army, had been taken well in advance of the invasion. He must have known that an opportunity to attack was possible. In the kind of war in which he believed, intelligence had a great role. Barrow has shown[29] how in this campaign he used contingents from the Lowlands; among these were men who came from the very area through which Edward was passing. From them would come the information he required. Nor would he be free of pressure from the nobles. Dunbar had taught them nothing; their inclination, like that of their English counterparts at Falkirk, was still to go on the offensive. Somehow, he had convinced them of the need for that restraint which not even harsh experience had shown them to be necessary. Wallace's own following, as will shortly be argued, was not inconsiderable. He may have used the threat of deploying it independently to force the nobles into agreement. It is equally possible, however, that he was forced to bargain with the nobles in order to secure their compliance. Their role, and, interestingly, that of the English nobles in the forthcoming battle, indicate that the relationship between leader and led was neither an easy one nor strong even in the heat of events.

The price of that restraint which Wallace urged on his noble allies was to prove a serious one. Because he fought at Falkirk it has always been assumed that he intended from the beginning to give battle to Edward. Wallace's own inclination, however, was the quick strike and retreat, the mounted attack and withdrawal before a counter-attack could be made. Even Stirling does not contradict this; it proves rather that he was adept at seizing the God-given moment. Wallace's great achievement in keeping a Scottish army in existence and, without committing it, almost bringing Edward's plans to frustration, has not been sufficiently recognised. No one has explained how Scotland was to be defended without any army; we cannot be sure that Wallace saw the existence of the army he raised solely in terms of pitched battles. The disaster at Falkirk – for such it was and not just in terms of numbers killed – has proved too tempting for historians. It fits too well into the theory that there, Wallace's period of supremacy was tidily if bloodily ended. What must be said is that no Scottish leader at this time would have scorned battle with the English, not least because of the practical difficulties of keeping an army unemployed in the field. Each would certainly have fought, and equally certainly, under more difficult conditions than those which Wallace provided for the Scots on 22 July.

The English advance was proving something of a disaster. If Edward's army was formidable in appearance and size, it was suffering both the consequences of a Scottish policy of scorched earth and the failure to maintain its own supplies. One version of events gives Edward at this point in the campaign some two thousand horse and an infantry force in the region of twelve thousand.[30] The cavalry were a committed unit, half provided by those same earls who had brought the country not long before to the verge of civil war, the rest recruited by commissioners of array. Of the infantry, the greater part did not share the patriotism of the earls nor the mercenary devotion of the other horse, for they were either Irish or Welsh and would soon show themselves unreliable. When, on 20 July, the army reached Temple Liston, Edward was forced to order the plunder of nearby Kirkliston, which belonged to Bishop Lamberton, in the hope of relieving the hunger of his soldiers. It was no more than a temporary expedient. The few transport ships which made their way to Leith brought wine, not corn.[31]

While Edward was at Temple Liston, a revealing incident occurred.[32] He dispatched Antony Bek, bishop of Durham, to seize certain castles held by the Scots. Bek's men had no food other than the peas and beans which they lifted from the fields. With such a weak force and without siege engines Bek could see no hope of carrying out his instructions. He sent to Edward for new instructions. Edward's reply was indicative of his state of mind; to Bek's messenger he said: 'Go back and tell the bishop that as bishop he is a man of Christian piety, but Christian piety has no place in what he is doing now.' To the messenger himself, Sir John FitzMarmaduke, Edward addressed these still more chilling words: 'And as for you, you are a bloodthirsty man. I have often had to rebuke you for being too cruel. But now be off, use all your cruelty, and instead of rebuking you I shall praise you. Take care you don't see me until all three castles are burnt.' It was as if Edward regarded the Scots as being fit only for the harshest of treatment even at this early stage. FitzMarmaduke carried Edward's answer to Bek. In fear of their king and with the lucky arrival of food ships to encourage them, Bek's troops dealt speedily with the castles.

The success of Bek's men was not enough to raise the morale of the English army for long. Food was still short. Many of the Welsh infantry were literally dying of hunger. Edward now committed one of those errors which so damage his reputation as a soldier. He ordered that the Welsh should be given wine. This, far from solving the problem, inflamed them. Drunk, they fought with the English and a number of priests were killed. Edward could not prevent his knights from attacking the Welsh. Of the latter, some eighty were killed and the rest put to flight. The Welsh spent the night apart from the rest of the army, threatening to change sides. Strangely, Edward claimed to be indifferent. For him the Welsh were still enemies, it seemed; let them join the Scots. 'With God's help', he said, 'we shall then defeat the whole lot of them in one go.' No doubt this was bravado. Nevertheless, for the great general he was held to be, Edward, on this campaign, appears vulnerable and inept. Whatever misfortunes attended the passage of the supply ships, he had relied too heavily on this source of provisions. He miscalculated the mood of the Welsh and neglected the elementary task of ensuring their loyalty. If it is true that he learned from his campaign and was never again to repeat the mistakes he committed there, it is also true that he was only rescued from his own blundering by outside intervention.

That intervention came on 21 July.[33] So desperate was the English position that Edward had decided to retire upon Edinburgh as a preliminary to abandoning the invasion. What happened is told in detail in Guisborough, our most complete source.[34]

It is ironic that it was two Scottish earls, Patrick of Dunbar and Gilbert de Umfraville of Angus, who brought to Edward the opportunity to redeem his reputation. Both had remained faithful to Edward, but the modern mind would find it less than easy to understand that allegiance. With them they had a scout or spy, it is not clear precisely which, who lifted Edward's heart with these words: 'My lord king, the Scots army and all your enemies are no more than eighteen miles from here, just outside Falkirk . . . They have heard that you intend to retreat to Edinburgh, and they mean to follow you and attack your camp tomorrow night, or at least to fall on your rearguard and plunder your vanguard.' The significance of this description of Wallace's intention, although taken from the account most often used by historians of the period, is overlooked. It tells us clearly that Wallace did not intend the pitched battle which followed but aimed to use the English retreat in the most obvious way, the way which, in other circumstances, Wallace, a master of improvisation, would have chosen.

But he was to be denied the fulfilment of his plan. He was not given the time to make the sortie from what we must see as a fortified camp at Falkirk. He had pulled the English forward to the point where, weakened and in retreat, they would offer an easy target for one of those mounted assaults at which he was adept. Edward was saved by the two Scottish earls. He did not hesitate. His words tell of his relief: 'May God be praised, for He has solved all my problems. The Scots will have no need to follow me, for I will march to meet them at once.' Telling his troops to arm themselves, but without, it seems, informing them of their destination, he led them in the direction of Falkirk. That night the English host camped on the Burgh Muir, to the east of Linlithgow.[35] Edward clearly still expected just such an attack as he had been warned of by the Scottish earls; his men were to rest with their horse beside them.[36]

During the night Edward was slightly injured when his own horse trod on him. The news of the accident was enough to panic his army which feared both betrayal and an attack by the enemy. Their reaction was so extreme as to suggest that had Wallace been able to carry out his first intention, he would have had little difficulty in inflicting severe damage on the English. Edward, however, despite the pain from his ribs, dealt more successfully with the panic than he had with the problem of the Welsh. At dawn the English marched through Linlithgow. They soon came in sight of the enemy; on the top of a hill they saw many spearmen. At this the English moved forward in the belief that what they had seen was the main Scottish army. The spearmen, however, retreated and were lost to sight.

This incident has not been considered worthy of much attention. Yet it may be of consequence to an understanding of the battle of Falkirk. What was this body of spearmen? It was large enough to cause apprehension among the English, who took it for the Scottish army. It could have been a late addition to Wallace's forces; if so, such an arrival would in all probability have been noted in accounts of the battle. In the absence of proof, it is possible to advance a tentative theory: that Wallace, in keeping with his intention, as expressed in Guisborough, of attacking the English while they were in retreat, had begun to move away from Falkirk with that in mind. The spearmen, therefore, would be a contingent sent from the fortified site or camp as part of Wallace's plan. This would be consistent with the argument that he was, as at Stirling, intent on improvisation rather than on a setpiece battle. The spearmen, on seeing the English army, would therefore retire on the main Scottish army, bringing with them the unwelcome news of Edward's approach. Thanks to the report he had received, Edward had quite literally stolen a march on Wallace. The latter was forced to abandon his original intention. His army was forced to fight on terms which he had not chosen. That it fought so well tells us that it had been trained with the utmost efficiency.

Wallace's army on the feast of Saint Mary Magdalene, Tuesday 22 July, was the product of two basic determinants. It was predominantly composed of infantry. Scotland was too poor to be able to afford the maintenance of a large force of heavy armoured cavalry on the English model. Such few heavy cavalry as were present were in the gift of the nobles. We shall return in due course to the vexed question of the role of the nobles and their cavalry. If Wallace had always relied after Lanark on mobility to create the maximum effect, his men's mounts must have been light, unarmoured, their function the ancient one of transport to the site of whatever action he intended. At Falkirk, given the circumstances in which he was now to fight, these skirmishers – they cannot properly be called cavalry – would be dismounted and integrated into the mass of the infantry. It was upon the infantry that the outcome of the battle would depend.

After his raid into England, Wallace had begun the long process of creating a standing army. To do so, he used the power of his personality, the requirement that every man between the age of sixteen and sixty serve in arms to defend his country, and that weapon to which he never scrupled to have recourse, fear. Once Guardian, he had the further advantage of authority. The numbers who accepted the call to arms cannot have been great, but their lack of experience, their indiscipline, and the natural fear of the conscripted soldier would make Wallace's task other than difficult. His was, it must not be forgotten, the role of a commander without professional training. No doubt he could employ willing officers, men who had seen service in the earlier part of the war. The question of whether these officers included a contribution from the nobles must remain moot. If, as Barrow says,[37] the earls of Atholl, Menteith, Buchan, Lennox, and Carrick were among the contributors to the Scottish army, it is a far step from that to assigning to them and their like the positive role of training the army. Responsibility for the training was Wallace's, as was the burden of defeat. The total number of troops available to him at the beginning of the battle is impossible to state accurately. We lack the kind of information which permits conclusions to be reached, as in the case of Edward's army, with any degree of confidence, and the figures given for the Scottish dead by English commentators[38] far outstrip any numbers open to Wallace. But we can say that the Scots must have been vastly inferior to the English in all component parts, cavalry, foot and archers. Of the three the foot were his supreme arm, and unlike the other two elements their contribution at Falkirk was exceptional. Over the foot he exercised the necessary control from the outset, and we need not rely on Bower's fanciful account[39] to understand that he had made good use of time to prepare the schiltroms which were the backbone of the Scottish army at Falkirk. The contribution of the Scottish cavalry and archers was, as we shall see, a different matter; their failure to carry out their role was crucial.

He had prepared the Scots, in a relatively short space of time, not only for the tactics at which he himself was so adept, but for exactly the test which now faced them.

That is, the army was to stand on the defensive to receive the principal English weapon, the heavy cavalry. His dispositions are well recorded in the account found in Guisborough. Wallace had divided the infantry into four schiltroms, the first known mention of what became a standard feature of the war with England but so obvious a tactic as certainly to be well-established. Each of the four, Guisborough tell us, 'was made up wholly of spearmen, standing shoulder to shoulder in deep ranks and facing towards the circumference of the circle, with their spears slanting outwards at an oblique angle'.[40] The hedgehog-like appearance of the schiltroms would be frightening, as it was intended to be. The schiltrom could be switched from the defensive to the offensive, as Robert I was able to do at Bannockburn. The twelve-inch, iron-tipped spears of the infantry were a powerful deterrent to the cavalry, and at Falkirk, as again at Bannockburn, inflicted severe injury on the horses themselves. If, as almost happened, the English cavalry charges were held, the infantry would be converted into an advancing force whose weaponry, once its momentum had gathered, would be irresistible.

The infantry's defensive position had been further strengthened by a fence of stakes. Each of the four schiltroms was surrounded by this enclosure, the stakes, linked by ropes, pointing towards the English. If these enclosures baulked the cavalry, they would then be thrown aside to allow the infantry to proceed to the second stage, the attack. We do not know how many men stood on this day in each of the schiltroms. As the Scottish army is unlikely to have exceeded that of the English, each of the schiltroms would scarcely have contained more than two thousand men. Wallace had with him a small body of archers, men from the Forest of

Selkirk. Archery was not a branch of warfare in which the Scots ever excelled. It does the men of Selkirk no disservice to say that their role at Falkirk, although an honourable one, was less significant than that of Edward's bowmen. These, Welshmen and others armed with the longbow and Genoese mercenaries using the crossbow, could only be effectively countered by cavalry. We shall see how the precaution which Wallace had taken to nullify the menace of Edward's bowmen was thwarted.

Wallace's fortified camp, now a battle formation, was well sited for its new purpose. Its rear was protected by Callendar Wood. In front was the Westquarter Burn. The Scottish position on the south-east side of a hill near Falkirk was rendered stronger still by a boggy loch between it and the advancing English.[41] Wallace's choice of site has been criticised.[42] If it was not ideal, and inferior to that selected at Stirling, it proved almost as successful as on the earlier occasion. We must assume from what we know of Wallace that had he meant to fight at this point in the campaign, he would have arranged matters differently.

When the English saw Wallace's dispositions, the more sensible among them must have appreciated its strength. In Guisborough we read that Edward himself was against an immediate assault.[43] Conscious as he was that his men had not eaten for some twenty-four hours, he proposed a halt. It is impossible to believe that he was not affected at least as much by what awaited him. His opinion was not shared by his subordinates. Edward, surprisingly, could not restrain them. The earls of Norfolk, Hereford, and Lincoln, among others, refused to heed their king. Ignorant of the water obstacle which lay between them and the Scots, the English vanguard moved forward but were forced to swing west round the bog.[44] They must have presented an attractive target to the Scottish archers stationed between the schiltroms. Since there is no mention of the archers at this juncture, the opportunity does not appear to have been taken. On the opposite flank the knights were as enthusiastic as the vanguard. The flavour of their mettle emerges from the words of Ralph Bassett to their nominal commander, Bishop Bek. The bishop, trying to ensure some discipline, was roundly told to mind his own business and to repeat the mass he had said before the battle.

The obstacle of the bog safely negotiated, the cavalry attacked the schiltroms. At the first contact the Scottish horse fled. The inevitable charge of treachery followed in Scottish accounts.[45] Whatever the motives of the cavalry, their flight was a disaster for Wallace. It was bad enough that they had not struck a blow. Worse, their absence was to allow free reign to the English archers. At Bannockburn Robert I kept in reserve a cavalry force of some five hundred under the command of the marshall of Scotland, Sir Robert Keith. Its task was to interrupt the work of the English archers. In the event Keith did more; he broke the lines of archers and they took to their heels. Their loss to Edward II was one of the turning points of Bannockburn. The presence of the future king of Scots at Falkirk is problematical.[46] He cannot have been ignorant, however, of its various phases. If Bruce learned much from Wallace, the use of horse against bowmen was one factor marked in his mind after Falkirk.

With the Scots cavalry gone, the schiltroms were isolated If the disappearance of Comyn and the horse removed from Wallace a potential defence against the English archers, his hopes were frustrated by the ineffectual Scottish archers. These were led by Sir John Stewart of Jedburgh, brother of James the Stewart. Sir

John had been a prominent figure in Scottish affairs for some time. In 1291 he had, with his brother, then a Guardian, and others such as Bruce, lord of Annandale, and Balliol, lord of Galloway, sworn fealty to Edward at Upsettlington. He is to be found on the Ragman Roll five years later. When the opportunity came in 1297, he joined in the unsuccessful magnate rebellion which came to an end at Irvine. His courage, and that of the men under his command at Falkirk, has ensured his reputation as a patriot.[47] He and they, and with them the men of Bute who perished at their side, are properly commemorated in a monument erected in 1877. There is no need to question the courage of Sir John Stewart and his men. They stood against, and fell, under the might of the English cavalry. They were as devoted to their cause, and as doomed, as the men in the schiltroms. But unlike the latter, there is, apparently, no positive role in the battle to be allocated to the archers under Stewart. It is widely accepted that they could not match the English in power or accuracy. The English longbow was indeed a fearsome weapon; its greatest days lay ahead, in the wars between England and France. But the role of the longbow at Falkirk has been pervasively challenged.[48] Slingers and crossbowmen participated on the English side, and to considerable effect.

What, then, had Stewart and his archers done as the battle unfolded? Their courage apart, there is no contemporary evidence to enlighten us. Wallace had placed them between the schiltroms, but to what purpose? The Scots, it will be remembered, had the advantage of a strong defensive position. Between them and the English lay an obstacle, of which the English were initially unaware. The English cavalry, halted in their headlong charge by water, must have been within range of Stewart's archers.

The Scottish bow, shorter than the English, is considered inferior. But the power of a bow depends on the pull exerted. The English archers pulled the bow to its furthest extent, to the ear, the Scots to the chest. This, of course, limited the range but it is not clear why, at Falkirk as on other occasions, the Scots did not follow the English lead. Wallace was a prudent, far-sighted man in military matters. It is not unreasonable to argue that he had given John Comyn the younger the role – of dealing with the archers – emulated by Bruce at Bannockburn. For whatever reason, Comyn left the field at an early stage in the battle and the opportunity to negate the threat posed by Edward's archers was lost to Wallace. What part had he, in his plan for the battle, given to Stewart? We do not know, but we can suggest that the archers, unlike the schiltroms, need not have adopted the passive role of awaiting the English assault. The first rush, under the headstrong earls, Norfolk, Hereford, and Lincoln, must have presented a tempting target to Stewart and his troops. But Stewart remained, as far as we are aware, detached from this phase of the battle. The English cavalry recovered, with devastating consequences for the Scots. Why did Stewart's archers not produce the necessary impact? As commander, Wallace must accept ultimate responsibility for this aspect of Falkirk, as with others. But we have no means of knowing what his relationship was with Stewart or whether Wallace had sufficient influence with the brother of James the Stewart to direct his actions. Sir James Stewart was emphatically no Comyn. He died heroically but his standing as a patriot depends on the manner of his death rather than on his contribution to Wallace's plan for the battle.

The English cavalry were still thwarted by the continued resistance of the schiltroms. Their weapons wrought much havoc on the English mounts.[49] They could offer no such resistance to Edward's archers. The English king, now in control of his forces, called back the cavalry. The Scots, their ranks already thinned by the brutal charges of the opposing horse, cannot have been ignorant of what was to come. It is easy to imagine their despair, as they stood, impotent, to await the arrows. It is possible, although by no means certain, that the recalcitrant and detested Welsh now joined the English in the missile attack.[50] That, their fate clearly sealed, the Scots did not break, argues well for the discipline which Wallace had instilled in them. They died in large numbers. One English chronicle celebrated the slaughter: 'They fell like blossoms in an orchard when the fruit has ripened.'[51] He goes on the relate that their 'bodies covered the ground as thickly as snow in winter'. These images, while hardly original, convey the horror of the battle as it was now.

When the archers and the slingers had done their work, Edward sent the knights against the broken, demoralised ranks of the schiltroms. Some of the infantry escaped the arrows and lances only to perish by drowning in the bog below their position. The numbers of Scots who had died on this long day which culminated in a massacre cannot be given with any hope of accuracy. The majority were of the common people who had been Wallace's strength from the beginning. One would not expect their names to be recorded.[52] If unknown, their courage mocked the conduct of their betters. Not all of the latter had betrayed them. The Stewart's brother, John, met the same fate as his men. Fordun, who found an explanation of the Scottish defeat in the flight of the nobles, especially John Comyn the younger, tells us that Macduff of Fife was killed at Falkirk[53] Guisborough relates that although the majority of the Scottish knights fled, a handful fought with the schiltroms.

Of the Scottish lords it is Robert Bruce, earl of Carrick and future king, whose role in respect of Falkirk is the most puzzling. He did not escape the censure of Scottish chroniclers. If their view that he led an English troop against the Scottish rear is dismissed as 'pure fiction' by one modern writer,[54] Bruce's most respected biographer twice admits to doubts about Bruce's part, even his presence at Falkirk.[55] Barron, who, in an impassioned chapter defends Bruce against the charge that he was implicated in the death of Wallace,[56] does not place Bruce at the battle.[57] Like another recent biographer of Bruce,[58] he has him working for the Scottish cause in the south-west at the time of Falkirk. The truth is that we do not know if Bruce was at Falkirk, but we can venture that it is unlikely. He was too important a figure not to be mentioned as present if he was there. His activity elsewhere is clear. As with John Comyn, his adversary, his motives elude us. His role in the war since its start suggests equivocation. At the time of Falkirk his support of the Scottish cause did not, it would seem, include subordination to Wallace. Bruce, as always, and again like Comyn, had his own plans and his own ambitions. Treachery, like patriotism, means different things to different men.

In an English chronicle,[59] Wallace is pictured uttering a memorable phrase to his army. Rendered into modern English from the original Scots, it reads: 'I have brought you into the ring: now see if you can dance.' The phrase may not, as has been suggested, be Wallace's own.[60] It hints at a despair which is not found elsewhere in his, admittedly few, recorded statements. It may be more realistic to interpret the sentiment as a recognition that he had done his best and that events must take their course. This would be more appropriate if, as has been argued, it was not his intention to fight at Falkirk. Once battle was joined, however, his ability to inspire as well as to prepare his army was demonstrated. His mistake was to rely on the support of the cavalry over whom he had not assumed control. Why he did not do so can best be explained by his unwillingness to alienate the nobles. He had not, of course, had experience of handling a force of heavy horse, but we know of no attempt by him to find a commander of horse sympathetic to his ends. Had he done so, the cavalry would, it may be argued, have been used as it was at Bannockburn. What the outcome of Falkirk would then have been must remain an intriguing mystery. He left the cavalry in the control of the lords, perhaps as part of that bargain by which they continued to tolerate, if not support, his tactics of withdrawal. Without that control and the opportunity for glory which, before the battle, it offered, they would have been less willing to continue with his army. Their defection at Falkirk was crucial, but it would be unreasonable to blame Wallace for failing to anticipate and then to prevent it. With that defection the English archers were free. Their work began the slaughter of Falkirk, a battle which brought to an end a campaign by Wallace which was a model for its time and a study for another celebrated Scot.

NOTES

1. Prestwich: *Edward I*, 478; Watson: *Under the Hammer*, 52.
2. Prestwich: *Edward I*, 478–79.
3. Watson: *Under the Hammer*, 49.

4. Ibid., 52.

5. Chap. 4 above.

6. Guisborough, 307–08.

7. Powicke, op. cit., 687; Prestwich: *Edward I*, 433–34 and 478; Salzman: *Edward I*, 141.

8. Prestwich: *Edward I*, chap. 16 for a detailed account of events.

9. Palgrave: *Parl. Writs*, i, 312–16.

10. Prestwich: *Edward I*, 111–12.

11. Guisborough, 324; *Cal. Docs Scot.*, ii, 1177.

12. Barrow: *Robert Bruce*, 140.

13. Wallace himself may not have found the saint's intervention unwelcome. His army must by this time have been in some disarray. The problems of carrying back to Scotland the booty which had been taken, the lack of control over the men of Galloway, and the knowledge that he was needed back in Scotland would have been troubling him.

14. The mood is reflected most clearly in Wright: *Political Songs*, passim.

15. Wright: *Political Songs*, 160–80, passim.

16. On the effects of the war on English society at this time and later, see Prestwich: *The Three Edwards*, 72–77; C. McNamee: *The Wars of the Bruces, Scotland, England and Ireland 1306–1328*, 1997 passim; Summerson, op. cit., vol. I chap. 4; J Scammell: 'Robert I and the North of England', *EHR*, lxxiii, 385–403.

17. Barrow: *Robert Bruce*, 98.

18. Prestwich: *Edward I*, 479.

19. Prestwich: *Armies and Warfare*, 117.

20. Ibid.

21. Ibid.

22. Ibid.

23. On the impact of troops on such a town as Carlisle, see Summerson, op. cit., vol. I, chap. 4, p. 197ff.

24. Prestwich: *Armies and Warfare*, 133.

25. Watson: *Under the Hammer*, 62, has 1500. Prestwich: *Edward I*, 479, suggests that 'the cavalry forces probably numbered some 3000'.

26. Guisborough, 324–25.

27. Ibid.

28. Barbour: *Bruce*, 330.

29. 'Lothian in the First War of Independence', *SHR*, Oct. 1976, 151–71.

30. The contrast here between Barrow's figure, Robert Bruce, 139, and that quoted above from Prestwich: *Armies and Warfare*, 133, is, of course, marked. But desertion was a potent factor, and as Prestwich himself says, op. cit., 128, 'under Edward I, armies in Scotland suffered a constant haemorrhage; indeed, desertions began the moment levies left their country muster point'. On the matter of desertion, see also Watson: *Under the Hammer*, 131 and 179, for further evidence of Edward's problems at a later date.

31. Guisborough, 325.

32. Guisborough, 324–25.

33. Ibid.

34. Ibid.

35. Guisborough, 326.

36. Ibid.

37. *Robert Bruce*, 143n.

38. In Wright: *Political Songs*, 176, we read in a 'Song on the Scottish War', 'the king subdues in the field near a hundred thousand'.

39. See chap. 4 above.

40. Guisborough, 327.

41. Ibid.

42. Salzman, 143, says: 'Wallace had not selected his position with any great skill'. Kightly, 178, writes that his position was 'nothing like so strong as the one he had occupied at Stirling'. Barron, 78, states that the Scots prepared to meet the English 'in a situation which had few natural advantages and, from which, in the event of misfortune, there was no easy means of escape!

43. Guisborough, 327.

44. Ibid.

45. Fordun, i, 330. Barrow: *Robert Bruce*, 144, acquits them of the charge of treachery and suggests that they were overcome by panic. He equates their conduct at Falkirk with their behaviour at Dunbar and Irvine. It might be thought that a succession of

such failure was in itself a form of treachery, the more so when in the case of Falkirk their role was crucial; they surely betrayed Wallace himself, if not the army, by their flight. Young, op. cit., 168ff, deals with the relationship of Wallace and Comyns both before and after Falkirk.

46. Neither McNair Scott nor Barrow can place Bruce at Falkirk on the Scottish side. Both evade the issue by concentrating on his activity after the battle. McNair Scott, 52; Barrow: *Robert Bruce*, 145.

47. Bower calls him 'most valiant'. He and his men were among those who were 'utterly destroyed'.

48. Prestwich: *Armies and Warfare*, 133. See also Bradbury: *The Medieval Archer*, 1985, chap. 5.

49. *Cal. Docs Scot.*, ii, 1007, 1011. See also below, chap. 7.

50. Prestwich: *Armies and Warfare*, 127 states that, for whatever reason, 'the Welsh showed little reluctance to be recruited into English armies'. But their role in the Falkirk campaign underlines how unreliable they could be and it is difficult to gauge their contribution to the English victory.

51. Rishanger.

52. Barrow: 'Lothian in the First War of Independence' should be consulted for some names.

53. Fordun, i, 330.

54. Kightly, 180. He does, however, add: 'if present at all, he was fighting on the Scots side.'

55. Barrow: *Robert Bruce*, 145. See also note 46 above.

56. Barron: op. cit., chap. 15.

57. Barron: op. cit., 77, 78, 181.

58. McNair Scott, 50.

59. Rishanger, 187.

60. Salzman, 143.

7

The Time of Sacrifice, 1298–1303

'Our beloved William le Walois of Scotland, knight'

Falkirk was the last opportunity which the Scots were to have to break Edward I's grip on their country. Over the next six years, until the submission of Comyn and his colleagues,[1] he tightened that grip inexorably. The campaigns which he fought between Falkirk and that submission were not uniformly successful; a mixture of inefficiency on the part of the English and dogged resistance by the Scots, both in the field and on the diplomatic front, combined to frustrate his design. What he had begun he found difficult to finish. But Edward was not to be diverted, and his unremitting pressure on the Scots, his permanent superiority in men and matériel, and in time the perhaps inevitable war-weariness of those who opposed him brought the conclusion he desired.

For the Scots all of this might have been averted had the outcome of Falkirk been different. It might well have been different. We are accustomed to thinking of Falkirk as a battle which revealed Wallace's inadequacies as a military leader. But it was also a battle which revealed Edward's inadequacies. He was saved by good fortune and a battle-plan which, though largely improvised, worked. Wallace's plan was the better and, as argued above, faltered and failed because of the defection of the cavalry and the feeble contribution of the archers. He could have foreseen neither of these eventualities. Even without these two basic elements in his plan, however, he was able to do serious damage to the English. We have noted the gloating English reports on the number of Scots who fell at Falkirk[2] but it is too easily forgotten that English losses were themselves far from inconsiderable. The cavalry was not the only factor in Edward's army, if the most highly regarded. Thus, the Master of the English Templars merits a mention as the only English casualty of note, in one account.[3] A second source, adds 'five or six esquires'.[4] This concentration on the fate of the élite arm in the battle tends to disguise the very heavy losses incurred by the English foot at Falkirk. Opinions vary as to the precise numbers of infantry slain by the Scots, but two authorities on the period, drawing on payroll records, indicate a figure of perhaps two to three thousand.[5] For what was not on the English side predominantly an infantry engagement, these were severe losses. The progress of the battle, furthermore, suggests that these losses occurred at that point when, with the Scots ranks decimated by the English cavalry and archers, the schiltroms were at their weakest, immediately prior to their final collapse. If that is so, it is testimony to the innate courage of the Scottish infantry, aided by the discipline brought about by Wallace himself. Like their Scottish counterparts the schiltroms, then, the English foot died unknown, their fate of little consequence to the chronicles. One hundred and ten horses were killed at Falkirk. This figure refers only to cavalry in Edward's pay. It has been shown that thirteen hundred men fitted into this category.[6] Unpaid cavalry might well have given Edward a total cavalry face of some four thousand.[7] We may therefore assume higher losses in horses.

Edward had won the battle but Wallace had inflicted serious damage on the English army and the king was forced before long to return to England. His activities between Falkirk and his arrival in Carlisle on 8 September point to a man in no position to benefit from victory. He sent the infantry ahead of him to Carlisle and with his cavalry looked for Scots where he might find them. Perth and St Andrews were burnt by Edward, but at Ayr he found that Robert Bruce, in his patriotic guise, had forestalled him by burning the town himself. As before Falkirk, so again were supplies problematical for Edward. He had no option but to retreat southwards. Something of Edward's mood may be ascertained from his destruction of Lochmaben as he moved through Annandale–Bruce territory. He had penalised a supporter, the elder Bruce who had never faltered even when insulted by Edward; it was the son, not the father, who was in rebellion.

At Carlisle further problems, redolent of his difficulties with the earls, awaited Edward. Of the earls, Roger Bigod of Norfolk, the marshal, and Humphrey Bohun of Hereford, the constable, were, as far as Edward was concerned, particularly obstreperous. Their adherence in the Falkirk campaign had been achieved only when Edward agreed to implement the arrangements made with Prince Edward in the king's absence the previous year.[8] It had required an oath sworn on the king's behalf by Warenne, Bek and others that he would carry out the arrangements if successful against Wallace. At Carlisle he prevaricated, to the displeasure of Norfolk and Hereford, then aggravated an already tense situation by a grant of Arran to Hugh Bisset of Antrim, without, as agreed, consulting the earls. Bisset's original intention had been to join the Scots, but Falkirk convinced him to change his allegiance, an action hardly likely to prove his loyalty in the eyes of Norfolk and Bohun. Pleading that their men were exhausted, the two left Carlisle.

Edward had come close to defeat at Falkirk and the outcome of the battle might well have swung Wallace's way had his army been larger, swollen by forces supplied by the likes of Bruce and the Stewart. If that had been the case, the Scottish cavalry would have been a more potent factor in the battle. It was not to be. We do not know what reasons prevented the magnates of Scotland from supporting Wallace at this juncture. We can only guess: jealousy, contempt, the politics at which they were more adapt than he, the pragmatism bred in them for generations, divided loyalties. It was left to Wallace to fight a battle which offered Scots their best chance to defeat Edward in the field.

Modern commentators are agreed that Wallace's resignation of the Guardianship was the direct and inevitable consequence of the defeat at Falkirk.[9] His reputation and therefore his hold on the office, it is argued, depended upon continued military success. Denied that, and lacking as he did the advantage of hereditary position or authority on which to fall back, he would thus have had no alternative to resignation. Whether he gave up his office willingly or otherwise is not known, but it is generally accepted that the opposition of the magnates to him

1. Statue of William Wallace at Dryburgh Abbey

2. John Balliol and his queen, Isabelle, from the Seton Armorial

3. Edward I (British Library, Cottonian MS Julius E iv, f. 6)

4. John Balliol pays homage to Edward I (from the fourteenth-century *Chronicles de France*)

5. The statue of Robert Bruce and the Wallace Monument. In real life, were the two men colleagues or opponents?

6. A contemporary battle scene (from the Holkham Bible Picture Book, British Library Ms Add 47 682, f. 40). At top, cavalry in action. Below, archers and infantry. The illustration mirrors elements in the battle of Falkirk.

7. Carlisle Castle, where Wallace was rebuffed in 1097 (© Michael J. Stead)

8. Newcastle town walls. A part of Wallace's body was displayed here in 1305 (© Michael J. Stead)

9. Hexham Priory, Northumberland, scene of a controversial incident in Wallace's invasion of 1097

10. Dirleton Castle, East Lothian, attacked by Edward I in the Falkirk Campaign, 1298 (© Michael J. Stead)

11. Urquhart Castle, assaulted by Andrew Murray, 1097.(© Michael J. Stead)

12. Lanercost Priory, a frequent target for Scottish raids. (© Michael J. Stead)

ECI DE ELLERSLIE

13. Portrait sketch of William Wallace by the eleventh earl of Buchan
(Scottish National Portrait Gallery)

and to what he represented contributed in some measure to his withdrawal from the leadership of the resistance to Edward. There is, undoubtedly, a certain appealing neatness about the sequence of defeat and resignation. It allows for the supremacy of Wallace to be seen as an episode, glorious in itself, but still an episode.

Wallace's resignation, however, and the reasons for it, cannot be so easily dismissed. Scottish popular tradition has long judged him with sympathy. The belief persisted that he was so outraged by the conduct of the Scottish lords at Falkirk that he no longer wished to associate with them and so decided upon resignation. We find this attitude in Fordun:

> But after the aforesaid victory, which was vouchsafed for the enemy through the treachery of Scots, the aforesaid William Wallace, perceiving by these and other strong proofs, the glaring wickedness of the Comyns and their abettors, chose rather to serve with the crowd, than to be set over them, to their ruin, and the grievous wasting of the people. So, not long after the battle, at the water of Forth, he, of his own accord, resigned the office and charge which he held, of guardian.[10]

It would appear, at first glance, that Fordun accepts the link between Falkirk and Wallace's resignation, although emphasising the treachery of his allies at the battle as crucial. Betrayal by Bruce as well as by Comyn cannot be discounted,[11] but it is unlikely to have been the main or the only explanation of Wallace's resignation. Fordun does, after all, mention other factors influencing Wallace. He tells us that Wallace preferred to return to his roots, to his own people, rather than to continue at their head, to their ultimate detriment. We need not question that he did indeed wish to make such a return. To do so was not to admit to failure but to act in a realistic and responsible manner. His departure from the field of Falkirk illustrates this clearly. To the English, not unnaturally, he had fled the battle. Celebrating the carnage among the Scots, the English sang of Wallace: 'Scared by the fear of punishment, the tyrant turns his back, whom the short jacket once pleased: faithless in the day of battle he flies like a truant . . . Wallace, thy reputation as a soldier is lost, since thou didst not defend thy people with the sword, it is just that thou shouldst now be deprived of thy dominion.'[12]

This judgement is, of course, preposterous. Wallace's courage was never at issue; it was not the least of his attributes, entirely to be expected of him. In this, if in no other way, he bears a strange resemblance to Edward II at Bannockburn. We read of that unhappy monarch bent on fighting to the death but advised to leave the field for reasons of state.[13] So it was with Wallace at the earlier battle. He could not permit himself the luxury of a death sword in hand; he was of value to his country and its cause only if he remained alive. He could no longer save the army once Edward had forced a breach in its ranks, but he could retire to prepare further his role in the defence of Scotland. Major rationalises his behaviour thus:

> There are those still living in our midst who will not suffer the word 'flight' to be used in reference to Wallace, and will only allow that he avoided a danger; for flight, they say, must ever bear an ugly meaning. But in this they err. To attack the attacker by waiting for him; to delay; yea, to fly – these too are branches of fortitude; for the greatest general that ever lived may fly but in a certain contingency is bound to fly. For better it is that he should be able to

keep himself and his men in safety against a fitting moment than by their death bring ruin quick and complete upon his country. Wherefore Wallace was justified in seeking safety for his men in flight.[14]

Like Pluscarden,[15] Major, further, has Wallace meet with Bruce after the battle and in a famous set-piece reply to the latter's accusation that he had acted above himself and his station. Wallace is made to speak in moving terms both of his reasons for resignation and of his confidence in the people whom Bruce so despises. If we accept that Wallace, as we are told in these and other sources, was intent upon severing his association with the lords and relying henceforth upon the people from whom he had sprung, we may be close to the real reason for his resignation of the office of Guardianship.

That reason cannot be understood unless one widely held assumption is looked at: that Wallace had no alternative to resignation. Modern opinion, as has been seen, stresses the inevitability of resignation. It is, however, interesting that early sources such as Fordun, together with tradition, imply that, for whatever reason, Wallace *decided* upon resignation; he had, that is, made a choice. We do not know when exactly he resigned; those who draw the connection between defeat and resignation do not offer a firm date for the latter.[16] It is possible, therefore, that Wallace pondered his decision for some time, perhaps over a period of weeks. He had learned patience as Guardian; the army which he marshalled, trained, and brought to Falkirk was the product of months of work as was the co-operation, however fragile in the event, which he had forged with the likes of Comyn and Bruce. He had become a wiser, if now a sadder, man. That being so, it is not unreasonable to suppose, lacking as we do any irrefutable proof to the contrary, that he must have debated the possibility that he could, despite Falkirk, retain power.

This is less of a fanciful suggestion than it may appear. There is no evidence that Wallace left the battle alone – quite the contrary – nor can it seriously be argued that his departure proved prejudicial among the people. Others, as we know, left either with him or about the same time.[17] It is probable that the Scottish lords, whose ranks had by no means been decimated, made their own way without Wallace, to avoid what they saw as the taint of association with him. But Fordun tells us that Wallace escaped 'to save himself and his',[18] a vague formula, it is true, open to more than one construction. Pluscarden, on the other hand, limits those who accompanied him to 'but few'.[19] Major writes of the 'surviving remnant of his army' which he took with him.[20] If we cannot be precise as to the numbers with him, Wallace had some kind of force with him and, despite the slaughter at Falkirk, it would be of some consequence. If we return, briefly, to Wallace's role in the battle, we may find support for this theory. He would have had with him on the day a nucleus of adherents upon whom he had come to rely greatly, such as had been with him from the early days, men who formed – and this was not contrary to established practice – a bodyguard. They would, through their attachment to their leader, be tried and proven soldiers. And can we lightly dismiss the thought that Wallace had foreseen the need for some such group, a need demonstrated beyond argument by the defection of others?

Two factors must be considered in this context. The first relates to the famous remark attributed to him as he addressed the Scottish army before Falkirk.[21] If there is any truth in it, it shows a man who believed that he had done the best he could for those under his command,

and that now, with his preparations completed, he would put his talents to use wherever circumstances dictated. He would not have allocated himself to a place in the schiltroms. It follows from this that, second, he would not have remained stationary, an obvious and attractive target to the enemy, as the battle progressed and the superiority of the English became evident. With his own group – his household troops, as it were – he would have moved about the field, to encourage, to support, to prompt. Not all of those with him can have been killed.

When at length he withdrew from the battle, he had about him, therefore, a force still capable of striking at the enemy. There is an account of a pursuit of Wallace by some of the English which seems to make this very point.[22] While this is romanticised by Major[23] in that Wallace himself turns upon the pursuers and kills one who has been unwise enough to outstrip his companions, the account does ring true. The departure of Wallace can hardly have gone unremarked by the English, and the subsequent pursuit could have involved a more general action than that reported, albeit a limited one quickly over. It is perhaps significant that Sir Brian le Jay, who with Sir John de Sawtry is the only English casualty of importance to be named by the chronicler,[24] is said to have been despatched by Scots when his horse plunged into a bog. The story has all the elements of a classic ambush with the foolhardy Englishman, and possibly others with him, lured to his death, and the episode is reminiscent of the death of Normans in 'the Malfosse' at Hastings.[25] Wallace was not a man to miss such an opportunity. The death of the master of the English Templars has the mark of Wallace. It would have proved that he and his men, far from being demoralised by defeat and concerned only with saving their skins, were to be reckoned with. There is no further mention of pursuit at this time. Nor can we be certain that Edward, with victory his, was concerned with Wallace's capture in the immediate aftermath of the battle. Indeed, his subsequent movements do not suggest a man with a plan to follow up his success. The fatal pursuit of Wallace was the act of a knight, adrenaline-driven, bent on individual glory. Warenne had fled from the catastrophe of Stirling Bridge, with Scots on his tail. Edward II was led away from the field of Bannockburn, then rode for his life, with James Douglas allocated the task of either capturing or killing him. But Edward seems not to have mounted a similar hunt for Wallace. No battlefield is tidy, after as well as during the actual engagement itself. Falkirk was no different in this respect. Prestwick has argued[26] that for all his experience, including defeat at Lewes and victory at Evesham, as well as action in Wales, the Continent, and the Holy Land, Edward fought only one true battle – Falkirk. There, Edward's control of his army had not been perfect at the time of the first encounter with the enemy. The contest had been fierce and long, without any of the agreed pauses to be found in some other battles. Even with the Scots broken, exhaustion must have set in among the English and Edward, wisely in the light of the fate of Sir Brian le Jay, may well have decided that pursuit of Wallace was not a priority. It is not impossible that, naturally elated with his hard-won achievement, Edward expected Wallace to seek terms. Used to a different set of rules from that of Wallace, Edward had misjudged his man.

Events were to show that Wallace, the popular hero, survived the battle even if his position as Guardian was called into question. As was the case to the end of his life, he was able to attract followers; Falkirk was not enough to destroy the devotion he had inspired. Once, like other survivors, he had disappeared into 'the woods and castles'[27] north of Falkirk, he succeeded in moving quickly enough and with sufficient support to constitute a threat to the English as they advanced, tentatively and, it may be, reluctantly. The burning of Stirling and Perth to deny succour to the English has been attributed to him.[28] No one argues that Edward had won Scotland with his victory at Falkirk, but Professor Barrow has stated that the resistance to Edward was immediately taken over by the nobles.[29] But Wallace was still capable of playing a significant role after Falkirk. He continued to enjoy the sympathy of the people on whom he would have drawn for reinforcements, and was as committed as ever to the cause which dominated his life. It may be suspected also that, as he had done before,[30] he dragooned the unwilling to join with him. By his presence he was menacing, and not only to the English.

Wallace was powerful enough to refuse to give up the office of Guardian. If this be doubted, one question must be faced: who was to replace him? There were obvious candidates and, as time would prove, no shortage of them. Let it be remembered, however, that from the little we know, Wallace was not replaced at once. The defeat at Falkirk surely rendered that impossible. If Wallace had left the field for his own good reasons, others of note had either fled or beaten a tactical retreat. Survival was more urgent than discussion. Although we do not know when Wallace resigned, it would have required a formal meeting of the Scottish leadership for the decision to be taken. No such meeting would be possible without preparation; our sources indicate that the Scots leaders must have scattered after the battle.[31] Once they were reunited, hard bargaining would have been a feature of the meeting no less than recriminations, and Wallace would be in a position, if he so elected, to influence that bargaining – and in no little measure. He would not have come alone, any more than would Bruce or Comyn, and his supporters would have watched over the negotiations, a reminder of what he represented. Nor would he have risked a further betrayal, the chance that he would fall a prey to his enemies in the Scottish camp. A defeated leader is a likely prey for those who have been less than enthusiastic in his support. There was no lack of Scots passively opposed to him before Falkirk. His failure there and his decision to vacate the office of Guardian would surely have encouraged their hostility. The Scottish magnates continued volatile, even a year after Falkirk,[32] and we cannot discount the possibility of recrimination and accusations of treachery as a catalyst for an outburst of violence when the Scots came together after the battle. For that reason, we can assume that Wallace would have looked to his own protection and that he had with him a following considerable enough to deter any attempt on him. He cannot have been other than a potent figure at the time of his resignation.

That resignation, and his replacement in the Guardian-ship, has never been placed more accurately than within the period July to December 1298. Our deplorable lack of certainty on this subject allows it to be argued that negotiations over both were protracted. Wallace's resig-nation would therefore not have been immediate, and his role in this period would be a more important one than is usually conceded to him. He would want to ensure his own position but, more crucial to him, to ensure if possible a satisfactory outcome to the negotiations. If that is so, it is significant that those who accepted, even pressed for, his resignation, were unable even at a time of the gravest danger for Scotland to agree on one man to take his place.

Instead, two were appointed, a clear acknowledgement of the problem caused by Wallace's departure from the Guardianship. Robert Bruce and John Comyn the younger of Badenoch together filled the office held formerly by Wallace himself. It is of course indisputable that the office was never considered to be the province of any one man, nor had it been so in practice.[33] But Wallace had laid a quite unique claim to it, and after his departure no other individual emerged with the necessary authority, either personal or inherited, to stand in his place. The alliance between Bruce and Comyn has been hailed as evidence of Bruce's patriotism[34] in that he subordinated his claim to the throne of Scotland, and as proof that the Scots were determined on the survival of the principle of Guardianship.[35] A more detached view of the relationship might be that the Scots lords were again unwilling to put aside their self-interest in the cause of their country. Bruce would not entrust the office to Comyn who, for him, represented the Balliol faction, although Balliol was, legally, still king. Comyn, for his part, was equally suspicious; he was not prepared to concede that Bruce might be the better choice to lead the Scots in the struggle against Edward.

It does not require hindsight to believe that the alliance between Bruce and Comyn was an unlikely one and doomed not to last. In an incident to which we shall return, the two men were at blows in the course of a meeting at Peebles in August 1299. It was a sordid affair unrelated to the safety of Scotland but underlines the tension and mistrust between the Guardians. Bruce resigned possibly as early as November 1299 and certainly not later than May of the following year, when his place was taken by Ingram de Umfraville. The joint Guardian-ship of Bruce and Comyn, that is, lasted at most no more than eighteen months, and from its inception was ill-founded. Wallace could not have been unaware of this. He knew both men well, had striven during his tenure of the Guardianship to reconcile them, and had suffered from their selfishness. He was astute, as he must have been to hold together the disparate elements in Scotland in the months after he assumed the Guardianship. He was a man of great presence, with a partisan and hardened following, in numbers perhaps the equal of those follow-ing either Bruce of Comyn. Given all this, is it not possible that he could – by recourse to a simple expedient – have remained either as sole Guardian or as one of a number of Guardians, and therefore able to influence if not dictate policy and events?

Wallace need have done no more than enter into a pact with Bruce or, perhaps more plausible because of their common allegiance to Balliol, with Comyn. To each he would have brought his personal army, his name, his popularity, and that unique determination which led him on. If he had chosen to remain at the forefront of the struggle at this time, are we seriously to believe that he would have been rebuffed? He could not be ignored if he insisted on a leading role; he had with him veterans who were out of sympathy with the Scots lords after Falkirk and capable, unless restrained by him, of turning on those same lords. He was, in all, far from the negligible figure that is the alternative if we concede that Falkirk was as destructive of his reputation as is generally held to be the case. To the argument that neither Bruce nor Comyn would have tolerated Wallace in authority because of Falkirk one need only cite, again, the self-interest of both. Each was, and would continue to be until the murder of

Comyn almost eight years later, suspicious and jealous of the other, to the extent that the adherence of Wallace must have been welcomed. An alliance with either would have offered Wallace a respectability which would have protected him if circumstances forced an accommodation with Edward. But Wallace withdrew. There is no evidence that he sought to hold on to power. He resigned and thus began that time of sacrifice which condemned him to Edward's justice.

It follows from this that Wallace had rejected the other alternative open to him, that is, of surrender to Edward. To suggest that he had ever considered the possibility is thought heresy, but no matter how unpalatable, it merits investigation. The argument that Edward would not have taken his enemy into his peace is not insuperable. At Wallace's trial in 1305 a reference to an offer of mercy by the king to Wallace was read into the indictment.[36] The approach came after Falkirk, and Edward was claiming at the trial that the prisoner had refused the offer of mercy seven years before. However hollow the proceedings were in 1305, Edward's charge may have had a foundation in fact. It is, of course, true that Edward was intent on blackening Wallace's name before judgement and on showing himself as one disposed to be reasonable to such as admitted the error of their ways and came into his peace. But in 1298 he had not yet become the violent and vicious destroyer of those who opposed him; he had not put to death Scots who defied him nor had he invoked the law of treason against them. Edward, after Falkirk, may have believed, as perhaps Bruce and Comyn did, that Wallace was a spent force; such damage as he did immediately after the battle may have been seen as a last desperate flourish. Had Edward been able to convince Wallace of the wisdom of surrender, it would have produced a greater psychological effect upon the people of Scotland than even the king himself could achieve. If mercy could be extended to Wallace, the great popular hero, and if Wallace accepted it, Edward's hold on Scotland must have been tightened. With Wallace would have come, surely, his supporters; the rift between the magnates and the lowlier members of the Scottish resistance would have widened. Wallace did not come into the English king's peace, but we do not know what form the rejection of the offer took or when he decided to continue the fight in his new role. What his frame of mind was in 1298 it is impossible to say, but he cannot entirely have escaped despair. And if he realised the futility of co-operation with the magnates, he may well have been tempted to look elsewhere in the hope of salvation for Scotland.

The theory that Wallace contemplated continuing the struggle against Edward other than militarily gains credibility when we look at the current political situation and at Wallace's own actions. He remained a convinced and committed adherent of Balliol, and in 1298 the latter's position was improving slightly. Wallace had been instrumental in securing the election of William Lamberton as bishop of St Andrews in November 1297.[37] The bishop's devotion to the Scottish cause was not in doubt, and when he journeyed to Rome for his consecration, which took place on 1 June 1298, he would have worked hard to convince Pope Boniface VIII to seek a betterment of Balliol's situation. On his way back to Scotland, Lamberton stayed in France, where, with other Scots already there he had the opportunity of gaining the ear of Philip IV. At that period, June and July 1298, when Lamberton was first in Rome then in France, both pope and king wrote to Edward. They called on him to free Balliol and to

leave Scotland in peace.[38] Although the release of Balliol
was not achieved until a year later, when he passed under
the protection of the papacy, Wallace would have known
in 1298 of the pressure on Edward and shared in the
hope of an eventual Balliol restoration. As Barrow has
so clearly indicated,[39] that hope had never entirely disappeared among the Scots, and after Balliol's transfer to
papal protection in 1299, it re-emerged, greatly strengthened. By his decision to go abroad in the service of
Scotland, the most intriguing action of his career, Wallace
was demonstrating a belief that the way to achieve the
freedom of Scotland now lay in diplomatic rather than
military activity.

As with the suggestion that Wallace would ever
consider surrender to Edward in 1298, the idea that he
might be prepared to tolerate some kind of arrangement
with him whereby Balliol would be restored as king is
likely to be received with hostility. But neither the
surrender nor the accommodation with Edward should
be disregarded. The first would reflect Wallace's dis-
enchantment with the magnates, the second his hope
that Scotland would have its own king once more. To
this end he would have gone abroad to argue for the
return of Balliol. Such an event could not have been
possible without the agreement of Edward; neither
Wallace nor any other Scot engaged in diplomatic work
could have pretended otherwise. With any such agreement would have gone conditions imposed by the English
king, but conditions, it might be, overseen by such independent authorities as Wallace could convince. It would
not be wholly different from the situation accepted by
the Scots in 1292. Why Wallace went abroad in the first
place has been variously explained,[40] but all commentators are of one mind: his mission was a diplomatic one.

Such a mission does not preclude the possibility that, however indirectly and however painful the thought, he and those like him were seeking just that kind of solution which would allow Balliol's restoration with Edward's agreement. Wallace was not the romantic figure he subsequently became in the popular imagination, an outlaw with the trappings so often acquired with the passage of time. He was a patriot realistic enough to understand what could be achieved and what could not. He is not diminished by the proposal that he would work for a resolution of what was otherwise an intractable problem.

If Balliol was to be restored, Edward could not be ignored. Wallace would have faced that fact with his habitual honesty. Edward was not the man to be persuaded by pope or king to give up his claim to Scotland. He saw it as both legal and valid. As Wallace knew better than most, Edward would fight for that claim. He would have been under no illusion as to the English king's determination to hold on to Scotland; nor would he have deceived himself into believing that military victory over Edward was in any way certain in the foreseeable future. But an accommodation, a restoration of Balliol under some form of English sovereignty, a buying of time – that might be another matter. Wallace was never to be deflected from his support of Balliol; he turned to diplomacy as a more subtle means of working for his restoration. It was further evidence of his honesty, of his capacity to adjust. It cannot have been easy.

There is no precise date to be given for Wallace's departure from Scotland. The incident at Peebles, touched on above, does, however, provide us with some guidance. The events of that day in August 1299 bear relating for what they tell us of Wallace's situation and of the fragile nature of the Scottish leadership without him. A spy in the pay of Robert Hastings, Edward's constable of Roxburgh, was among the Scots present at Peebles and informed Hastings of what had happened there. Hastings in turn passed the information on to his master in a letter written on 20 August, twelve days after the developments he described:

> At the council [that is, of the Scottish leaders] Sir David Graham demanded the lands and goods of Sir William Wallace because he was leaving the kingdom without the leave or approval of the Guardians. And Sir Malcolm, Sir William's brother, answered that neither his lands not his goods should be given away, for they were protected by the peace in which Wallace had left the kingdom, since he was leaving for the good of the kingdom. At this the two knights gave each other the lie and drew their daggers. And since Sir David Graham was of Sir John Comyn's following and Sir Malcolm Wallace of the earl of Carrick's following, it was reported to the earl of Buchan that a fight had broken out without their knowledge; and John Comyn leapt at the earl of Carrick and seized him by the throat, and the earl of Buchan turned on the bishop of St Andrews, declaring that treason and lèse-majesté were being plotted. Eventually the Stewart and others came between them and quietened them . . .[41]

An examination of this extract from Hastings' report is revealing. The sad fact of the recurrence of trouble between Bruce and Comyn may be passed over; little excuse was needed by either for an outbreak of violence. Although Wallace was not present at the council, we do not know why, he had not yet gone abroad. His absence can be explained in several different ways, of course. He could have been barred by those attending, although if that were the case, it would be difficult to understand Malcolm's role. He could have chosen to remain apart from his former colleagues, being disillusioned or despondent. He might have been planning his journey. He might equally by this time have fallen out of sympathy with the continuation of the war in its present form; such an attitude would be in keeping with the argument that he was now committed to a diplomatic resolution of the war. We cannot neglect the fact that, unlike Malcolm, he had played no part in the recent raid mounted by the Scots across the south of Scotland. At one time such an opportunity would have appealed to him, and one cannot but wonder that he did not participate. The raid would have been a reminder to him of those days, the year before, when, before Stirling, he had struck at Lanark, raced to Scone with Douglas to surprise Ormsby, and then hurried to assault the defences of Dundee. It may, indeed, be argued that it was precisely this sort of undertaking for which, by experience and temperament, he was most suited. Yet he did not share in it. His failure to do so unless, in contradiction of Hastings' account, he was already out of the country, is both strange and significant, indicative of his adjusting to the unfamiliar and perhaps unpalatable role he was about to play.

If, for whatever reason, Wallace was not at Peebles, his interests were well guarded. Malcolm Wallace was swift to answer on behalf of his brother and ready to protect both his name and his possessions. What Malcolm is reported to have said is not without its own interest. He asserted that his brother had left the kingdom in peace. That can only mean after Falkirk and at the time of his resignation. Malcolm's remarks may be dismissed as those to be expected of him. But that is not entirely wise. Falkirk was a defeat but it did not end the war in

Edward's favour. On the contrary, even with much of the Scottish army destroyed, Edward was unable to consolidate his position, was forced to quit Scotland within two months of the battle, and would not return until July 1300. Wallace must be allowed some credit for that relatively happy state of affairs; it has not been demonstrated beyond debate that he resigned as Guardian before Edward left Scotland in September 1298. Scotland, thus, in that sense, had been left in peace.

Lamberton, too, was at Peebles. He had returned from the Continent in time to join in the raid, and his continued devotion to Wallace is not to be questioned. According to Hastings, the earl of Buchan rounded on the bishop. Whether this implied violent intent is not clear, although it is not unlikely. Buchan saw in Lamberton a supporter of Bruce and, as Hastings makes plain, Wallace and Bruce were linked through the former's brother. Lamberton was a powerful figure in the Scottish leadership and can safely be assumed to have added his voice to that of Malcolm on behalf of Wallace on this notorious occasion. It is not easy, lacking evidence, to say the same of Bruce. He was concerned, it would appear, more with his own than with Wallace's affairs. Such words as he may have uttered in defence of Wallace would be indirect, originating in his own opposition to Comyn or to anyone who, like Graham, was associated with Comyn.

It is, of course, possible that any indifference felt by Bruce towards the absent Wallace was the result of Wallace's lack of sympathy for those now leading (since his resignation) the Scots. That lack of sympathy is substantiated by Hastings. He reported to Edward that Graham had charged Wallace with leaving Scotland without permission from the Guardians. Wallace was acting as he thought fit and setting out to argue the Scottish case abroad. It makes sense therefore to believe that, once he had decided upon this journey, he was not to be deflected and did not consider the opinion of Bruce and Comyn to be of relevance or consequence. It is also reasonable to assume that he would have spoken with Lamberton before, at length, beginning his journey. If that is indeed so, he would have listened closely to what the bishop had to say on the mission, and the two would have entered into some form of agreement regarding what Wallace was to do. It is quite impossible to accept that Wallace, although enjoying an international reputation because of his achievements as Guardian, would ever go abroad without having the advantage of both Lamberton's knowledge and of written letters of introduction from him. The subordination of his natural aggression to diplomacy notwithstanding, Wallace was too strong a personality ever to be content with the humble role of messenger ascribed to him by McNair Scott, but he would not have neglected to insist on the blessing and the fullest support of the Church, through his constant friend and ally Lamberton, and no doubt also through Wishart. That enigmatic figure, whatever the vagaries of his relationship with Wallace, cannot have done other than wish for the success of the forthcoming mission.

At some unrecorded date, either about the time of or soon after the meeting at Peebles, Wallace left Scotland for the Continent. Again, interestingly, we find ourselves deprived of precise details of his movements and his activities. If he does not entirely disappear, he fades, not from the popular memory, but from the accounts of the chroniclers. Such slight information as we have suggests that he may have visited Norway, France, and Rome, probably in that order, and if we despair of learning the truth we can, as always, turn to Blind Harry to elaborate on Wallace's adventures – for such they must have been – with his customary invention. Thus, if Harry is to be believed, Wallace fought with the French pirate, Thomas Longueville the Red Rover, who, recognising superior virtue as much as strength, became his companion, and with the Englishman, Thomas Lyn, not to mention his epic defeat of an enraged lion. Major[42] is not alone in questioning Harry's fabrications, but in the course of his extended wanderings Wallace would most certainly have had the opportunity of proving his courage in the simple interest of staying alive. Why, therefore, should not Philip IV have sought to enlist Wallace in his service, as the tradition would have us believe? Philip was nothing if not intelligent; an ally of the experience and stature of Wallace was not to be overlooked. That same tradition has the Scot decline the honour, and the rewards of serving the king of France for that love of country which was, finally, to destroy him, but we cannot confidently state that Wallace was not approached by Philip or his agents.

The evidence for a visit by Wallace to Norway lies in a safe-conduct issued to him in the name of Haakon V. This document, together with others of perhaps greater significance, was found on Wallace's person at the time of his arrest by Menteith[43] but, like them, has disappeared. Whether Wallace met Haakon we do not know, and what such a meeting, if ever it took place, was intended to achieve is equally unclear. Certainly, any kind of military alliance between Scotland and Norway was unlikely if not impossible. Norway would remain for some considerable time, as it had always been, an important if unreliable factor in Scottish politics. Had not Eric II, father of the Maid, been among the original competitors for the throne of Scotland, no matter how insubstantial his claim? Largs and the treaty of Perth both lay well within living memory. Not until 1468 would Shetland and Orkney become part of the Scottish kingdom. The Scots, however desperate they thought their situation at the time of Wallace's departure, would not have sought to bring to their shores a Norwegian force whose friendship could never be taken for granted, even if Haakon had been willing to supply it. It may be that, as Barrow suggests,[44] Wallace went no further into the possessions of the king of Norway than the Orkneys; such a journey would still have entailed a safe-conduct. Wallace would in any case be more drawn to Germany than to Norway, to those towns such as Hamburg and Lübeck with which he had been anxious to establish contact in the course of his association with Murray. There is no reference to his going to Germany, but such a visit makes at least as much sense as one to Norway. If indeed he went to Germany, he would first have gone north in order to lessen the possibility of interception and capture by the English, whose ships would have rendered hazardous a crossing of the North Sea by the direct route. Wallace would have been anxious to convince any German towns which he did in fact visit of the continued wisdom of trade with a Scotland still independent of England.[45]

We can speak with more authority when we turn to the question of Wallace and France. That he came to the attention of Philip IV is indisputable, although the exact circumstances seem to puzzle the chroniclers who tell us of the vicissitudes suffered by Wallace at this time. One account has him seized with his companions on the orders of the French king who was ready to turn him over to Edward.[46] Wallace may here have been the victim of a temporary cessation of the feud between the two

184

kings from which the Scots had for long sought to benefit. In June 1299 at Montreuil-sur-Mer a treaty was agreed for the marriage of Edward with Philip's sister, Margaret, which took place on 4 September. Edward, in thanking Philip, merely asked him to retain Wallace in France, a peculiar circumstance to which it will be necessary to return.[47] Whether or not Wallace subsequently impressed Philip by deeds such as those Blind Harry describes, the French king proved to be not unsympathetic to the Scot. Devious as he was, Philip was not the man to allow the marriage of his sister to interfere for long with his quarrel with Edward, and almost four years were to pass before Philip made with Edward that treaty which helped to break the Scottish resistance to Edward. In the meantime, Philip had Wallace in France, a possible source of embarrassment to Edward. It is not beyond the bounds of possibility that he was as impressed by Wallace as Blind Harry would have it, but Wallace was not to be seduced from his mission. On his behalf Philip wrote to Rome to instruct the French representatives at the court of Boniface to aid Wallace, whom he chooses to describe as 'our beloved William le Walois of Scotland knight', in the work he was about to undertake there.[48] Philip's letter is dated 7 November 1300 and therefore heralds Wallace's departure for Rome. What he hoped to achieve there it is difficult to say, for he was about to become involved in a debate of a kind for which he was eminently unsuited, in what was in essence a trial of the question of Scotland before the papal court.[49] At the time at which Philip's letter was written, Wallace had been away from Scotland for more than a year. It cannot have been an easy year for him but, as was his way, he sacrificed himself to the cause of Scotland wherever that cause took him. In his absence, Bruce had resigned the Guardianship, Edward had invaded Scotland in a campaign from which neither he nor the Scots could claim great satisfaction, and a truce of seven months had been agreed. To these and other events in Scotland we must now turn.

NOTES

1. See below, chap. 8.
2. Chap. 6, above.
3. Rishanger, 188. His successor as Master of the Scottish Templars, John of Sawtry, also perished at Falkirk.
4. Lanercost, 191.
5. Watson: *Under the Hammer*, 67, describes the English losses as 'the silent, but significant, casualties of an English victory'. Prestwich: *Edward I*, offers a figure of 'approaching 2000' casualties in the English infantry.
6. Watson, op. cit., 62, suggests that 1500 men-at-arms 'actually served'.
7. Prestwich: *Edward I*, 481, states that there were 'probably' as many as two to three times as many unpaid as paid cavalry under Edward's command.
8. Above, chap. 6. On the oath sworn for Edward, see Prestwich: *Edward I*, 482.
9. C.f. Kightly: *Folk Heroes of Britain*, 181; R. McNair Scott: *Robert the Bruce King of Scots*, 53; Barrow: *Robert Bruce*, 146; Barron: *Scottish War of Independence*, 84.
10. Fordun, 102.
11. Above, chap. 6.
12. Wright: *Political Songs*, 176.
13. Barbour: *Bruce*, 434; *Salacronicon*, 142–43.
14. Major, Book IV, chap. XIV.
15. Major, Book VIII, chap. XXVIII.
16. C.f. Barrow, 146–7; Kightly, 181.
17. Rishanger, 387; *Pluscarden*, Book VIII, chap. XXVIII.
18. Fordun, 101.

19. *Pluscarden*, Book VIII, chap. XXVIII.

20. Book IV, chap. XIV.

21. Rishanger, 187.

22. Rishanger, 188.

23. Major, Book IV, chap. XIV.

24. Note 3, above.

25. On Hastings, and on 'the Malfosse', the reader is referred to McLynn: *1066 The Year of Three Battles*, 1998.

26. *Armies and Warfare*, 306. In the same paragraph, after stating that 'full-scale battles were not frequent', Prestwich points out that Hastings was probably William the Conqueror's 'sole experience of commanding a major set-piece battle' and that 'Henry II was not present at a single one'. Wallace had experience of two, Stirling Bridge and Falkirk, in a much shorter military career.

27. Rishanger, 387.

28. Kightly, 181.

29. Barrow: *Robert Bruce*, 146.

30. Chap. 4, above.

31. The small force of cavalry had fled; the Comyn faction, according to Fordun, had deserted; what Bruce did is unclear; Wallace himself left the field.

32. For evidence, see below on the event at Peebles.

33. On the development of the Guardianship, see N. Reid: 'The Kingless Kingdom: the Scottish Guardianship of 1286–1306', *SHR* LXI, 2, no. 172, 1982.

34. McNair Scott, 53.

35. Barrow: *Robert Bruce*, 147.

36. Chap. 10, below.

37. Chap. 5, above.

38. Rishanger, 185.

39. *Robert Bruce*, chap. 6.

40. Kightly (182) sees his mission as of his own making; McNair Scott (53) makes him Lamberton's messenger to France; Barrow: *Robert Bruce*, 165, recognises that his work abroad was more important. Reese: op. cit., 107–08, mentions Lamberton in this context. Young, op. cit., 171, links Wallace with Matthew

Crambeth, bishop of Dunkeld, and others in France and Rome. For Crambeth see Barrow: *Kingdom of the Scots*, chap. 8.

41. *Cal. Docs Scot.*, ii, 1978, in Public Record Office, London. Young, op. cit., 169, states that the incident at Peebles demonstrates the continuing 'animosity' between Wallace and the Comyns which, he argues, had begun with Lamberton's election to St Andrews.

42. Major, Book IV, chap. XIV.

43. See Barrow: *Robert Bruce*, 164 n. 4.

44. Ibid.

45. Barrow, 14–15, traces briefly the German interest in trade with Scotland.

46. Rishanger, 387.

47. Chap. 10, below.

48. Stevenson: *Documents Illustrative of Sir William Wallace, his Life and Times*, 163.

49. On the proceedings in Rome, see Barrow: *Bruce*, 166–69; Barrow: *Kingdom*, 244–45; McNair Scott, 59 and 241–42.

8

The Time of Doubt, 1303–1304

'For God's sake do not despair'

The date of Wallace's return to Scotland from the work he had undertaken on the Continent is not known. Nor do we have details of the means whereby he re-entered his native land. The fact that he was able to do so apparently unhindered argues for either English ineptitude or a reduction in surveillance. Wallace's role in France and at the papal curia was an important one. In the case of his time in Rome, his function has been described as 'the Scottish counterpart of the powerful English delegation'.[1] This was led by Henry Lacy, earl of Lincoln, and Hugh Despenser, father of the favourite of the future Edward II. Their brief, ostensibly the matter of Anglo-French disharmony, may have been widened to lay the ground for Edward's rebuttal of Boniface VIII's bull of June 1299, '*Scimus fili*'. Carried by Archbishop Winchelsey, Boniface's rebuke to Edward over Scotland did not reach him until the following summer, in Galloway.[2] The embassy by Lincoln and Despenser is seen as the first step in Edward's response.

The departure of the English embassy to Rome is contemporaneous with Philip IV's letter of commendation for Wallace. It is likely therefore that Lincoln, who had fought against Wallace at Falkirk, would have the opportunity to discover whether Wallace was as fine an advocate for his cause as he was a soldier. Wallace's reception in France, whether we rely on the admittedly limited facts available to us or draw on Blind Harry, indicates that he was seen for what he was, a courageous and reputable agent for his country. There is no reason to suppose that he was viewed differently in Rome. If that is so, Edward cannot have been left in any doubt of the situation by his representatives on the Continent, such as Lincoln and Despenser. It would be quite wrong to imply that Wallace had the necessary forensic skills to take the leading role in the presentation of the Scottish cause at the papal curia. That honour belonged to Master Baldred Bisset.[3] Bisset and his colleagues, Master William Frere, archdeacon of Lothian, and Master William of Eaglesham disposed of one of Edward's arguments in words which must have appeared to Wallace, himself a powerful presence in the Scottish diplomatic endeavours. Edward's claim to have 'full possession of Scotland' was thus refuted; it was stated by the Scots that he held 'only certain places in the dioceses of St Andrews and Glasgow'.

The Scots must have felt that they had cause for this robust rejoinder to the English king, for also contemporaneous with Wallace's time on the Continent was a gradual but important improvement in the status of John Balliol. From July 1299 until the summer of 1301 he was kept in papal custody. He was then placed by Philip of France in the family home at Bailleul-en-Vimeu in Picardy. Even Edward, within months of Balliol's move to Picardy, was drawing the conclusion that Balliol's restoration as king was possible. With France and the papacy supporting Balliol at this period, Edward was driven to concede that 'Scotland may be removed out of the king's hands (which God forbid) and handed over to Sir John Balliol and his son'.[4] The Scots were to be disappointed in their hopes, but the possibility of a Balliol restoration had its effect on the thinking, and loyalties, of Robert Bruce, the earl of Carrick.[5]

If Wallace was a significant voice on Scotland's behalf, in Paris and Rome, then it is surely inconceivable that Edward's envoys abroad omitted to keep their master informed of Wallace's activities and his movements. He who had led Scottish resistance in battle was now achieving another kind of success. Intelligence gathering was by modern standards unsophisticated and under-developed but could at times be effective.[6] The report on the gathering of the Scots leaders at Peebles in August 1299 has already been noted.[7] The English, for their part, were suspicious of the Scots in this regard; secrecy was enjoined on Warenne and others when they were summoned to a war council in York before the Falkirk campaign.[8] Edward, of course, had cause for concern, at least in his own mind; the celebrated case of Thomas de Turberville, executed for working on behalf of the French government, lay only a few years in the past.[9] Within Scotland itself Edward's agents were constantly on the alert. Simon Fraser was one who was viewed with considerable doubt. In 1299, Sir John Kingston, keeper of Edinburgh Castle, made his feelings known; Fraser, he said, in a report on the Scots, 'is not of such good faith as he ought to be'.[10] Both Fraser and Wallace were to learn that their movements were watched, and detailed, even by their fellow countrymen.

The English king was always keen that his enemies fell into his hands, if at all possible, through their fellow countrymen. He had learned the value of bribery in his Welsh wars. On at least two occasions in 1282, Edward paid spies for surveillance on the Welsh prince, Llywelyn ap Gruffyd, and his brother, David. Llywelyn was spared the death of a traitor, being killed, unrecognised, in battle. His brother was far less fortunate. Handed over to Edward by the Welsh, he suffered the agonies of hanging, drawing and quartering at Shrewsbury. A price of £100 was put on the head of Rhys ap Maredudd, who met his fate at York. Another rebel, Madog ap Llywelyn, escaped capture by Welshmen only through the power of his oratory.[11] He was not long at large; the Welshman, Enyr Fychan, claimed responsibility for Madog's capture, although an Englishman, John de Havering, did insist that he was the real captor of the Welsh rebel.

What had happened in Wales, Edward hoped for in Scotland. But Wallace, returning to Scotland, was neither intercepted nor betrayed at this time. Reports on his travels must have reached Edward, and it is not unlikely that elements in the English fleet were given the task of seeking him out as he travelled from the Continent. Edward's use of his fleet in the war with Scotland was almost entirely for the purpose of moving supplies north.[12] On the east coast, ports such as King's Lynn, Yarmouth, and Hartlepool fulfilled this function. Ireland catered to the west. The hostility of France ensured that the Cinque Ports in particular had a defensive role in English strategy. But while Wallace was, to our knowledge, still abroad, the defeat of Philip's army by the Flemings at Courtrai in July 1302, and the rapprochement between him and Edward culminating in the treaty of the following May,[13] eased somewhat the need for cross-channel vigilance by the English. In theory, that would have freed ships to watch for Wallace, if Edward so intended. The Cinque Ports alone could provide, when required, some fifty ships. Numbers for royal ships were fewer, but still considerable; Edward had ordered the building of thirty galleys in 1294.[14] These figures suggest that Edward would have had at his disposal ships enough to mount patrols on routes open to Wallace.

But was Edward bent on the capture of Wallace? Defeated at Falkirk, with the Guardianship lost and himself absent from his native country and remote from developments there, Wallace may well again have seemed a broken reed to the English king. Edward, after all, was dismissive of the Scots as a race, an opinion shared by his people.[15] The ease with which Berwick was captured, and the fiasco of Dunbar, offered evidence to support Edward's remarks to Warenne in 1296. Falkirk, in Edward's eyes, had more than avenged Stirling Bridge and implied to him a return to the natural order of things. He would be aware of Wallace's involvement on the Continent but, for Edward, the role of diplomat was of less consequence than that of the soldier. While Wallace was in France and in Rome, he was, to Edward, not the threat he had been as Guardian. It is not inconceivable that in these circumstances Edward who, it will be remembered, had spurned Philip IV's offer to hand the Scot over to him,[16] no longer had an interest in Wallace.

All that changed with Wallace's decision to return to Scotland. What motivated him to do so is unclear. An appeal to his patriotism by Lamberton or Soules, a longing for his native country, a conviction that he still had a part to play there, the inbred fatalism of the martyr – these are possibilities. When he did return, it was to a subordinate position in a Scotland different from the one he had left. The balance of power had shifted and the ordering of affairs was, in terms of the Guardianship, in new hands. If Wallace was unique in his achievements, he was not, of course, unique to the independence of Scotland. The armies which he led at Stirling and more particularly at Falkirk were filled with men of like persuasion. Unnamed and in any other context viewed as unimportant, they were ready to lay down their lives at his command. They stood to the end at Falkirk, helpless against the missiles and the final cavalry attack. Alongside them, if not always in battle at least possessing a special kind of expertise in government, must be placed those without whom independence was impossible to accomplish. It was with them that authority had resided since Wallace's decision to resign from the Guardianship. Superior to him in origins and social class and often lacking his resolution, they followed their own path, parallel to his but sometimes crossing it. They were the people who carried out the complicated diplomatic manoeuvres and maintained the government of Scotland as the response to Edward's repeated assaults.

By the beginning of 1301 necessity had forced the Scots to accept that a return to the concept of a single Guardian was unavoidable. The combination of Bruce and Comyn, already noted,[17] could not survive the clash of personalities and ambitions. The addition of Bishop Lamberton, Wallace's choice for the see of St Andrews in 1297, to the combination of Bruce and Comyn, could only delay the inevitable. Comyn held on to office while Bruce chose resignation. Whether Bruce, in resigning, was planning that defection to the English which ultimately took place in January or February of 1302 is open to debate. As long as Balliol retained that place, however unjustified by his person or by events, which made his restoration

194

the continued obsession behind Scottish diplomacy, the defection of Bruce was a matter of time. Ingram de Umfraville replaced Bruce as Guardian on 10 May 1300 at the parliament of Rutherglen, but the triumvirate which he formed with Comyn and Lamberton did not last a year.

If the Scots then concluded that they must select a sole Guardian because dissension prevented an alternative, there was no outstanding candidate. Comyn's apparent failure to work with others was open to criticism, while his conduct at Falkirk must still have rankled. Bruce was not free of the suspicion of inconstancy and personal ambition. He would in any case be opposed by Comyn, as he himself would have opposed the other man. Umfraville had a long and distinguished career in the war but, in the context of the Guardianship, did not match the standing of Bruce and Comyn. Lamberton, as a bishop, was unlikely to be considered. Wallace, the first sole Guardian, and despite Falkirk, neither forgotten nor disregarded by the people, had disqualified himself and was absent on the Continent. It would be idle to suppose that, had he been in Scotland, he would have been considered by those whose voices carried most weight; he had been relegated, as far as they were concerned, to the lower ranks.

We are ignorant of the process of selection and of the means by which the choice of John de Soules was arrived at. Although he emerged as Guardian as a compromise, he should not be undervalued. Soules was a moderate in the sense that he was not bound to the Bruce or the Comyn faction. If his name appeared as one of the auditors acting for Robert Bruce the Competitor in the protracted search for a king after the death of Margaret of Norway, he was to maintain a certain distance from the family's later activities. It is true that he did not escape future censure,[18] but the source of the censure, the chronicler Fordun, was not impartial. Soules' relationship, through the marriage of his nephew into the Comyn family, with John Comyn, Bruce's opponent, surely counted more with Fordun than it did with those who sought a Guardian for Scotland in early 1301. It has been written of this neglected, virtually unknown, man that his 'record of constancy in the patriot cause can stand beside that of Wallace'.[19] Given Wallace's unshakeable hold on the public imagination and Soules' relative anonymity, that statement, however reasoned, is not well supported. Unquestionably, he made no impact comparable to that of Wallace. But of the period 1296 to 1305, it might be said that no one did. Soules made no end as a martyr on an English scaffold as did his more celebrated contemporary. But if Soules died quietly, it was as an exile in France, a determined fighter for Scotland. How he was seen by the English can be deduced from their treatment of him when, with Wallace and Simon Fraser, he refused to submit to Edward in 1304. Soules, unlike Wallace, was not pursued to the death by Edward, but Edward nevertheless appears to have looked on him as one of the more dangerous of his Scottish opponents. At this time, Edward, although generally in a conciliatory mood, decreed that 'The Stewart, Sir John de Soules and Sir Ingram de Umfraville are not to have safe conducts nor come within the king's power until Sir William Wallace is given up'.[20] Unlike the Stewart and Umfraville, Soules stubbornly refused to come into Edward's peace, a stance of which Wallace, with whom his connection is evident from Edward's decree, would have approved.

Wallace and Soules, then, were both the victims of the relentless, almost pathological, hostility of Edward I. It is an intriguing thought that that monarch, to whom the motto *Pactum serva* or 'keep faith' has been ascribed, failed so signally to see its virtue in others. For him, the character of Robert Bruce, that most inconstant of men, was more appealing. In him perhaps he recognised himself. He forgave Bruce where he could not bring himself to let Wallace live or grant Soules his peace other than on conditions which he must have known Soules would reject. As they shared the enmity of the English king, so did Wallace and Soules share the belief that the independence of Scotland was linked inexorably with the restoration of Balliol. They maintained to the end that it was for the Scots themselves to choose to keep or replace that pathetic man. Although Soules from his exile in France would support Bruce when the latter had murdered Comyn and made himself king, he was Balliol's man while the possibility of a restoration existed. In this his constancy was the equal of Wallace's own. We may doubt the wisdom of their continued allegiance to Balliol. He was not a man to inspire devotion. He had lost his throne in the most ignominious of ways and, once removed from Scotland, was content to allow others to risk their lives and lands on his behalf. But Wallace and Soules were not romantics. They were under no illusions as to Balliol's quality. Hard-headed and practical, they saw in Balliol a symbol of choice and therefore of freedom.

Under the Guardianship of Soules the Scottish efforts to secure the restoration of Balliol were intensified. At Rome, to which Wallace had made his way, the papacy had continued in the person of Boniface VIII that policy of sympathetic understanding of the Scottish cause which dated at least as far back as 1294. This was in large part due to the debating skill of the Scottish delegation which, with Master Baldred Bissett an exceptional advocate, made such an impression at the papal court. It was from Soules that this delegation, of which it is possible Wallace was a member, derived its authority.[21] The Scots, confident that their success over Edward's representatives at Rome was an important step towards the return to Scotland of Balliol, appeared to have deceived themselves into thinking that Edward would concede it. He had, of course, no such intention. Certainly, he would never allow Balliol or any other king of Scotland to rule without imposing his own conditions. But there is no evidence that he had any concession in mind. Soules and the Scots could argue as they would, Edward would be bound by no will other than his own.

The Scots under Soules were faced by the unpleasant fact that only the death of Edward was likely to end the war. There was no sign of that in 1301. In the summer he campaigned in Scotland with his usual vigour, but with as little success as in the previous year. He brought with him his son, Prince Edward, to whom he entrusted the submission of the south-west. It was the king's wish, it is said,[22] that the prince should have 'the chief honour of taming the pride of the Scots'. The prince was as un-successful as his father, but learned something of his intransigence. Edward spent the winter of 1301 to 1302 at Linlithgow, but if it was his capital, he was in no sense the master of Scotland. Soules knew better than to offer Edward the opportunity of a decisive battle, but his tactics of harassment wore the English down and Edward was forced to agree to a truce of nine months on 26 January 1302.

The truce had not rid Scotland of the English presence. Nor could it have had any effect on two significant events of 1302. Bruce defected to the English, the possibility of the restoration of Balliol no doubt a strong factor in his calculations.[23] If that is so, it says much for the power of Scottish propaganda both in Rome and at the court of Philip of France, into whose custody Balliol had been released in the summer of the previous year. Bruce, a realistic man when compared to such as Wallace, must have been affected by the general Scottish mood. What damage his defection did to the Scottish cause it is impossible precisely to say. It must, certainly, have been a counter to the Scottish propaganda and it made Edward's position in the south-west easier.

More serious for Scotland was the change in the fortunes of Philip of France, which occurred after his defeat at Courtrai in July. The arrogance of the French nobility was as great as that of the Scots, and as at Dunbar produced the same outcome if with greater slaughter. Thereafter Philip was less able to support the Scots, even if he had wished to. Unsentimental as he was, the French king, also distracted by his notorious embroilment with the papacy, was looking with a less sympathetic eye than before at the situation in Scotland. He had to assess what the Scots could offer; it is not surprising that he saw no profit in the alliance with them. Soules did not fail to recognise the danger and himself went to France in the autumn. With Lamberton, James the Stewart and Umfraville, among others, he argued in vain. If Rome in 1301 was a happy arena for the Scots, Paris in 1302 was not. The interests of France alone dictated Philip's answer.

On 20 May 1303, a treaty of peace was signed between France and England at Paris and ratified on 10 July by Edward, who was then at Perth. Scotland, excluded from the treaty, was open to him. Hostilities had resumed with the end of the nine-month truce and Edward had wasted no time in ordering his lieutenant in Scotland, Sir John Segrave (later to bring the captured and doomed Wallace to London), into action. It is with these events that Wallace once more enters the picture. What he had been doing since his work on the Continent we do not know and it is, simply, idle to speculate. For one English chronicler of the period, however,[24] there is no doubt as to his role. Wallace, 'their commander and captain', was at the head of the Scots. This is plainly incorrect. He could not re-emerge in authority. With Soules in France, affairs in Scotland had passed into the hands of John Comyn,[25] the former Guardian who assumed the position for a second time. It is not credible that Comyn should have allowed Wallace the position with which Rishanger credits him. Enemies they may not have been, but Comyn, as at Falkirk, was no admirer of Wallace. That apart, as well as Wallace's suspicion of Comyn, again the legacy of Falkirk, there is no record of any achievement by Wallace since his resignation of the Guardianship which could, in military terms, have entitled him to command. He had passed from the forefront if not from the minds of the people.

This is not to say that he did not throw himself into the struggle and that he did not, by example, animate the Scottish resistance. He would always do that. But again it is difficult to allot him a precise place in what was happening. It is impossible to state categorically that he was present at the success the Scots achieved at Roslin on February 24 1303.[26] Sir John Segrave, on the instructions of his king, who was still not ready to assume command in person in Scotland, was leading a large force of cavalry on a reconnaissance to test the Scottish strength west of Edinburgh when he was set upon by Scottish troops. These, mounted, had come from Biggar in an action in which it is tempting to see the hand of Wallace. Learning of the English advance, they had scorned the darkness and surprised Segrave, whose force suffered badly in the attack.[27] A number of English knights were killed, more were captured, and Segrave himself, at the head of the first brigade of horse, was badly wounded. He was rescued soon enough, but had almost met with disgrace. But Wallace was not the leader of this Scottish attack. If he took part, it was under the command of the Guardian, John Comyn, and Simon Fraser. Roslin was not a great victory – it made no difference to the course of events, but it proved that in the tactics of which Wallace was such a master lay the best chance of success for the Scots.

The arrival of Edward himself in Scotland, as so often, swung control of the war away from the Scots. He had summoned his host for May and by the middle of that month had crossed the Border. He was at Roxburgh on 16 May, Ascension Day. He again gave his son a command in the south-west. With the prince went Richard de Burgh, earl of Ulster, Robert Bruce's father-in-law. Edward moved through the east of Scotland in what was a copy of his progress of 1296. Although it was less of a formality than on the previous occasion, he met little resistance. He had chosen to avoid Stirling with its castle, held by Sir William Oliphant, another of those lesser but still worthy Scots who defied Edward almost to the death. Edward was a master of detail, prepared to employ whatever methods were best suited to his purpose. His army was able to cross the Firth of Forth and thus bypass Stirling on three prefabricated bridges which he had had ferried up the east coast from King's Lynn. In the following year he would take Stirling with the help of siege engines which the Scots were never able to match.

Of course Edward had to find the money for these and the other massive expenses which this and similar campaigns entailed. Edward could never forget this, nor was he allowed to by the magnates and the clergy upon whom he had continued to make the kind of demands which had brought civil war close in the period before Falkirk. Edward could never entirely reconcile himself to the fact that the Scots were as determined as he, and he therefore found an excuse for his failures in Scotland in the shortage of ready money. He had made plain when he wrote in 1301 to the exchequer:

> And you can be certain that if it had not been for a lack of money we would have finished the bridge which was started to cross the Scottish Sea and you must understand for sure that if we had been able to cross this season, we would have achieved such an exploit against our enemies that our business in these parts would have been brought to a good and honourable conclusion in a short time.[28]

The conquest of Scotland would have offered Edward a partial solution to his financial problems. His failure to achieve that conquest may in part explain his growing impatience and, ultimately, violence. But in 1303, while he could not forget the need for money, he was able to enjoy his progress through Scotland. Only at Brechin, where he arrived at the end of July, did he face serious opposition.[29] Barron tells us that he found the castles of Urquhart and Cromarty defiant and their capture involved heavy fighting.[30] Edward was at Kinloss in September and then returned to Dunfermline, intending to winter there.

It is impossible to say if Wallace was able to make any attempt to interfere with Edward's progress through the eastern half of Scotland. There is little likelihood that he did, for he had retired into the Forest of Selkirk, so often his lair in the past. The dangers involved in an assault on the powerful and confident army which Edward commanded were too great. The territory over which Wallace would have had to travel to carry out an attack was held by the English. The shelter of the forest, with the opportunity it offered for regrouping and planning away from the threat of harassment by the enemy, could not be ignored. Wallace, therefore, now returned to that form of warfare by which he had first made his name – the raid.

The long-established belief, to which Trevelyan, among others, gave expression, that 'Wallace was a guerrilla leader of genius',[31] has been challenged with great authority by Barrow.[32] Wallace's use of large armies, at Stirling and Falkirk, appears to support Barrow's argument. The skill with which he trained and then handled these armies in battle shows that he was confident in the set-piece. But he was adept in the command of the smaller as well as of the larger unit. Stirling and Falkirk are evidence of his talent for improvisation rather than of that conservatism of which Barrow writes. It was a talent which he shared with his enemy, Edward I. However meticulous his preparations, Edward excelled in the change of direction, the shift of emphasis, the taking advantage of an opening. He did not defeat the Scots at Falkirk because of his attention to detail. He could not even dictate the course of the battle; his subordinates disregarded him, where they did not disobey him. He did, however, see the weakness of the Scots once the cavalry had fled, and he did not hesitate to bring into action the one branch of his army to which the Scots now had no answer. It may be that genius in war lies in that one quality which Wallace and Edward had in common. In 1303 Wallace was denied an army. He

203

therefore fell back on the tactics of the guerrilla. Since Falkirk the Scots, wisely, had not used the call to arms which produced a large and, if badly handled, an unwieldy force. For Wallace there was no alternative to the raid.

We thus find him issuing from the forest to strike into Annandale and Liddesdale and as far south as Cumberland. He was not, however, in sole control of the considerable force of infantry and horse which was employed on this occasion.[33] The raid of June 1303 is of interest for two particular reasons: the leadership and the intention behind the sortie. With Wallace were associated Comyn and Fraser. His relationship with them could not have been easy, for by this time they did not share Wallace's own attitude to the continuation of the war as such. Balliol, especially after the Anglo-French treaty of 20 May, no longer had any realistic hope of restoration. He himself had settled for a life of retreat, far from the scene of action, and might not have welcomed a return to Scotland. Comyn and Fraser knew this; their submission to Edward was a matter of time. Comyn was still in arms in the autumn, a threat to the English, but a reduced one. Like Bruce, he was not a simple man but as inclined as his opponent to consider his own future. Whether he, again like Bruce, had ambitions to replace Balliol as king, albeit under Edward's tutelage, is a mystery, but he saw himself as second to none in the Scottish hierarchy. Fraser died in 1306 and, if he is remembered at all, it is as a Scottish martyr. But he could never match Wallace's resolution. As recently as 1300 he had fought on the English side at the siege and capture of Caerlaverock. His subsequent move into the Scottish camp was never forgotten or forgiven by Edward, whose terms to Fraser were severe. Were Comyn and Fraser at the time of the raid already considering submission? There is no means of answering that question. But the raid was the final throw of the Balliol party, so strongly represented by Wallace, Comyn and Fraser.

If Wallace and his colleagues hoped by their raid into Cumberland to force Edward to turn to its defence and thus relieve the pressure on Scotland, their secondary task must have been to punish Bruce for his defection by striking at his home territory of Annandale. Bruce's value to the English cause in 1303 and 1304 was not merely one of propaganda. Even those who argue for him must concede that he was active in Edward's service.[34] Comyn therefore, for his part, did not need the excuse of a family feud to attack Annandale. As for Wallace, we can assume that he saw in the raid a legitimate method of exacting revenge upon one whom he would consider a traitor. It was not in his nature to equivocate when the question was one of loyalty to Scotland. He applied throughout his career one elementary test, and that Bruce had failed.

The raid, of course, did not succeed in its primary aim. In that respect, if not desperate, it was from the beginning hopeless. Edward was not to be diverted; in his present campaign lay the best chance of the final subjugation since 1296. In May, despite the blow of the Anglo-French treaty, the Scots, at least those in Paris, were optimistic enough to believe that Edward might again concede a truce.[35] Such an attitude was ill-conceived and ill-founded. The facts argued against it. Edward swept through the east; Bruce was his man, Comyn was beginning to weaken. However volatile he might be, Edward was always capable of patience when, as in late 1303, he could see an end in sight. He waited, secure in the knowledge that those who had defied him would, at length, come to him. He was not entirely a cynical man, rather an experienced one. He could categorise the Scots with a fair degree of accuracy and had done so from the start of the proceedings to find a king of Scotland. Wallace, unlike the others, defied Edward's calculations.

He would have no part in the negotiations which led to the general Scottish submission in February 1304. He may have been strengthened in his resolve by outside influences. At various stages throughout the long war the Scots showed themselves capable of the most sublime sentiments, expressed in letters and documents. If the most celebrated example is to be found in the Declaration of Arbroath, there were others too often overlooked. One such was a letter written on 25 May 1303 on behalf of the Scottish delegation then in Paris with the thankless and fruitless task of dissuading Philip IV from an alliance with England.[36] We do not know who was responsible for the drafting of the letter, whether it was Soules or Lamberton, or, no less likely in the circumstances, a clerk imbued with their spirit but better able to put their thoughts into words. The letter urges constancy and offers hope. To those for whom it was destined it said: 'For God's sake do not despair. If you have ever done brave deeds, do braver ones now. The swiftest runner who fails before the winning-post has run in vain.' These words might have been written *of* Wallace rather than *for* him and those who persevered with him. The letter may never have come to his notice, but how appropriate it was. Tragically, he would fail well before the winning-post, but by that failure he did prove the letter wrong. In late 1303 and early 1304, as Comyn and the other leaders of Scottish resistance were seeking first a respite and then to come into Edward's peace, he did not swerve from his duty and the task he had set himself. The claim by one

English chronicler that Wallace sought terms at the beginning of 1304 does not ring true. The reason is not one based on emotion but on one element of the supposed approach to Edward. Wallace, we are to believe, requested of Edward, through intermediaries, that he be allowed to 'submit to his honest peace without surrendering into his hands body or head'. This is a standard formula. It is when we consider the words which the chronicler puts into Wallace's mouth that we are forced to dismiss the possibility that Wallace really meant to submit. Wallace, in this account, was either so naïve or so arrogant that he proposed that 'the king grant him of his gift, not as a loan, an honourable allowance of woods and cattle and by his writing the seizure and investment for him and his heirs in purchased land'. Not surprisingly, Edward is reported to have been affronted and offered a reward for the death of Wallace. The Wallace we read of here, the Wallace who is also supposed to have made a similar plea to come into Edward's peace the previous year'[37] is neither the Wallace of history nor of tradition.

He was now increasingly alone and isolated. Edward had not wavered in his determination to take him. We cannot put a date to Edward's decision that Wallace should not be pardoned. It may have been as early as Lanark. Stirling and the destructive raid into the north of England which followed the battle would add to the enormity of Wallace's crimes. Yet it is possible, as the indictment of 1305 relates,[38] that after Falkirk Edward was willing to accept Wallace into his peace. Furthermore, the English king, as has been seen,[39] turned down Philip IV's offer to surrender Wallace to him. Wallace's reappearance on the Scottish side in 1303 after his embassy on the Continent, and in despite of what Edward took to be his generosity, may have shaped the king's future attitude.

Edward used whatever means came to hand in his pursuit of Wallace. Those who hunted down the Scots were guaranteed reward; Edward did not expect his helpers to have high motives. Something of this emerges from an undated document from the period of 1297 to 1303. The document, as becomes clear, carries a sting in the tail:

> The king by his letters patent grants to his chief valet Edward de Keith, all goods and chattels of whatever kind he may gain from Monsire Guilliam le Galeys [Wallace] the King's enemy, to his own profit and pleasure. Provided, however, that if the said Edward by chance under colour of this gift takes anything from other people at the King's peace, he shall duly answer to those from whom such are taken.[40]

The king did not deceive himself, then, as to the quality of those he employed, but he himself was not swayed by niceties. To capture Wallace he would scorn no opportunity, send away no man who offered his services. The number of these increased with the submission of 1304.

Edward spent the months of November 1303 to February 1304 at Dunfermline with his second wife, the Frenchwoman Margaret. There he was accessible to the many Scots who now sought to make their peace with him. He was more gracious, in this hour of triumph, than he had been in another, in 1296. His son, less than successful in the south-west in the summer and autumn, had established himself at Perth by Christmas, and it was to him that Edward entrusted the negotiations for the Scottish surrender, for such it was. Comyn, still technically Guardian and in the absence of Soules the obvious choice for the distasteful task, acted for the Scots. Edward was disposed to be generous, even tolerant; the statesmanlike qualities so much admired in the past had not entirely deserted him. He could afford to indulge the Scots; he was their master and they knew it. But nevertheless Comyn conducted himself with an authority and a confidence surprising to us, given the circumstances. He was not Balliol, nor was he required to be. Neither he nor those he represented would be stripped of honour and dignity. Edward understood and accepted that there was no question of unconditional surrender. He knew the importance of this concession if he was to gain and keep the support of the Scots for his plan for their country.

On 9 February Comyn, with eleven associates, surrendered at Strathord near Perth. The terms which he had been able to obtain from Edward need not concern us here.[41] Wallace was not among those who submitted to Edward. He had excluded himself from the negotiations and was, in turn, with Soules and Fraser, excluded from the terms accepted by Comyn. There is no indication in any source that Comyn or Bruce or any of the Scottish leaders now in Edward's peace interceded for his life. Even Robert Wishart, the bishop of Glasgow, said by the English to have been the instigator of Wallace's first actions, did not speak up for him at this moment of reconciliation with the English king. Wishart was not a young man, his courage did not always stand the test, and he was still viewed with suspicion by Edward, who insisted on his brief exile. Lamberton and James the Stewart, the former Wallace's appointee, the latter the man who in English eyes had instigated his rebellion in 1297, returned from France to make their peace. No doubt they were, like others, glad to have it. No doubt they could claim that no one was capable of influencing Edward's attitude towards Wallace. The sad fact remains that the Scottish leaders cannot be exonerated of the charge of, at best, indifference to Wallace, with whom they had served and with whose sentiments they had claimed to sympathise. In the eighteen months left to Wallace after the surrender at Starthord, we can find no evidence that his former colleagues, some of them friends, made one positive move to save him from the fate which became increasingly inevitable once Edward was free to concentrate on him. They made no intervention at Edward's court, they entered no plea, they offered no bargain, and at the end they cannot satisfactorily be cleared of possible complicity – through their neglect if for no other reason – in his death. They left him to Edward. A foretaste of what that could mean came with the fall to the English of Stirling Castle.

NOTES

1. Barrow: *Robert Bruce*, 116.

2. Winchelsey, archbishop of Canterbury from 1293 to 1313, was less than eager to confront Edward on this occasion. He was also unhappy at the prospect of travelling through Galloway with its hostile population and landscape. In the event, he was well enough received by Edward at Sweetheart Abbey, but his relations with the king were not always amicable. See Prestwich: *Edward I*, passim.

3. Watson: *Under the Hammer*, 143–44; Barrow: *Robert Bruce*, 118–9; Prestwich: *Edward I*, 495.

4. Watson, 144; Prestwich, ibid.; Barrow: *Robert Bruce*, 116–19.

5. Below, note 23.

6. Prestwich: *Armies and Warfare*, chap. 8, particularly 211ff.

7. Above, chap. 7.

8. Watson, 61.

9. Wright: *Political Songs*, 278ff; Prestwich: *Edward I*, 38–83.

10. Stevenson: *Docs*, ii, 301–03.

11. Prestwich: *Edward I*, 221.

12. Prestwich: *Armies and Warfare*, chap. 11, for Edward's use of the navy.

13. Prestwich: *Edward I*, 397.

14. Prestwich: *Armies and Warfare*, 268.

15. As, for example, in Langtoft's Chronicle, excerpts in Wright: *Political Songs*, Appendix, 273ff; Wright, *Song on the Scottish War*, 160ff.

16. Chap. 7, above.

17. Ibid.

18. Fordun, i 331.

19. Barrow: *Robert Bruce*, 162.

20. *Docs Illus. Hist. Scot.*, 276.

21. On the delegation, see Barrow: *Robert Bruce*, 166ff.

22. *Cal. Docs Scot.*, ii, 1191.

23. He had, of course, never accepted Balliol as king. On his motives see Barrow: *Robert Bruce*, 172–75, and McNair Scott, 60–61.

24. Rishanger.

25. Wallace's relationship with Comyn is as difficult to judge as that with Bruce. Comyn, of course, suffered, as Bruce did not, from Scottish chroniclers, but in his apparent dislike of Wallace he cannot have been unique, any more than in his wish to see him toppled.

26. He would undoubtedly have been mentioned had he been present, especially in the light of Rishanger's comment.

27. Fordun, i, 333–35.

28. Prestwich: *The Three Edwards: War and State in England 1272–1377*, 1980, 50.

29. *Cal. Docs Scot.*, ii, 1687, 1386. The siege of Brechin ended on 9 August with the death of the constable, Sir Thomas Maule, and the surrender of the garrison.

30. Barron, op. cit., 193.

31. *History of England*, 1945, 218.

32. Robert Bruce, 130.

33. *Cal. Docs Scot.*, ii, 1374.

34. He was in charge of the garrison of Ayr and took part in the attack on the Scots at Peebles.

35. As circumstances had altered since the truce of January 1302, the Scottish confidence was surely misplaced. Perhaps the view from Paris was a more favourable one, and king Philip was adept at saying what the Scots there wanted to hear, despite his treaty with Edward.

36. Barrow: *Robert Bruce*, 128.

37. Watson: op. cit., 212, takes issue with this conclusion. I am afraid that I have not changed my view. Bellamy: *The Law of Treason in England in the Later Middle Ages*, 1970, 33, deals with the question of Wallace's supposed approaches to Edward.

38. See chap. 10 below.

39. Chap. 5, above.

40. *Cal. Docs Scot.*, ii, 1424.

41. *Foedera*, i, 974–75. See also Young: op. cit., 186ff; Barrow: *Robert Bruce*, 129–30 and 132–33.

9

The Time of Betrayal, 1305

'The king will take careful note of how
each conducts himself'

Stirling Castle was held for the Scots by a young and, as
Edward was to discover in the high summer of 1304,
courageous man. Sir William Oliphant was of a family
which had come to the attention of David I when he was
earl of Huntingdon. An early member of the family, David
Olifard – the original spelling of the name – saved the
king's life at the battle of Winchester in 1141, when the
latter was fighting for his niece, Matilda, in the struggle
against King Stephen. Oliphant or Olifard was granted
lands by his grateful monarch in Roxburghshire and
prospered under David I and his successor, Malcolm IV,
under whom he was justiciar of Lothian.[1] No Oliphant
served Scotland better, it might be argued, than Sir
William in 1304.

Oliphant appears to have been guided by a more
esoteric code than that to which Wallace subscribed. That
is not in any way to decry his contribution to the patriotic

cause by his defiance of Edward. That cause, like any other, needed heroes, even martyrs; as constable of Stirling Castle, Oliphant was the former and came near to being the latter, along with his colleagues. Two incidents, however, illustrate that not all Scots were motivated in the same way as Wallace. Yet their role, as in the case of Oliphant, cannot be disregarded. The submission of the Scots in February 1304 had forced Edward to carry out what might nowadays be called mopping-up operations. One such, albeit a great undertaking, was the siege of Stirling Castle. It is in connection with this event that we find the evidence to demonstrate how Oliphant's attitude differed from that of Wallace. By 1304 it was Oliphant rather than Wallace who represented the face of Scottish opposition to Edward.

The castle had been left alone by Edward in the campaign of 1303. The reason, according to Guisborough, was that, if held by the Scots, it would act as a deterrent to potential deserters from Edward's army.[2] If as illustrious a knight as Giles d'Argentan could desert, as he did, then Edward clearly had a point.[3] But in 1304 Edward was ready for Stirling; with him, having redeemed himself, was the same d'Argentan.[4] Stirling stood as a stronghold but, perhaps of more moment to Edward, it represented through Oliphant's stubborn refusal to surrender the kind of obstacle to the king's total subjection which Wallace personified. When he began the siege of Stirling in May 1304, therefore, Edward was in no mood to be tolerant of any opposition. This was at once made evident to Oliphant. Custom dictated that before the siege proper could begin, negotiations should take place. In action which today strikes us as strange, Oliphant asked permission to seek the advice of Sir John Soules who, as Guardian, had put the care of the castle into his hands.[5] Oliphant required to know of Soules, he argued, whether he should fight or surrender. Soules was in France and Oliphant's gambit was surely no more than a tactic to gain time. We can hardly be surprised if Edward, no mean prevaricator himself when circumstances demanded, saw it as such. Yet it is Edward's rejection of Oliphant's proposal which has aroused comment.[6] Oliphant's manoeuvre marks him out from Wallace; for the latter, to contemplate communicating with Edward rather than offering defiance, as before Stirling, would surely have seemed incomprehensible. Unquestionably, Oliphant was a man of great heart, who subscribed to a set of values which however had no place in Wallace's reasoning.

Oliphant's later career offers a further example of the distinction between the two men. A prisoner in Rochester after the battle of Dunbar in 1296, Oliphant was in English hands from the fall of Stirling until 1308. The English valued his courage and experience; it was by agreeing to fight for Edward II against Robert I that he obtained his freedom.[7] In October he was in command of the English garrison in Perth, the town in which one part of the dismembered body of Wallace had been displayed on the orders of Edward I.[8] Thus, two Scots – Oliphant, was a Perthshire man – had defied Edward. Now, after 1308, one fought on the English side and was in no way condemned by contemporaries for doing so. Wallace died for the same cause that Oliphant had embraced, and then, to save himself, forsaken. Oliphant had been a Balliol man at the outbreak of war but that, apparently, was a less than firm commitment. He would later give his allegiance to Bruce, who had for so long striven against the Balliols. Oliphant was not by any means unusual in his interpretation of loyalty. We need not turn to Bruce for an example. Sir William Douglas, as we have seen, was prone to changes of heart; nor can his son, the Good Sir James, entirely escape censure in this regard. Relatively few paid with their lives for such behaviour. One who did after a career of equivocation was Sir David Brechin, executed by Bruce for his part in the Soules plot of 1320.[9] Even so notorious a man as Brechin could, however, raise sympathy; the sentence passed on him by the 'Black Parliament' so angered Ingram de Umfraville, a former Guardian of Scotland, that he left Scotland never to return. Brechin had fought both for and against the Scots. So too had Oliphant, the heroic defender of Stirling. The thinking of Brechin and Oliphant and their equals was not for Wallace; he would surely have dismissed it. But in the summer of 1304 he and Oliphant were comrades-in-arms against Edward.

It took Edward three months to capture Stirling. He used the siege to demonstrate and experiment with the most advanced technology of the age. Thirteen siege engines, including two from Brechin and one from Aberdeen, were deployed. Robert Bruce supplied his own engines for Edward's benefit. Crossbows and bows and arrows were ordered from a number of sources; in this regard the mayor of Newcastle was particularly assiduous.[10] Some kinds of explosive devices were prepared for use against the defenders of the castle. Edward's favourite weapon at Stirling was the 'Warwolf', built on the site. The Scots, in the long term, could not hope to succeed in the defence of the castle. Their only siege engine proved ineffectual. Even so, Edward narrowly avoided death from a springald. The spectacle of the siege was watched by Edward's queen, Margaret, and her ladies. On July 20 the garrison was allowed to surrender after Edward had used the castle with them inside for a day's target practice for 'Warwolf'. The king was only dissuaded from hanging and disembowelling the garrison by the intervention of those about him, notably his wife.[11] Oliphant and the survivors of the siege were sent to various prisons in England.

The siege of Stirling was in its way as much of a show-piece, designed to impress and overcome the Scots, as would be the trial of Wallace in the following year. Edward's treatment of Oliphant and the Stirling garrison could leave no further doubt of the reception which awaited Wallace upon capture. Edward had been guilty at Stirling of a breach of that code of chivalry which, like Oliphant, he claimed to hold dear. To act so, Edward must have been dominated by an extreme passion. It came, perhaps, from frustration, from that rage which he had inherited from his Plantagenet forebears, from inherent defects at which we can only guess. While it would be foolish indeed to eliminate these from the attempt to explain his behaviour towards Wallace, it may well be that Edward was colder, more controlled in his pursuit and execution of Wallace than is generally believed. Certainly, as will be argued,[12] the trial of Wallace was not merely contrived but directed by a man not swayed by emotion alone.

It would be easy, that is, to see in Edward no more than the anointed guardian of that hatred of Wallace which is found in popular form in, for example, Lanercost:

> The vilest doom is fittest for thys crimes,
> Justice demands that thou shouldst die three times.
> Thou pillager of many a sacred shrine,
> Butcher of thousands, threefold death be thine!
> So shall the English from thee gain relief,
> Scotland! be wise and choose a nobler chief.[13]

Edward would undoubtedly wish to be associated with these sentiments; he gave expression to them, in legal terms, at the trial in 1305. That he was paranoic or had become so in the course of the war is also indisputable. But he was a subtle man, as well as devious. It is possible that in his treatment of Wallace there may lie a greater subtlety than that with which he has hitherto been credited. The surrender terms which Edward offered to the Scots in February 1304 were never open to Wallace. Edward was categorical: 'As for William Wallace, it is agreed, that he shall render himself up at the will and mercy of our sovereign lord the king as it shall seem good to him.'[14] There were others of the Scots, of course, who were not permitted to capitulate on the same conditions as Comyn: Wishart, James the Stewart, Fraser and Soules were excluded. With time, however, they were to come into Edward's peace. Wallace could not. Why Edward was so utterly severe towards Wallace is an absorbing question. With Scottish resistance crushed in 1304, Edward's exclusion of Wallace from the peace terms seems vindictive to us. The matter may resolve itself into the simple answer of Edward's abhorrence of defiance and Wallace's intransigence. But in the case of Edward, the matter is more complex. Wishart, James the Stewart, and above all, Fraser, were guilty of treason, if Edward chose to regard their behaviour as such. English sources point to Wishart and Stewart as the prime movers behind Wallace's rebellion. Fraser, a member of Edward's household, was constantly under suspicion, and with reason. But it was not until they joined in Bruce's rebellion that condign punishment was visited on Wishart and Fraser. The former avoided death because of his calling. Fraser finally went to the scaffold, to suffer the same barbarous death as Wallace. James the Stewart, described by Bruce's biographer[15] as 'cautious and devious, possessed of a recognisably 'Stewart' canniness . . .', was under threat on various occasions but was allowed to live. All three men had broken their word to Edward, and more than once; Wallace had not, of course. Their opposition to Edward had not been as spectacular as that of Wallace, it had been rather more insidious, more calculating. It is this characteristic which makes them seem less attractive than Wallace. Whatever their contributions to the struggle against Edward – and Fraser, for one, could not have given more – they cannot stand alongside Wallace. Yet for Edward, however hard they tested his patience, they were worthy, for years, of his tolerance.

Not so Wallace, in whose case Edward repeated his theme of unconditional surrender in March in what appears to be a reply to a request for clarification from Alexander de Abernithyn:

> . . . and in reply to the matter wherein you have asked us to let you know whether it is our pleasure that you should hold out to William le Waleys any words of peace, know this, that it is not our pleasure by any means that either to him, or to any other of his company, you hold out any word of peace, unless they place themselves absolutely and in all things at our will, without any exception whatever.[16]

In the same letter Abernithyn is commended by Edward for his good work in keeping 'watch at the fords of Forth'. Here may be an indication that Wallace was in or expected to be in the vicinity. If so, he eluded the enemy, as he continued to do until August of the next year.

It is from material of this kind and from accounts of sporadic appearances by Wallace that we learn what little we know of his movements and activities between the surrender by Comyn and his capture by Menteith. He would be unable to rest for any length of time in any one place. If we can accept that he was given refuge by many unknown sympathisers, most drawn from the common people, we should not pretend that there were not Scots prepared to betray him into Edward's hands. This must have been especially true after the St Andrews parliament of March 1304. There the peace terms were confirmed. Edward, in the cases of Simon Fraser, the garrison of Stirling, and Wallace, called for them to be outlawed by due process under Scots law, and this was done. Again, as in the negotiations for the surrender in February and subsequently, the leaders of the Sots did not seek to divert Edward from his pursuit of Wallace. Both Fraser and the garrison of Stirling surrendered in July; Wallace alone remained.

The readiness with which the Scots consented to Edward's treatment of Wallace is cynical. It does, however, suggest that as early as the St Andrews parliament they were being led by the English king towards the settlement of September 1305.[17] For Edward the capture and execution of Wallace were essential not simply on the grounds of removing the most stubborn of his opponents. The Scottish leaders acquiesced, by default at best, in the execution with its gruesome details. The suspicion that the death of Wallace satisfied them and Edward alike by his symbolism, the end of the old Scotland of resistance and the beginning of a new Scotland of full collaboration, cannot be overlooked. Edward brought the Scots, not unwillingly, in this direction in the months between February 1304 and August 1305.

Wallace stayed ahead of pursuit but with increasing difficulty. If we lack detail, it is obvious nonetheless that the pressure on him was intense. Edward's servants in 1303 had been futile or, more probably, frustrated by Wallace's knowledge of the terrain and the network of relatives and sympathisers on whom he could rely. His own experience of the raid and the ambush were to his advantage when they were employed against him. On 15 March 1303, for example, Edward had rewarded with money certain Scots who had been involved in an attempt to ambush him and Fraser.[18] In the autumn of that year, another equally unsuccessful attempt was made on the two. Reimbursement was made by Edward on 10 September to the pursuers for two horses killed in the skirmish from which Wallace and Fraser escaped.[19] Wallace and Fraser were too wily to be taken easily. But it is evident that they cannot have survived without the help of many unnamed Scots; the temptation to surrender the two outlaws must have been great, but continued to be resisted by the majority.

Edward, with Wallace so elusive, had recourse in 1304 to what has been described as the 'unattractive notion, of forcing former friends and associates to take part in the search for Wallace.[20] If unattractive, it was, for Edward, logical. He believed that he knew the Scots. Indeed he did but, for whatever reason, his blackmail, for such it was, did not result in the capture of Wallace. That at least is to the credit of the Scots; it may be impossible to clear them of accepting Wallace's death, but at least those on whom Edward tried his blackmail are not proven to have succumbed to it. We have the names of those whom Edward sought to coerce into the betrayal of Wallace. The return of James the Stewart, Sir Ingram de Umfraville, and Sir John Soules to the court and the favour of the king were not to be granted with letters of safe conduct until Wallace was taken.[21] Of the three Guardians, Soules never came back to Scotland from France, while the others, each with his own code, do not stand accused of action against Wallace to secure the safe conducts. The lengths to which Edward would go can be more readily seen in another document.[22] In this he is more specific in the pressure he brings to bear: 'Sir Simon Fraser, Sir John Comyn, Sir Alexander Lindsay,[23] and Sir David Graham[24] are to exert themselves until twenty days after Christmas to capture William Wallace and hand him over to the king. And the king will take careful not of how each conducts himself, so that he may show most favour to the one who takes him with regard to mitigation of his sentence of exile or fine.'[25] Not content to exert pressure on the four, Edward was setting one against the other with the promise of a reward in the form of an easement of the penalties under which they had already laboured.

Wallace himself, if on the run, was not entirely on the defensive. He was carrying on the war as best he could. We have seen evidence of his escapes from ambush. A much larger force threatened him in September 1304. This was led by Edward's trusted and able soldier, Aymer de Valence. In the company of some three hundred archers and with the banner of St George to protect him, Valence met up with Wallace '. . . under Earnside'.[26] Wallace had not lost his skill. Although his own force could not equal that of Valence, he inflicted casualties on the mixed Anglo-Scottish troops and their horses and got away.[27] The English claimed that he had been put to flight, but that would count for little with the increasingly irate and demanding Edward. Such an encounter as this with Valence tested Wallace, and we have no way of knowing how close on this and other occasions he came to capture. But he was too astute not to leave himself a means of escape, the more so in the face of a large rather than a smaller force. In the circumstances, victory for Wallace was escape. That is not to say that he was inevitably successful in this last year of his life. We do not know. He had been resoundingly defeated on at least one occasion in 1304, at the time of the negotiations for submission to Edward. From his winter quarters at Dunfermline Edward ordered a raid into the forest of Selkirk and areas of Lothian. It was a powerful force which he dispatched under the command of the experienced soldiers, Segrave, Clifford, and Sir William Latimer. With them was Bruce. The intention was to lay hands on the Scottish leaders. In this it was unsuccessful, but there is no question that at Happrew, west of Peebles, on Fraser's own territory, Wallace and Fraser were defeated. Edward was less impressed by what the raid had achieved than by its failure to capture Wallace.[28]

There was one respect in which Wallace, as time ran away from him, had not changed. He struck at any with English sympathies or connections. This we can see from a document dated 24 March 1305 from Westminster; it is worthy of being reproduced in its entirety:

To the helper, captain and justice of the water from the water of Forth to Orkeneye, or to him who supplies his place. The abbot of Redyng has besought the king to restore to him his island of May and the manner of Pednewen in that bailiwick, which were conferred upon the church of Redyng by former kings of Scotland and were delivered to the abbot as a cell of his church by the rebellion of John de Balliol, late king there, and which the abbot held peacefully as a cell of his church from the time of that delivery until William le Waleys and his accomplices, lately insurgents against the king in those parts, ejected the abbot and his men from the said island and manor; the king orders them to cause the abbot to have such seisin of the island and manor as he had before the commencement of the late war, and not to permit him to be disturbed by any one as to his seisin, so that after he has had seisin he may answer to everybody as he ought.[29]

It is not merely in the reference to Wallace that the interest of the document lies. It is to be found more in the assumptions which are behind it and which find expression there. Scotland is Edward's; the war is over; Wallace has no army, only accomplices; he and they are insurgents. With none of this, of course, could Wallace agree. If technically the war could be said to be over with the submission of the Scots in February 1304, Wallace continued to set his face against any such acceptance. In his own mind, since he was Balliol's man and since Balliol alone was king of Scotland, there could be no question of insurgency, of rebellion. But it was not Wallace who wrote the documents or the law, and it was the law that he was an outlaw, to be hunted down, and, in Edward's view, a traitor. It mattered little now what Wallace thought, except that he was able to give brief expression to it at Westminster in August 1305. It mattered more what he did, and of that we have insufficient knowledge. We can only guess. The picture is one of desperate evasion, of emerging from one bolt-hole only to be driven into another by relentless English pressure, of hunger always and starvation sometimes, of unrecorded brushes with English and Scottish enemies, of the solace to be found in and with a few devoted friends careless of their own lives, of the comfort of religion, above all of that spirit peculiar to him which, somehow, sustained him to the end. We can visualise the increasing desperation with which Wallace fought on, perhaps even in that desperation seeking a clean, swift death, sword in hand. That he was not to have.

It would be gratifying to be able to think that Wallace's continued defiance of Edward, even in the sordid circumstances in which he existed, stirred his people to further rebellion against Edward. But there was no such outcome. As he flitted from one hiding-place to another, Wallace, we may be sure, would speak to those he met with that same fierce commitment to the Scottish cause he had always had. Perhaps he gained adherents. But he could never again raise a force large enough to represent a genuine threat to the English. There is no dignity in suffering, and the Wallace who sought succour from the people from whom he had sprung must have been far from the man he once was. His words would carry conviction, but now, in the last months of his life, he needed the nobles as he had not in 1297. They, if they had not forgotten him or found him an embarrassment as they made themselves amenable to Edward, had different values and priorities. These last months of Wallace's life have to be set against the background of Scottish indifference to the English occupation, if not of active collaboration. With Wallace reduced to a fugitive and therefore, in practical terms, impotent, where was the leadership to come from? Comyn and Bruce, in an alliance of whom most hope of a national revival lay, could not work together. It is true that when Wallace was captured, Bruce was no more than six months away from the murder of Comyn and the subsequent seizure of the throne of Scotland. At the time of the execution, no one could possibly foresee such a sequence of events. The 'band' into which Bruce had entered with Lamberton on 11 July 1304 has been interpreted as evidence that the security in which Edward believed he held Scotland was deceptive.[30] But if this was so, more than a year after the band, at the time of Wallace' death, Bruce had risked nothing and, like Comyn, of whose motives and intentions we know even less, had not been inspired by Wallace's resistance to the point of emulating him. No doubt there were whispers of abhorrence for Edward and his policies; these would be the staple of Scottish conversation. No doubt some among the Scots leaders, as they prepared for Edward's parliament of September 1305, were genuinely shocked by the horror of Edward's treatment of Wallace. But there was no more than that. Neither his last resistance nor his execution roused his countrymen.

The end for Wallace came suddenly. He was captured in or near Glasgow on 3 August. A monument at Robroyston marks the place at which, traditionally, he was seized. His capture fell to Sir John Menteith. As a subject of Edward, Menteith had no reason to think of Wallace as other than an enemy and his capture as an honour. From an early date, however, the belief grew that Wallace had been taken by treachery, and it is upon Menteith that the odium has fallen. Blind Harry did not spare him,[31] and Menteith's reputation never recovered from the criticism. Not satisfied with making Menteith an English sympathiser, in itself crime enough, Harry has him betray the closest of friends in Wallace, godfather to his children. To treachery therefore was added betrayal of a friend for money. Recent commentators, however, while they can never hope to rehabilitate Menteith in the popular mind, have sought to excuse him if not to exonerate him. As will be argued,[32] contemporary opinion may very well have understood Menteith's conduct. Originally a firm supporter of the Scottish cause, Menteith, son of that Walter Stewart who had held the earldom of Menteith by right of his wife,[33] had come into Edward's peace at an unknown date. It may have been between September 1303 and March 1304.[34] Like so many Scots, Bruce and Comyn not excepted, Menteith had no apparent difficulty in changing from one side to the other. His was the fervour of the convert. He was rewarded for his defection to the English cause by Edward, who made him sheriff of Dumbarton and keeper of its castle. It was natural that having given his oath to Edward, he should, again like others among his countrymen, see no shame in participation in the pursuit and capture of Wallace. If Menteith was guilty of treachery, it is impossible to believe that, given the opportunity which fell to him, others would not have acted in the same manner.

What Wallace was doing in Glasgow we do not know. He was, apparently, alone, although one English chronicler would have us believe otherwise. It is Peter of Langtoft who regales us with this story: 'We have heard news among companions of William Wallace, the master of the thieves; Sir John de Menteith followed him close at his heels; and took him in bed beside his strumpet.'[35] When taken, alone or not, he had in his possession documents, since lost, which might have explained his presence there. The possibility that they implicated certain Scots with him may be doubted. Their seizure, as far as we can tell, led to no arrests. Edward, although he had good reason to think the Scottish question settled, was suspicious by now of all about him. He would not have hesitated to act if the papers in Wallace's possession had given him cause.

It is conceivable that Wallace was in Glasgow in the hope of taking ship; if so, he can hardly be blamed for seeking a respite from the intolerable strain of the pursuit by the agents of the English king. One question, among many, is why Wallace, as far as we can tell, had not already attempted to escape from Scotland. That even in the direst straits escape from Edward was possible would be illustrated by Bruce after his rebellion.[36] Wallace himself had accomplished his return from the Continent, although almost certainly knowledge of his whereabouts had been relayed to Edward. By 1305 the position had, of course, changed; Wallace would have been conscious that the hands of Scots as well as English were turned against him. Bruce, Comyn, Wishart, all of whom had played their part in the resistance to Edward, were now his men. Fraser had countered the outlawry imposed at the 1304 St Andrews parliament with surrender to Edward four months later. Fraser had been forgiven, if not forgotten, by Edward. Wallace was isolated; Edward was implacable, colleagues had become enemies. Flight abroad was an option, and not an impossible one. Yet Wallace did not exercise it. Perhaps he had accepted his inevitable fate and was in Glasgow, bent on finding allies for yet another strike at the English. Whatever his reasons, they have not come down to us.

As we are ignorant of his reasons for being in Glasgow, the circumstances surrounding his capture are equally uncertain. English accounts stress that he was taken by his own countrymen. We need not be surprised by this; true or not, the belief that they had betrayed him to Edward isolated him still further from what the English claimed was Scottish acceptance of their rule. A particular Scot is named in connection with the capture of Wallace. This is Ralph de Haliburton. He came from a family close to Wallace at the beginning of his adventures in 1297. Ralph de Haliburton himself was a member of the garrison of Stirling Castle under Sir William Oliphant, and upon its fall in July 1304, was sent into imprisonment in England. On 28 February 1305 he was released on condition that he helped to capture Wallace.[37] He was released into the custody of a Scottish knight, Sir John Mowbray, who became responsible for him. Mowbray, himself taken a prisoner to England after the battle of Dunbar, was yet another Scot who changed sides. Whatever his precise part in the capture of Wallace, Mowbray, unlike Menteith, has escaped criticism, as indeed has Haliburton for whom he was responsible. What exactly the released Haliburton did to ensure Wallace's capture or whether he was, as has been suggested, Wallace's supposed servant, the mysterious Jack Short, we have no means of knowing. It is tempting in the search for an answer to revert to the traditional account, that treachery was indeed how Wallace was taken. Blind Harry has him allowing himself to be bound by Menteith on the incredible excuse that in this way Menteith would be able to smuggle him, supposedly already a prisoner, through the English lines.[38] That Wallace, for so long a master of self-preservation, should be so deceived is both ludicrous and insulting to his memory. He was captured either through a well-laid trap – for an escape along the Clyde was a possibility of which the English would not be ignorant – or his presence was reported to Menteith who carried out his duty for which he was rewarded with land by the English king.

Wallace was at once sent south. There is no record of an attempt at rescue, although his capture cannot have gone unremarked. He was transferred into the custody of Sir John Segrave for the crossing into England. His fate was already decided, as he must have known, but it is unlikely that he could have suspected that Edward intended to give him the formality of a trial and even more unlikely that he could have suspected its purpose.

NOTES

1. On the family see Black op. cit., 637; Barrow: *Kingdom of the Scots*, passim; Duncan: *Scotland, the Making of the Kingdom*, 1989, passim.

2. It could equally be argued that as deserters from Edward's army, they might be welcomed by the Scots!

3. For the activities and antics of this knight see Prestwich: *Armies and Warfare*, 234–35.

4. Ibid.

5. Negotiations were an essential preliminary to a siege. In this case both Oliphant and Edward appear to have outlined their positions in lengthy statements of justification.

6. Perhaps because of Edward's subsequent treatment of the garrison.

7. Barrow: *Robert Bruce*, 194.

8. Below, chap. 10.

9. Barbour: *The Bruce*, ed with trans. by A.A.M. Duncan, 698ff; Barrow: *Robert Bruce*, 309–10; Nicholson: *Scotland, the Later Middle Ages*, 1974, 102–03.

10. Prestwich: *Edward I*, 501.

11. One would like to think that Scottish leaders present at Stirling would be among those pleading for Oliphant and his men. If so, they were to be less sympathetic to Wallace in the following year.

12. Chap. 10 and Conclusion, below.

13. Lanercost, Maxwell trans., 176.

14. *Cal. Docs Scot.*, ii, 1444–1445 and 1463.

15. Barrow: *Robert Bruce*, 81.

16. *Cal. Docs Scot.*, ii, 1463.

17. For a different verdict on the relationship between Edward and the Scottish nobles, see Barrow: *Robert Bruce*, chap. 8. Watson,

op. cit., 190, confirms that the parliament 'marks the transformation, admittedly still incomplete, of the English presence in
Scotland from a military regime to a peacetime administration'
and reminds us that the outlawry of Wallace and other was
approved by Scots.

18. *DNB*, 569.

19. Ibid.

20. Kightly, 185.

21. *Cal. Docs Scot.*, ii, 1563.

22. Palgrave, Docs, 276

23. Sir Alexander Lindsay, of Barnweill, near Ayr, rose with
Bruce in 1306 and was present at the murder of Comyn.

24. It will be remembered that it was Graham who played a
leading role in the fracas at Peebles in August 1299. He it was
who laid claim to Wallace's lands, thus setting in train the quarrel
between the Scottish leaders. See chap. 7 above.

25. Whether any of them inclined to carry out Edward's wishes
we do not know for certain. None of them took part in the actual
capture; for that reason, if for no other, they must be exonerated.

26. *Cal. Docs Scot.*, iv, 477. Valence's later career, see J.R.S.
Philips: *Aymer de Valence, earl of Pembroke 1307–24*, 1972. Barbour,
op. cit., 90, describes him as 'wise, brave and a noble knight in
his deeds'.

27. *Cal. Docs Scot.*, ibid.

28. *Cal. Docs Scot.*, ii, 1432.

29. *Cal Close Rolls*, 24 March 1305, Westminster.

30. Barrow: *Robert Bruce*, 184–85.

31. Eleventh Book.

32. Conclusion, below.

33. He was still engaged on the Scottish side in September
1303: Stevenson *Docs Illustr. Hist. Scot.*, ii, 453. He was Edward's
man at the latest by March of the next year. *Cal. Docs Scot.*, ii,
1474. His reward for the capture of Wallace, generally given as
£100 of land, is found in Stevenson: *Wall Docs*, 101–02, 147.

34. He was keeper of the castle of Dumbarton.

35. The failure of other chroniclers to use this story is perhaps
indicative.

36. Bruce's adventures are described by Barrow: *Robert Bruce*, chap. 10.

37. We are left to guess why he was considered especially likely to accomplish the task. With him, as with others in the story of Wallace's capture, it is not easy to understand how Wallace came to trust him or, indeed, others after years of pursuit.

38. Eleventh book.

–10–

The Time of Glory, 1305

'Lasting bliss'

Wallace reached London on Sunday, 22 August, and was led through streets filled with jeering, abusive citizens to the property of one William de Leyre, an alderman and former sheriff, in the parish of Fenchurch, where he spent the night. Early the next morning he was brought on horseback to Westminster Hall through streets thronged once more. He formed part of a procession, directed by Segrave and his brother Geoffrey, which included those named by Edward to sit in judgement on him, as well as sheriffs and aldermen of the city. Inside the hall, at the south end, a scaffold had been erected, and there Wallace was made to stand. On his head his captors had placed a crown of laurel, to mock him, it was said, for his boast that one day he would wear a crown in this place.[1] It is unlikely that Wallace would ever make such a remark. Neither before Stirling nor Falkirk did he act the braggart, although he was not above the use of a title when he felt it justified.[2] The placing of a crown on his head was part of a deliberate policy of humiliation. The practice was not unique. In the following year, his old ally and companion, Simon Fraser, in London to suffer the same fate as Wallace, was crowned with a garland of periwinkle.[3]

The commission which Edward had empowered to deal with Wallace was a formidable one.[4] The principal legal figure was Peter Mallore or Mallory, justiciar of England, whose name is frequently found in the records of the period. He was especially active in 1306 in the aftermath of Bruce's seizure of the crown of Scotland. Mallore condemned, among others, Christopher Seton, who had seconded Bruce in the murder of Comyn and had himself cut down Comyn's uncle; Alexander Scrymgeour, standard-bearer of Scotland and an associate of Wallace when the latter was Guardian, and John Strathbogie, earl of Atholl, the first of his station to be executed for treason since Waltheof was beheaded by order of William I in 1086. With Mallore sat another judge, Ralph de Sandwych, a man of vast experience under Edward and his predecessor. He would later sentence Simon Fraser to death. As constable of the Tower of London he had been responsible for the custody of some notable figures of the war with Scotland, among them the earls of Menteith, Ross, and Atholl, after the battle of Dunbar. The mayor of London, John le Blunt, represented the city, while a fourth member of the commission was John de Bacwell, who would meet a melancholy end, suffocated to death at the coronation of Edward II in February 1308. Finally, there was Segrave. Of those who faced Wallace on that day in Westminster Hall only Segrave, a soldier, would, we may guess, be assured of his respect. Segrave had long served Edward. He was one of those who volunteered to go with Edward on crusade, despite his opposition to the royal cause in the war with Simon de Montfort. A veteran of the Welsh wars, Segrave subsequently had a distinguished career against the Scots. He brought a large contingent of troops to the Falkirk campaign and was present at the sieges of Caerlaverock and Stirling. Edward entrusted him with a number of posts in Scotland. When Edward returned to England in February 1302, Segrave remained behind, acting with Bruce and others in Scottish affairs. He was constable of Berwick castle in 1302 and captain of Northumberland in January of the following year. Segrave was not always successful in Scotland. He was wounded and captured by Simon Fraser at Roslin in February 1303 but later rescued. It had been an inglorious episode, but Segrave gained some revenge in defeating both Fraser and Wallace in a clash at Happrew, near Peebles. By 1304 Segrave was responsible for the whole of southern Scotland. His primary concern became, on Edward's instructions, the capture of Wallace. As we shall see, Segrave was not to be free of Wallace even after the execution.

Two factors have served to obscure the nature of the proceedings in Westminster Hall, The first is the undoubted horror of the sentence on Wallace, the second the charge of treason laid against him. To concentrate on these is to misunderstand Edward's intention. He meant to destroy Wallace in body and in reputation and to that end brought him to trial as an outlaw as well as a traitor. In that context, the sentence was in accordance with the law as it stood not merely in England but in Scotland. Edward was a master in the use and abuse of the law. This characteristic had been noted long before at the time of the rebellion of Simon de Montfort when, as Prince Edward, he had prompted this comment on his behaviour: 'The treachery or falseness by which he gains his ends he calls prudence; the way he arrives at his object, be it ever so crooked, is reputed to be straight; when wrong serves his ambition it is called right; he calls lawful whatever he wills, and thinks himself above the law.'[5] Wallace was now to discover the truth of this. For Edward the form was important if the outcome was itself already decided.

To speak of a trial in modern terms is inaccurate. Wallace was permitted no jury. No witnesses were called. There was no plea. Wallace was given no opportunity to defend himself, although he did succeed in making one interruption. Mallore read the indictment and Segrave the sentence. There was no appeal. Wallace was immediately led to execution. While shocking to us, the whole procedure was in keeping with contemporary practice.[6] It is crucial to an understanding of the treatment of Wallace to remember that he had been outlawed at the St Andrews parliament in the previous year and, in all probability, at least once prior to that. Nor should it be overlooked that the outlawing of Wallace had been by due Scottish process in 1304. An outlaw, once proclaimed, had no entitlement even to the formality of a trial. His life was forfeit, and the hand of every man was turned against him. If the law was in a sense admitting its inability to deal with the criminal, it was at the same time, as in the case of Wallace, making his crimes manifest to the public and thus making summary justice possible. If taken, therefore, the outlaw could expect only that the judgement would be carried out against him with or without the formality of a trial. The status of a man did not protect him from this harsh aspect of outlawry. In the reign of Edward II, his cousin Thomas, earl of Lancaster, was outlawed with various of his confederates. When he fell into Edward's hands, Lancaster was at once convicted and executed.[7] In respect of the summary, not to say sham, nature of the proceedings in Westminster Hall, Wallace was treated no worse than any other outlaw.

Edward was, however, careful to emphasise that the decision to outlaw Wallace had followed upon a refusal of clemency. Wallace was shown to be not merely an outlaw but an obdurate one. There is a clear indication of this in the indictment.[8] The reference was to events after Falkirk. It would be easy to dismiss this offer as a formality and its appearance in the indictment as evidence of Edward's hypocrisy. We should not too readily assume this. The offer may mark a stage in Edward's approach to the problem of Wallace which has not perhaps received adequate attention. He had not always vindictively sought Wallace's death. His decision not to accept custody of Wallace from Philip of France has already been touched on.[9] It was a peculiar episode for which we have no explanation, but it does suggest that at the time Edward saw little threat in Wallace and no need to put him to death then. Edward's behaviour towards Bruce and other Scottish leaders demonstrates that he sought an accommodation until he felt himself utterly betrayed. Once he had reached that point he became demonic in pursuit of those who had spurned him. This was so in the case of Wallace. It was not until February 1304 that Edward took the ultimate step of refusing to Wallace that clemency which he had just held out to the other Scots. From there it was, in legal process, but a step to St Andrews and thence to Westminster Hall.

The list of crimes with which Wallace the outlaw was charged by Mallore was an impressive one.[10] It included killings, arson, destruction of property and sacrilege. These crimes relate mostly to the period between the start of his rebellion against English rule and the close of his invasion of the north of England. Then, indeed, he had burned villages, towns and religious establishments and, Mallore stated, spared neither the young nor the old, nuns nor priests. None of this Wallace could deny. This part of the indictment illustrates how well he had carried out his intention to wage war against the English. The more undisciplined of his followers committed atrocities in England which stain his name, but their savagery was the currency of war at the time. He had too as a matter of policy attacked the representatives of the English Church, which for him threatened the Scottish cause. All of these crimes constituted a standard accusation, one which might with equal truth have been made against Edward himself. Wallace was after all repaying like with like. The accusation was designed to prove that Wallace's crimes were common knowledge or notorious in the public mind and therefore beyond doubt or defence. Once more, in this, Edward was calling upon precedent. In 1287 he had had the Welshman, Rhys ap Maredudd, declared a notorious criminal. Wallace, a public outlaw, was cited for crimes which were of themselves public knowledge.

The one specific charge against Wallace in this section of the indictment was the murder of Heselrig. The motives behind the murder have been a source of debate but not the deed itself.[11] Had it been the sole crime laid against Wallace, it would have been sufficient to bring the death penalty – by hanging – in a Scottish as well as in an English court. The symbolic importance of the murder may however have led Edward to include it at Westminster. With the murder Wallace had emerged as a leader of the resistance; the blow to English prestige must therefore be avenged.

The outlawry and the murder were of themselves overwhelming. The case based on them was irrefutable, and for each there was an accepted penalty. When, however, we turn to the question of treason, Edward's argument in less secure. It was the charge of treason which brought from Wallace his only recorded contribution to the proceedings. He denied – we may safely assume that he did so with the utmost vehemence – that he was a traitor. He had never sworn allegiance to Edward. That we know to be a fact. Where the likes of Bruce and Comyn, and even Fraser, had given their allegiance, and their service, to the English king, and at various times throughout the war, Wallace had resolutely refused to do so. He might have saved his life by emulating these lords. He remained Balliol's man. Edward was not deterred by this.

It is difficult for us to comprehend how, if Wallace had never given his allegiance to Edward, the king could accuse him of treason. In a crucial sense, however, the definition of treason was the prerogative of the monarch. Edward had recourse in the case of Wallace to conviction on the king's record, a development in the law of treason which was of his own devising. It allowed him to bring Wallace before the court, to have the accusation rehearsed, and to secure the verdict he sought. He needed only to present his statement of the crimes with which he charged the prisoner; the judgement he demanded followed without delay or debate. The abuse possible under this system was to lead to public disquiet. It was the treason trials engineered by Edward II which, however, demonstrated the extent of that abuse. Appeals at the start of the reign of Edward III, for example those against the judgements in the cases of Thomas of Lancaster and Andrew de Harcla, prompted discussion. When parliament at length turned to Edward III for a definition of treason, he produced it in 1352; it is that statute which is still the basis for English law on the subject. But Wallace was, in 1305, quite literally dependent upon his enemy for the definition of treason as it applied to him.

What was that definition? Edward was, as always, careful to state it in some detail. He returned first to the surrender to him by Balliol of the kingdom of Scotland in 1296. This act, he argued, made the inhabitants of that country, whether or not they accepted Balliol's surrender and Edward's consequent sovereignty, subjects of the English king. To him Scotsmen of all degrees had at that time and afterwards sworn their loyalty. No Scot was in Edward's view excused from that loyalty by mere fact of not having sworn it. It is a wholly unacceptable argument to our way of thinking; our sympathies cannot but lie with Wallace.

The immediate question of allegiance thus settled to Edward's own satisfaction, the indictment as it deals with treason encompasses Wallace's rebellion, his assumption of the title of Guardian of Scotland, his convening of parliaments, and his seduction of the people of Scotland into seeking an alliance with France, at the time England's enemy. All these acts were hostile to Edward and by that token treasonable. Their inclusion in the indictment, as with the evidence relating to the waging of war, tells us of the impact made by Wallace in his struggle for the independence of Scotland. If he was a soldier, he was no less a statesman. In his anxiety to blacken Wallace's name, Edward was in the event providing the proof of his captive's achievements. There is one, and to us unusual, addition to the recital of treasonable acts given by Mallore. Wallace had displayed banners while in the field against the English. This was a charge frequently found in treason trials of this and other periods. It was raised in

1318 with Gilbert de Middleton and against Thomas of Lancaster and certain of his associates after the battle of Boroughbridge in 1322. As late as 1497, in the reign of Henry VII, Lord Audley faced a similar charge. To display one's banners while in arms was held to be a declaration of war against the monarch who was alone capable of instigating a just and legal war.[12] The court chose once more to ignore the fact that Wallace had never been Edward's man.

It will be seen that Edward had produced as damning an indictment against Wallace for treason as he did for outlawry. The case proven to the satisfaction of the court, Segrave read the sentence, which, as was customary, was implemented without delay. We recoil with horror from the details of the punishment, and rightly so. Edward's biographer remind us that 'clemency towards his enemies was not in Edward's character'.[13] Nor, Prestwich further illustrates, was he a man to show respect for a dead enemy. At the end of the battle of Evesham, Edward's troops almost certainly took their lead from him, when they grossly mutilated the corpse of Simon de Montfort.[14] When the head of Llywelyn ap Gruffyd was brought to him, Edward did not give it Christian burial with the rest of the body but had it displayed at the Tower of London. But Edward, although indisputably cruel from his youth, was not always consistent in his treatment of rebels. Among the Welsh leaders, Dafyd and Rhys ap Maredudd, for whose head, in a move similar for the hunt for Wallace, Edward offered a bounty of £100, suffered the ultimate penalty. By contrast, however, Morgan ap Maredudd, whose men at the battle of Maes Moydog were described as 'the best and bravest Welsh anyone has seen',[15] was spared, and later employed by Edward in his household.

A second rebel leader, Madog ap Llywelyn, lived out his life in the Tower of London.

Wallace, however, was not as fortunate as either Morgan or Madog. He was the first, and, until Bruce's rebellion, the only Scot to be executed by Edward. The king need not have ordered in the first instance the penalty on which he did decide for Wallace. To have hanged him upon capture, at some significant site in Scotland, would have been both humiliating and effective, a clear indication of Edward's contempt for Wallace and a warning to the Scots; Wallace was an outlaw in Scotland, the scene of his triumph at Stirling Bridge, and hanging was the appropriate and recognised punishment. Edward chose instead to have Wallace brought to London for a state trial; not even the Welsh Prince Dafyd ap Gruffyd had appeared in London to meet his end. With Wallace found guilty, Edward still had alternatives in determining the fate of the Scot. Historians are agreed that mercy for Wallace was out of the question. For them, the evidence that Edward was cruel, vindictive, and paranoiac brooks no argument.[16] Edward was all of these things, but he was also astute and manipulative; his record in respect of the matter of Scotland teaches us that. If impulsive, he could be calculating. It is not easy to believe that it was, from the outset, Edward's plan to have Wallace executed with all the severity of the law; that is, to have him 'barbarously done to death', as William Camden wrote of the punishment ordered for Anthony Babington and his fellow conspirators in 1586. Edward must surely have weighed the advantages to himself of a public and ostentatious display of mercy once the inevitable verdict of guilty had been handed down. Must we wholly discount the possibility that he rejected the option of mercy out of hand? A Wallace, incarcerated like Madog in the Tower of London, would have been a living symbol of Edward's magnanimity. The grand gesture was not alien to Edward. He spared the family of Dafyd ap Gruffyd, as he did the wife and sisters of Robert Bruce. We judge his treatment of Bruce's family as reprehensible but Edward's contemporaries would not necessarily agree.[17]

Wallace, reprieved and a prisoner, would have achieved no great posthumous reputation. Edward decided in favour of making an example of him. In this, he erred in our eyes, but we have the benefit of hindsight. The Scottish leaders, some of whom were almost certainly present in London in preparation for the parliament Edward had called for September, were silent, their fear of the king perhaps outweighing their pity for, or loyalty to, Wallace. Silent, too, were Lamberton and Wishart, the two bishops most closely allied with Wallace. Simon Fraser was once more Edward's man. John de Soules was in France, as stout in the cause of Scotland as when he had refused to submit in 1304. We are driven to the conclusion that, with the exception of Soules, the ruling elite of Scotland had left Wallace to his fate. This may have been the result of personality and policy. Wallace's relations with the ruling elite had rarely been easy; to them he represented a threat to the established order. In this, they shared a characteristic with Edward, with whom they were, at the time of Wallace's death, formulating a new policy for the governance of Scotland. It was obvious to the Scots that, having failed since 1296 to defeat Edward, they had to accept what he offered them. If the price was complicity in the execution of their erstwhile colleague, now perhaps an embarrassment, they seem to have accepted it. Edward had judged the Scots well.

For his treasons Wallace was drawn, tied to a hurdle – perhaps as in the case of Fraser in 1306, wrapped in an ox-hide – at the tails of horses to the place of execution. To be drawn was recognised as the mark of a traitor. Edward did not devise this aspect of the punishment for Wallace, not had it originated in the war with Scotland. It had been employed at least twice in the reign of Edward's father. Edward used it himself in the cases of Dafyd ap Gruffyd and Rhys ap Madedudd. Ten years before Wallace, Sir Thomas Tuberville was drawn to the place of execution. The use of the hurdle or the hide served to protect the victim and save him for the viler aspects of the sentence; he might otherwise have been ripped apart on the surfaces over which he was dragged. Wallace's journey to his torment at Smithfield took him from Westminster, through Eastcheap, past the Tower, to Aldgate, and onwards by a circuitous city route for more than four miles, to the delight of the populace.

By a strange and cruel coincidence the London through which Wallace was dragged to his death was in some measure the product of the efforts of another Wallace, Henry le Waleys. This holder of the name was highly regarded by his king. He was at various times mayor of London and Bordeaux and was no mean planner; he helped in the creation of the new town of Winchelsea and advised on the reconstruction of Berwick.[18] Some of those who now watched the melancholy and painful last journey of William Wallace had felt the harshness of Henry le Waleys as he implemented Edward's policies for the capital. Like his master, Henry le Waleys was a harsh man and his unpopularity led to his loss of office in London in 1284. He did not, however, fall in Edward's esteem.

At Smithfield the arrival of the hated William Wallace was greeted by a vast concourse of onlookers. Executions provided a spectacle enjoyed by all classes; the practice of viewing them continued for centuries. Samuel Pepys attended the execution of the regicide, Major-General Thomas Harrison, in 1660, and that of another parliamentarian, Sir Henry Vane the younger, in 1662. James Boswell in the next century thought executions 'a very great melancholy'. As late as 1757 English 'amateurs de supplice', were crossing the Channel to Paris, to witness the protracted and hideous agonies of the hapless Robert François Damiens, who had failed in a somewhat half-hearted attempt on the life of Louis XV. The presence of a lady of the court on that occasion aroused the disgust even of the intended victim himself.

The reaction of the public to an execution was not always straightforward; criminal could become victim if the circumstances were right. Prestwich tells how, upon the execution of Dafyd ap Gruffyd in 1283, in contrast to the citizens of London, York and Winchester, those of Lincoln would not accept any part of the dismembered body.[19] Their fastidiousness cost them the king's displeasure and a considerable fine. The fate of Anthony Babington, whose plot in 1556 to murder Elizabeth I and replace her with Mary, Queen of Scots, aroused great revulsion. As a consequence, the government ordered that those who were executed after Babington should either be hanged until dead or unconscious before being disembowelled. Jack Ketch, the executioner, having already botched the decapitation of Lord William Russell, narrowly escaped lynching when he did the same with James, duke of Monmouth, in 1685. A prisoner might exhibit remarkable composure. Pepys thought that, on the scaffold at Charing Cross, Vane was 'looking as cheerfully as any man could do in that condition'. 'Vane', he recorded, ' . . . in all things (he) appeared the most resolved man that ever died in that manner.' An executed man could be deemed capable of sanctity, able to perform miracles; even such a despicable incompetent as Thomas of Lancaster fell into that category after his death at Pontefract in 1322. The crowd was capable of astonishing behaviour, if moved. The Jesuit, Father Henry Garnet, was about to be cut down from the rope while still alive, when members of the spectators prevented the hangman from carrying out the more gruesome aspects of the execution. Some pulled at Garnet's legs until he was 'perfectly dead'. The hangman was then allowed to carry out his remaining duties undisturbed. It seemed that even the most remarkable occurrence was possible at a public execution. Sir Everard Digby, one of the 'Gunpowder Plotters', was reported to have called out, 'Thou liest!' when his heart, plucked from his body, was held aloft by the executioner with the words, 'Behold the heart of a traitor.' But there was no guarantee of the public's reaction. Sir Thomas Graham, the murderer of James I of Scotland, had boasted at his trial that he would be remembered for ridding the country of a tyrant. Instead he went to his death at Stirling universally vilified. James, increasingly loathed for his rapaciousness and severity, had become a martyr, once dead.

There was no pity for Wallace, no revulsion as to what was done to him at Smithfield. The English had been conditioned to see him in the most extreme terms. For Matthew of Westminster, who was present at the execution, Wallace was 'a man void of pity . . . more hardened in cruelty than Herod, more raging in madness than Nero'. Wallace's death was 'justly deserved', not merely in keeping with the verdict but 'with additional aggravations and indignities', Matthew gloated. There is no reason to suppose that Matthew was exaggerating the strength of English feeling against Wallace; those with him in the crowd undoubtedly shared his sentiments.

For the murders, robberies and other felonies he had committed, both in his own country and in England, he was hanged, as standard a punishment as drawing was for treason. He was cut down while still alive so that he might be spared none of the bestialities ahead. He was disembowelled and in all probability emasculated, although the official record makes no mention of this. Matthew of Westminster relates that Wallace was 'mutilated', a clear reference to what was commonly inflicted on traitors.[20] For his sacrilege, the burning of religious establishments and relics, his heart, liver, lungs, and entrails were cast upon a fire. From these, it was believed, issued the thoughts which led him to sacrilege. That disembowelling and the burning of entrails was a fitting punishment for sacrilege was well established; it appears to have been first used in the case of David ap Gruffyd. Not even his royal blood had saved him from this particularly revolting aspect of the judgement. Wallace was decapitated for his outlawry. Strangely, decapitation of itself was considered a not dishonourable death, used throughout the centuries for nobles convicted of treason or other crimes. Waltheof had died thus, as did Lancaster.

But Edward was not finished with Wallace, even now. His head was placed on a pole on London Bridge, no doubt that those who passed that way might marvel at Edward's justice. His body was hacked into four pieces. One quarter was sent to Newcastle upon Tyne and there exhibited above the common sewer, to the delight of those who recalled Wallace's brutal invasion of the district in 1297–98. A second part went to Berwick, that town of so great and tragic a significance in the war which had made his name and brought about his death. A third

247

part was hung at Perth, the town of St John, of such strategic value to Scots and English alike, where, according to Blind Harry, Wallace performed some of his most spectacular deeds. There is some dispute as to the destination of the fourth part. Lanercost differs from the official version in giving Aberdeen for Stirling. Both towns were familiar to Wallace. The former had witnessed one of the more calculatedly brutal episodes associated with him: the hanging of a number of Scots who had defied him. Stirling was the scene of his great victory. For that reason is may be the likelier choice, in keeping with Edward's intention to blacken Wallace's memory. It was Segrave who was commanded to see to the transportation of Wallace's quarters to their destinations. For this he was paid fifteen shillings.[21]

Thus Wallace perished, horribly if memorably. Edward had removed his most persistent but not, as time would show, his most dangerous enemy. In doing so, as time would also show, he had made a colossal blunder. It became, and remained, an article of faith in Scotland that Wallace had died a hero and a martyr. Hero he undoubtedly was, by any measure. From the moment of his appearance at Lanark, he was a hero in personal, military and political terms, brief though his supremacy was. And Edward, although he did not live to learn this, had made him into a martyr on 23 August 1305. Blind Harry tells us that by his death at the hands of the English Wallace entered into 'lasting bliss'.[22] He had entered into glory, his eyes fixed, Harry says, on his most beloved possession, his psalter, held before him by Clifford.[23] And it was into a kind of glory that Wallace indeed had gone. His name survives in the popular memory, where those of others, with a crucial or melancholy role in the War of Independence, have not. The name of Simon Fraser means little today. Yet he served the Scottish cause well, fought with Wallace, did not betray him when it might have been to his own advantage, joined Bruce in 1306, and met the same ghastly end as Wallace. Alexander Bruce, brother of Robert, was executed at Carlisle by Edward. Dean of Glasgow, Alexander had been known at Cambridge for his scholarship and his character. He too fought for the cause, although incompetently, and fell before Edward's violent and uncertain temper. But who speaks now of Alexander Bruce? Christopher Seton, husband of Christina Bruce, perished at Dumfries, where he had helped in the murder of Comyn. Seton is forgotten. Like his brother, John Wallace was taken to London and there put to death. Not even his relationship with William has saved John Wallace from anonymity. Not one of these, or any of the long list of Edward's victims, not even one of the standing of the earl of Atholl, has as lasting a fame or as firm a hold on the imagination of the people of Scotland as William Wallace.

What cannot easily be demonstrated is when Wallace's reputation, the one he has come to enjoy, was first established in Scotland. The indictment presented on Edward's behalf at Westminster Hall would appear to suggest that he meant not only to destroy Wallace's body – which was his to dispose of – but his reputation. That he failed to do the latter in the long term has perhaps led us to overlook the possibility that in the short term he did succeed in his aim. Wallace had been stigmatised as an outlaw and a traitor. It is difficult to argue that the verdict would have been radically different in a Scottish court, whether dominated or not by Edward, had the charges been those used at Westminster. There was a frightening unanimity in both countries on the subject of the outlaw and the traitor. Nor would the sentence have differed. For confirmation we may look to the Scone or 'Black' parliament of August 1320. There the members of the so-called 'Soules conspiracy' were brought to justice. On that occasion Robert Bruce did not scruple to use the full severity of the law if he thought it warranted. It is true that unlike Edward he did temper justice with mercy in certain of the sentences.[24] But a famous figure of the period, Ingram de Umfraville, was so disturbed by Bruce's execution of David of Brechin – both the judgement itself and the manner of punishment – that he withdrew his allegiance to Bruce and returned to his estates in England. All this took place when Scotland was secure from the English menace. Not even as humane a king as Bruce could entirely escape from his own temper and the cruelty into which it led him.

What then was the reaction in Scotland to the death of Wallace? It is here that we are perhaps most unfortunate in our lack of contemporary Scottish evidence on which to draw. We do know that the death of Wallace did not prevent the Scottish lords from advising Edward on and in some cases participating in the new form of government for Scotland which emerged from the parliament of Westminster in September 1305. While it is correct that discussions on the new council for Scotland had been taking place before the capture and death of Wallace, it is equally correct that, one month after his execution, men with whom he had fought were prepared to assist Edward's lieutenant in Scotland, John of Brittany. Not even Bruce can be entirely cleared of this association, despite at least one strenuous defence of him.[25] It would be comforting to draw a connection between Wallace's death and Bruce's rebellion of 1306, but it would be to fly in the face of reason. Bruce had long aspired to the throne and had been plotting to achieve his aim – whether or not with the help of Wallace we cannot tell.[26] But whatever the motive behind the murder of Comyn – whether Bruce feared betrayal by Comyn or was thwarted by him in his plans – it was a rash and unconsidered act. It tells us that, when provoked or baulked, Bruce possessed the more extreme reactions of his grandfather, the Competitor, rather than the more equable temperament of his father, the earl of Carrick. Bruce's subsequent moves, which involved him in rebellion against Edward, were the consequence of the murder; he was not driven by any desire to avenge Wallace.

Bruce's whole relationship with Wallace was a strange one,[27] but it may well be that the clue to the question of Wallace's reputation is to be found in certain of Bruce's actions once he became king. It must be remembered that, prior to the murder of Comyn, Bruce's behaviour had always been dictated by a degree of self-interest absent in Wallace. His family had always stressed the strength and legitimacy of its claim to the throne. Bruce himself fought for years to establish that legitimacy against the claims of Edward II. It might not serve his purpose in this struggle to have his name linked with that of Wallace, a convicted traitor and outlaw. This question of legitimacy may explain the otherwise surprising omission of Wallace's name from Barbour's account of Bruce. Even in the famous speech which he puts into his hero's mouth at Bannockburn, Barbour can find no place for a mention of Wallace. Uplifting though Bruce's address is, noble as its sentiments are, he does not in Barbour's report call upon the name of Wallace to inspire his army. It may not be irrelevant that after the completion of his work Barbour received first a gift of money and then a pension from Robert II. There was again war with

England. Barbour would thus fulfil the role Blind Harry gave himself at the time of James III, if with different motives; to produce a story which would stir and unite a people governed by a weak king in the face of the enemy. If this argument is correct, it makes Barbour's treatment of Wallace the more striking.

More significant, however, because of the firm evidence, is Bruce's attitude to Menteith, the traditional villain in the story of Wallace's capture. It was noted earlier[28] that Menteith, in seizing Wallace, was acting on the instructions of Edward, to whom he was bound by his oath of loyalty. It is entirely possible that Comyn, Lindsay, or Graham might have played Menteith's role had opportunity offered. But that opportunity, and with it the loathing of posterity, fell to Menteith. If in the capture of Wallace Menteith had been acting by reason of his oath to Edward, he was not averse to an attempt to lay hands upon the possessions of those who had joined Bruce in 1306.[29] Yet, in 1309, Bruce accepted Menteith into his peace and bestowed lands upon him. Menteith's name, further, was one of those associated with the Declaration of Arbroath. Menteith, first for the Scottish cause, then Edward's man, and finally a supporter of Bruce, did not suffer in the latter's eyes because he had handed Wallace over to the English any more than he did by his shifts of allegiance. If four years after Wallace's death, Menteith was received by Bruce and was subsequently so to be established that he was involved in the Declaration of Arbroath, we are entitled to wonder whether it was Wallace's reputation rather than that of Menteith which had suffered in those years.

If this is indeed the case, it may explain, along with Barbour's omission of Wallace from his tale, the reticence of his contemporary, Fordun, on the matter of the inspirational nature of Wallace's reputation. If Fordun tells us how Wallace learned of the meaning of freedom and casts Menteith as the villain who betrayed Wallace to the English who tore the hero apart in London, we have to wait for Andrew Wyntoun for the quintessential and lasting Scottish view of Wallace:

> In all England there was not then
> As William Wallace so true a man.
> Whatever he did against their nation
> They made him ample provocation
> Nor to them sworn never was he
> To fellowship, faith or loyalty.[30]

Wyntoun's description of Wallace, embroidered by Blind Harry, has prevailed. The English account of Wallace is ignored. Yet neither is wholly satisfactory. Only by utilising both sources, together with such documentary evidence as we possess, can we hope to achieve an understanding of this remarkable man.

NOTES

1. Stevenson (ed.): *Documents Illustrative of Sir William Wallace*, 189.

2. Guisborough, 142. Wallace summoned Carlisle to surrender under the title of 'the Conqueror'. Given his recent victory and his almost unimpeded progress through the north of England, however, the title may be said to be not undeserved. See chap. 5 above.

3. Wright (ed.): *Political Songs of England*, 218.

4. *Calendar of the Patent Rolls*, 18 August 1305. Stubbs (ed.): *Chronicles of the Reigns of Edward I and Edward II*, i, 139, includes Geoffrey de Segrave among the judges.

5. Wright, op. cit., 94, in 'the Battle of Lewes'.

6. For a contemporary account of the trial, see Stubbs (ed.): *Chronicles*, i, 139–42. Modern commentaries appear in Bellamy: *The Law of Treason in England in the Later Middle Ages*, 34 et seq and Keen: 'Treason Trials under the Law of Arms' (*EHR*), passim.

7. Brie (ed.): *The Brut*, i, 222. Phillips, op. cit., 224–25.

8. Mallore read: '. . . and offered you mercy if you surrendered, you did despise his offer, and were outlawed in his court as a thief and a felon according to the law of England and Scotland . . .'

9. Chap. 7, above.

10. The indictment is printed in Stubbs (ed.): *Chronicles*, i, pp. 139–42.

11. Blind Harry, sixth book, for the traditional story. Kightly, op. cit., chap. 6, summarizes the various accounts. Reese, op. cit., 43–44, likewise offered some variants.

12. See on this Bellamy and Keen. Also Keen: *The Laws of War in the Later Middle Ages*, 105 et seq.

13. Prestwich: *Edward I*, 202.

14. Ibid., 51.

15. Ibid., 223.

16. Watson, op. cit., 213, calls him 'bloodthirsty' and refers to 'a degree of vindictiveness which does Edward no credit'. Barrow: *Robert Bruce*, 137, says that Edward, 'the greatest of the Plantagenets . . . appears small and mean. He is measured against one of the great spirits of history and found wanting.' For Prestwich's commend on Edward's attitude to his enemies, see note 13 above. But see his mitigation of Edward on p. 503.

17. Barrow: *Robert Bruce*, 162; Prestwich: *Edward I*, 109 and 508–09.

18. Prestwich, op. cit., 265–65

19. Ibid., 203

20. Mathew of Westminster: *Flores Historium*, iii, 123–24

21. *Calendar of the Patent Rolls*, 29 September 1305.

22. Eleventh book, 1406.

23. Eleventh book, 1397–98.

24. Barrow, *Robert Bruce*, 429–30.

25. Barron: *The Scottish War of Independence*, chap. 15.

26. The documents found on Wallace at the time of his capture, had they survived, might have answered the question.

27. The ingrained belief that Bruce drew on Wallace for inspiration, found in Bower, for example, surfaced in the film *Braveheart* in 1995.

28. Chap. 9.

29. Barrow, op. cit., 448.

30. Wyntoun: *Oriyginale Cronykil of Scotland*.

Conclusion

A Man for All Times?

Alone among his contemporaries, William Wallace has made the transition from one millennium to another in a positive manner, with his reputation intact, even enhanced. His are attributes which defy the passing of the years to remain inspirational today. In the eyes of some, he is worthy of canonisation on the model of Joan of Arc.

Wallace has thus left behind in their own time the major figures of the war of 1296, whether Scots or English. John Balliol, for example, we know only as a feeble incompetent, forever 'Toom Tabard', stripped of his title and his dignity. John Comyn, likewise, has all but disappeared from our ken, a victim of Bruce violence and pro-Bruce propaganda, the aspirations of his line extinguished with the death of his son on the English side at Bannockburn and that of his grandson two years later. Comyn deserves more of us, but his reputation went with his murder in 1306.

Taller by far than either Balliol or Comyn looms Edward I. Crusader, lawmaker, builder, arbiter in

European affairs, he crushed the Welsh and might have done the same to the Scots had not his body betrayed him. But it is not merely his treatment of Wallace which alienates us from this feared and fearsome monarch; his adherence to a code of chivalry at once romantic and brutal anchors him firmly in a remote past. Robert Bruce has fared somewhat better. The courageous survivor of years of suffering for himself and his family, the victor of Bannockburn and beneficiary of an influential life by John Barbour, Bruce is assured of respect and affection, but, as in his own day, he cannot be exonerated of expediency. In this sense, he is still yesterday's man because, unlike Wallace, to us his motives are suspect, his loyalties questionable. Even the greatest of Scottish kings is somehow diminished when judged alongside Wallace.

The Wallace of today is an exceptional, unique man. But we would do well to consider that the Wallace of today is not, and cannot be the Wallace of 1305. No contemporary would be wholly at ease with our version of his life. There would be agreement, of course, on certain of his qualities, courage – constancy, strategic and tactical ability, leadership – among them. Two aspects of his life, however, would preclude reconciliation of the Wallace of 1305 and the Wallace of today. Both are challenging but reflect the contemporary view of Wallace and cannot be discounted if we are to see him as he was. We must, therefore, strive to strip away the accretions of the centuries.

Wallace died a failure and a traitor in 1305. To rid his country of the English and to see it sovereign, with its own king, these were the twin ambitions of Wallace's life after Lanark. He achieved neither. At the time of Wallace's death, Edward I was master of Scotland and about to promulgate, in the forthcoming parliament at

Westminster, an ordinance whereby Scotland, no longer allowed the status of a 'realm' but now merely described as a 'land', was to be governed. John Balliol, for whom Wallace had fought to the death, had not been restored to the throne which he had lost, perhaps to his own relief, nine years previously. His expected return to Scotland, which prompted English fears and Scottish hopes in 1302[1] and which lay behind Bruce's defection to Edward,[2] had not come about. Scotland had reverted in 1305 to its condition in 1296, before Wallace's first re-corded appearance in the war with England. It was an occupied and defeated country, its people repressed, its affairs in the hands of a foreign monarch. When, many years after Wallace's death, Scotland was finally free and with its own king, that was the work of a man with whom his relationship had been at best an uncertain one. It is too readily forgotten that had Wallace survived Edward I and lived to witness an independent Scotland, it would have been as an opponent of Bruce; Balliol's man, Wallace would not have changed his allegiance.

The fact that Wallace died alone is too readily for-gotten. He was butchered as a punishment and as a spec-tacle for the populace of London and for those Scots present in the capital in anticipation of the parliament. To them and to the English sympathisers still in Scotland, he was a rebel and a traitor. They had condemned him as such at the St Andrews parliament in March of the preceding year. There is no evidence to suggest that they had changed their minds about him in the period leading up to his capture and trial. We need not charge Bruce, Comyn, Lamberton and the others with complicity in Wallace's end. They viewed it with apparent indifference, the indifference of the collaborator. It is an ugly and emotive word, but unavoidable. Wallace had become an embarrassment to them. He represented the old, stern Scotland, that of resistance. Edward had offered them a new Scotland, that of collaboration, and they had accepted it. Bruce, Comyn, and Lamberton, all three like Wallace Guardians, were nominated to occupy important positions in the government which Edward had established for Scotland. They were not the only Scots for whom he found a place. It is idle to speculate about the thoughts of these men, whether they whispered against the sentence on Wallace, whether they planned rebellion or not at some stage in the future. We can only judge them by their actions. They collaborated with Edward in the dispositions he was making for Scotland. Wallace's execution, for them as for Edward, was a symbolic prelude. It marked a beginning.

Wallace thus went alone to his death; there would be no slaughter of his adherents, as happened in the aftermath of Robert Bruce's uprising in the following year. It could hardly have been otherwise. Well before his capture by Menteith, Wallace had already become something of an anachronism in the landscape of Scottish politics. He who for a brief but momentous period had represented all, at the end stood only for those who now had no voice, the impotent majority unable to influence events. For long enough, there had been no place for him as of right in the councils of the Scottish leadership. Other concerns, other ambitions, pre-dating those to which he had given expression, once again dominated.

When exactly he had been marginalized by the leadership must be a matter of interpretation. He had been with them in the struggle against Edward but arguably, even when knighted and Guardian of Scotland, not of them. We read of the two bishops Lamberton and Wishart in association with Wallace but that relationship did not stand the test of time; Lamberton, for one, had turned to Bruce in 1304.[3] William Douglas 'le Hardi', not a natural ally, rode with Wallace in the raid on Scone in 1297 but that connection was soon broken by Douglas' return to the political environment in which he was most comfortable. Robert Bruce was in rebellion in 1297, at the same time as Wallace, but distinct from him. Malcolm Wallace was with the Bruce faction in the confrontation at Peebles in 1299[4] and thus opposed to John Comyn. It is difficult to judge what conclusion to draw from this alignment because Malcolm's relationship with his brother was not straightforward. The confident and aggressive manner in which Sir David Graham sought to obtain William Wallace's possessions at Peebles on that occasion suggests that the awe of Wallace, so crucial in his attempt to unite the Scots in Balliol's cause, had faded. As Graham was in the Comyn camp at this time and indeed, as has been noted,[5] was at odds with Wallace's brother, Malcolm, we may suppose that Wallace and Comyn were no longer acting in concert on Balliol's behalf. The roots of this estrangement perhaps lie in an event two years previously, when Wallace, as the victor of Stirling Bridge, was acting as de facto leader of the Scottish resistance to Edward. It has been argued that his nomination of Lamberton to St Andrews was one cause of the rupture, breaking as it did the Comyn hold on the see.[6] If this is so, then Wallace could rely neither on the Bruce nor the Comyn faction, each with its own agenda but both resentful of Wallace's anti-establishment stance.

The accepted starting-point for the disassociation of the Scottish leadership from Wallace is his defeat at Falkirk. But we cannot be sure that Wallace was forced to relinquish the Guardianship by the weight of magnate opinion. It is as likely, if not more so, that he chose to

resign.[7] If the act of an honourable man, his resignation
was a mistake. It removed him, unnecessarily, from the
forefront of affairs. He was never again to be allowed to
exercise his undoubted military talents to the full. That
was Scotland's loss. The view of one English chronicle
that upon his return from the Continent he became the
'commander and captain' of the Scots and the inspiration
behind their resistance[8] is now discredited. It does, however, indicate the strength of his reputation in English
minds as the only Scot to have inflicted a major defeat in
the field against the enemy. Wallace was, at best, one of
several leaders, as in the raid of June 1303 into Annandale,
and he is absent from the list of those involved in the
celebrated engagement at Roslin in the previous February.[9]
Thereafter, Wallace was simply a peripheral figure.

By 1304, Edward was finally in control of the Scottish
problem. Comyn's resistance came to an end in February.
Edward understood the motivation of Comyn and those
associated with him. The relationship between Edward
and the Comyn family was of long standing and of mutual
benefit.[10] The submission terms imposed by Edward
reflected, at least in part, the value to him of that association. The penalties levied on the Scots in 1304 fall
short of those inflicted on Welsh rebels and as far short
as those inflicted on Wallace. The thinking behind the
1304 terms was not dissimilar to that of Henry III and
the Prince Edward, as he then was, at the end of the
Barons' War in 1265, when the maximum penalty inflicted on any supporter of Simon de Montfort was to
redeem his lands at seven times their annual value.[11] In
1304, even as obdurate an opponent as Wishart was
required to pay no more than three times the value of his
lands. Ingram de Umfraville, once joint-Guardian and
less astute perhaps than Wishart in reading the signs,

had to find five times the value of his lands because of his dilatory submission.[12]

Like his father, Edward appears magnanimous, a king bent on reconciliation with a defeated people. He was even prepared to forgive, if no longer fully to trust, the likes of Fraser and Thomas Boys, who had been in his service.[13] It is not, however, by his generosity in 1304 that Edward is remembered but for his treatment of Wallace. It has earned him opprobrium but it had its own logic, and not only in Edward's eyes. Just as Edward excluded Wallace from the general submission, so Wallace continued in his defiance of a king who, to others, had conducted himself in the negotiations with Comyn in a tolerant and tolerable manner. Things had moved on; Wallace, it must surely have seemed to the Scots themselves, had not, or perversely, would not. 1304 perhaps offered Wallace his best chance, however slim, to enter Edward's peace; he chose not to take it. Had he submitted, would he have been as leniently treated as Fraser and Boys? It is not impossible; Edward was not wholly incapable of the grand gesture.[14] Had Wallace associated himself with Comyn in the general submission of 1304 and not stood apart, he might have survived, despite everything, in an atmosphere conducive to reconciliation.

It did not happen. Wallace had a different vision from those who submitted with Comyn. In modern terminology, he had embraced the cause of independence for Scotland, Comyn, Bruce and their equals a form of devolution. It was this which led them to collaborate with Edward in his plans for Scotland, promulgated in a parliament at Westminster, attended by some of them at least, in the month after Wallace's execution. They may well have considered that they had no alternative. As a practical proposition, independence had ceased to exist at Falkirk, the last opportunity in Wallace's lifetime to achieve it. When it was revived, it was not because of the circumstances of Wallace's death, but as a consequence of the murder of Comyn by Bruce. Wallace, an anachronism at the time of his death, was an irrelevance at Comyn's.

The second aspect of Wallace's career to which we must turn our attention, and one more contentious even than his inability to achieve his twin aims of freeing his country of a foreign yoke and restoring to it its rightful king, John Balliol, is the charge of treason brought against him at Westminster. His denial of that particular item in the indictment rings down over the centuries, heroic, splendid, clear and authentic. Wallace would have found no shame in admitting to the other crimes laid at his door; on the contrary, he would have taken them as acknowledgement by the English themselves of the blows he had dealt against them in a short space of time, little more than a year. The murder of Heselrig at Lanark, whatever the motives behind it, was a fact. The invasion of the north of England and the destruction it wrought, for this too he was responsible. Under him, assemblies had been convened, proof of his defiance of Edward. Killings, robberies, felonies, these were the inevitable consequence of war; Wallace could not pretend that they had not occurred.

But his reaction to the accusation of treason was quite another matter. His rejection of it was personal. Can we be certain that it was not also a political statement, however brief? For Edward the question was a simple one; Balliol's submission to him in 1296 encompassed his subjects. It did not count that Wallace had neither given homage nor sworn allegiance to him. Like other Scots, Wallace had had opportunity to do so but did not take it.

In 1304 the Scots had once again submitted to Edward, accepting his sovereignty and his law. What that meant was made evident in the month after Wallace's death when, at the parliament in London, Scotland ceased to be a 'realm' and was referred to as a 'land'. Had Wallace been astute enough, in his last public utterance, to use his trial as a platform to remind his fellow countrymen where their duty lay?

If so, he went unheard. As we have already noted, his death aroused no protest from the Scottish leadership; they accepted it as a preliminary to the settlement drawn up by Edward. Nor was the news of his death in London, and in the wake of that news the gruesome sight of his severed limbs on public display at various places in Scotland, to lead to unrest in the country, let alone violence against the English. No spontaneous demonstrations or uprising in protest at the treatment of Wallace are recorded. Such apparent passivity is intriguing. The English delight at Wallace's end is to be expected; the accounts we have linger over the details of the execution and reflect the general elation at the just punishment meted out to the Scot described as 'an unworthy man'. But what of the Scots, a nation which only eight years previously he had energised and to which in its darkest days he had given back its pride? Without firm evidence, we may nevertheless make some assumptions. In the winter of 1296–1297, within a few months of Edward's departure from Scotland after his humiliation of Balliol, there were uprisings over a wide area against English rule. They ranged from the north to the south-west. If at first uncoordinated, they had a common purpose. Scotland then was defeated but not cowed. Support for action came from all sections of the population. In 1305, Scotland was, we may suppose, both defeated and cowed,

264

incapable of resistance, even to avenge Wallace, the lost and, we would wish to think mourned, leader. But a long war had taken its toll, there was a general desire for a return to normality, at the price of English occupation. There was to be no second Wallace or Moray in 1305, drive by that same powerful force which had manifested itself in the past.

Does this passivity on the part of the Scots in 1305 mean more than a broken spirit? If so, were they, like their leaders, complicit in the new dispensation for their country and, by extension, in the death of Wallace? He had been the first Scot to suffer under the English law of treason and there must have been many in Scotland who fervently hoped that he would be the last. The casualties of 1296 had been incurred in what was obviously a war. The submission of 1304 had ended the war, and now Edward had taught the Scots, through Wallace's death, what defiance of him might entail for the perpetrator, if the English king was so inclined. It was a salutary lesson, the more effective because without precedent in the war. With a single act of savagery, as merited to his mind as the sack of Berwick, Edward had effectively and efficiently shattered Scottish illusions as to the nature of the law under which they were henceforth to be governed. Worse would certainly come in response to Bruce's rebellion, a still greater betrayal for Edward than Wallace's, but in 1305 the example made of Wallace was more than enough. At this remove, we prefer to believe that the execution, with all its attendant horrors, had failed in its primary purpose. This cannot have been the case. When it was ordained that the laws of Scotland would be examined with a view to ensuring that any element 'openly contrary to God and reason' was removed, the Scots could be in no doubt as to what this signified. As with

Wallace, Edward would be both prosecutor and judge; his will was the law.

At this remove also, we tend to shirk one other possibility: that in Scotland itself there may have been a wide acceptance, not limited to the leadership, of the validity of Edward's judgement on Wallace. Wallace the outlaw of the St Andrews parliament would not alienate the Scots. Quite the contrary; there was, and of course still is, something romantic about the outlaw. The anti-English and anti-establishment hero – that too the Scots would accept. But treason was another matter altogether. Wallace, 'a Scot born in Scotland', had, of course, been tried, judged, and executed under English law. But Scots and English law alike reflected an abhorrence of treason, of sin and sinner. There is no shortage of evidence to illustrate this. Robert I acted with the utmost severity against those implicated in the Soules conspiracy of 1320.[15] Sir Robert Graham and the other assassins of James I perished horribly; in the words of one writer, 'the fiendishness of the punishment inflicted upon them . . . on this unique occasion even surpassed English practice'.[16] The royal birth of Walter, earl of Atholl did not spare him as accomplice of Graham in regicide and treason. Graham's confident assertion that he would be remembered for the 'great good' he had done for Scotland was not borne out by events, so heinous was the crime thought to be.[17]

There was, in effect, no limit in either England or Scotland to what might be done to a traitor in an age of instant and savage retribution. A work from the reign of Edward I offers the standard view: 'the judgement for lese majesty against the earthly king is executed by torment according to the ordinance and will of the king and by death.'[18] Inevitably, there were excesses. The vengeance exacted by Edward II in 1322 against the supporters of Thomas of Lancaster provoked outrage.[19] In the reign of Edward IV, the activities of John Tiptoft, earl of Worcester and constable of England, gained him a reputation for cruelty.[20] The trials of James Hamilton of Finnart and Janet Douglas, Lady Glamis, were not untainted, and the burning of the latter aroused horror.[21] Such public reactions were, however, unusual.

The principles behind the various elements in the English punishment for treason were understood in Scotland. Drawing and hanging were imposed on some of the Soules conspirators by the 'Black Parliament' of 1320 to emphasise that as well as traitors, they were common criminals; like Wallace to the English, they were 'unworthy'. The nature of Wallace's own death was not lost on Scots. In a revealing passage, Bower tells us that Edward 'thought to destroy the fame of the noble William for ever, since in the eyes of the foolish his life seemed to be ended with such a contemptible death'. Bower's use of the adjective 'contemptible' here is instructive. The word itself is open to interpretation but the context in which it appears points us in the direction of Bower's own meaning. Writing a century and a half after the events he is relating, he goes right to the core of Wallace's punishment, to present it as Edward is envisaging it.

Was Bower unique in this stance? We do not know. Elsewhere, he is fulsome in his praise of Wallace. In a biblical allusion, Wallace is a 'second Mattathias', the Jewish priest who led a revolt against the Syrians in the second century BC. As the 'hammer of the English', Wallace is a 'mighty arm' and 'a salvation in time of trouble'. His activities are a 'celestial gift'. We are nearer here to the Wallace of today, our Wallace. Present also in Bower are other themes which we have inherited – the perfidy of the Comyns on the field of Falkirk, the envy with which Wallace was met in sections of the Scottish people, and, most seductive of all perhaps, the liberating effect of Wallace on Bruce, on opposite sides at Falkirk. 'Like one awakening from a deep sleep,' Bower informs us, 'Bruce henceforth became every day braver than he had been.' Notwithstanding the use of 'contemptible' in his reflection on Wallace's death, Bower assures us that Edward misjudged the impact of the execution, for 'the sudden death of a just man after a good life does not lessen his merits if he dies thus'.[22]

This theme, that Wallace's reputation was not destroyed in 1305, is yet another embraced today. Bower was not writing in a vacuum; he could draw on a hundred and fifty years, if he so desired, of oral tradition, and with it its concomitant invention. But in Bower's case we are still concerned, primarily, with history.[23] He and Fordun and Wyntoun, both of whom preceded him, are the Scottish counter-balance to the English verdicts on Wallace. All three were written after their English counter-parts. Fordun's *Chronica Gentis Scotorum* is the nearest in time to Wallace, dating from the 1370s. Wyntoun's *Orygynale Cronykil of Scotland* was completed fifty years later. Some twenty years separate Bower's work from that of Wyntoun, but the link between the three is strong. Their view of history has been challenged with some force in recent years.[24] Their Wallace may be a man of exceptional powers, but does not our certain knowledge of him lead us to that same conclusion? We need not rehearse his achievements to see that this is the case.

Yet these achievements have not been enough. The generations which followed on Wallace have looked for, and found, each in its own way, something more in him. It has been argued above that in 1305 Wallace was both failure and traitor. The Wallace of today is far removed from that bleak verdict. When did the transformation, or rehabilitation, of Wallace begin? How did the hero become superhero? There is a temptation to believe that the process was prompt, almost immediate.[25] This is not evident if we look at the earliest extant Scottish accounts. The heroic, patriotic, inspirational Wallace of Fordun, Wyntoun, and Bower bears a resemblance to the Wallace of the years 1297 to 1305. What were their sources? Fordun, as the first of the three, had recourse to the English chronicles. Wyntoun admits to other sources, lost to us. He says, 'of his [Wallace's] good deeds and manhood, great accounts I heard say are made'. It is possible that Wyntoun had available to him the life of Wallace by John Blair. Bower, as the last of the three, had both the advantage of Fordun's work and the opportunity to consider the value of the oral tradition which had been building.

It is in their treatment of that oral tradition, and its concomitant, invention, that we can distinguish Fordun, Wyntoun and Bower from the most celebrated and influential of Wallace's biographers. We may dispute their interpretation of events, however influential it has been.[26] With Blind Harry we move irrevocably from interpretation to creativity. No other life of Wallace can match the enduring appeal of Harry's work; the film *Braveheart* is Harry's account transferred to the screen. Harry is as little known to us as Wallace and the subject, perhaps, of as much investigation.[27] Even the question of his blindness has received attention. John Major, a contemporary, is forthright about Harry's blindness and about his work:

There was one Harry, blind from the time of his birth, who, in the time of my childhood, fabricated a whole

book about William Wallace, and therein he wrote down
in the native tongue, of which he was a master, the deeds
commonly ascribed to Wallace – however, I give only
partial credence to such writings. By recitation of his work
in the presence of men of the highest rank, he obtained
food and clothing, which he well deserved.

This passage, with its influence on academic evaluation
of Harry's reliability, is interesting in more than one
respect. On the matter of Harry's blindness, the subject
of considerable debate,[28] Major is emphatic: Harry was
born blind. Of more consequence is the period Major
assigns to Harry's biography of Wallace. Major was born
perhaps as early as 1467 or as late as 1470. His reference
to his childhood at the time at which Harry was com-
posing his biography therefore bears out McDiarmid's
conclusion on the date of Harry's 'Wallace'.[29] This is more
important than the question of Harry's blindness. A
Scottish Homer or not, Harry flourished at a time of
renewed anti-English sentiment.[30] The perceived pro-
English policy of James III was arousing opposition in
Scotland, For some no doubt the proposal of a marriage
between James' son, Prince James, and Cecilia, daughter
of Edward IV, evoked memories of a similar proposal of
a marriage between Margaret of Norway and Edward of
Carnarvon, when Scotland's future hung in the balance.

We have evidence in payments made to him by the
Lord High Treasurer that Harry was known at court,
but it was among those hostile to the king that he found
his patrons. Two such were Sir James Liddale of
Halkerston and Sir William Wallace of Craigie. These
were powerful men, and Harry may have had access to
one more powerful through the former. Liddale was
steward to Alexander Stewart, duke of Albany, brother

of the king. Relations between James and Albany and his other brother, John, earl of Mar, were difficult.[31] Disagreement manifested itself publicly in the case of Albany over the king's policy towards England. Albany, it became clear, had pretensions to the throne. Imprisoned, he escaped and fled to France, whence he returned in due course, with the support of Edward IV, as a potential Alexander IV. It has been suggested that Albany, seemingly a more regal figure than his brother as a fine horseman and the possessor of 'a very awful countenance', made use of Harry's 'Wallace' as propaganda in his disagreements with the king.[32] One authority on the period has demonstrated that opposition to James III's pro-English stance was almost entirely based in the south of Scotland.[33] Wallace of Craigie and Liddale were both southern knights. Among the southern nobility, Albany was the most prominent. The prospects of an Anglo-Scottish rapprochement, towards which James III was moving, would not have appealed to such as Archibald Douglas, earl of Angus, notorious as 'Bell-the-Cat'.[34] Angus was not alone in profiting from the disturbed conditions in the Border, something which James III's plans threatened.

For such as those Harry fashioned an epic violently anti-English from its opening lines.[35] Major, as already noted, concedes Harry's skill in pulling together 'the deeds commonly ascribed' to the hero of the work. But he adds a rider; Major does not entirely accept Harry's version of events. The power of Harry's epic does not derive, as Major hints, from historical accuracy. Here, accuracy is sacrificed to effect. Harry is, for example, contradictory in the matter of Wallace's date of birth.[36] He has Wallace defeat Edward I in a battle in the vicinity of Biggar in the summer of 1297. The size of Edward's army, and the number killed, are both ludicrously high. If, as has been argued, Harry muddled Biggar with the later engagement at Roslin,[37] his accuracy in matters of detail is further open to question.

We must assume that this counted for little to the audience for which Harry was performing his epic. The point has earlier been made[38] that *Braveheart* is Harry's 'Wallace' transferred to the screen. There is the same violence, presented with refinements which Harry might have envied, the same rampant xenophobia. Wallace is in both cases a one-man fighting machine, the effects of the blows he inflicts on the English every bit as appalling as those dealt to the infidel by Roland and Charlemagne's paladins in an earlier epic. Wallace's love for Marion Braidfute is common to Harry and to *Braveheart*. The author of the screenplay, Randall Wallace, surely comes close to conjuring up Harry's own thought with these words:

> Historians agree on only a few facts about Wallace's life, and yet they cannot dispute that his life was epic. There were times when I tried myself to be a fair historian, but life is not all about balance, it's about passion, and this story raised my passions. I had to see through the eyes of a poet.[39]

Randall Wallace's debt to Harry is indisputable. But from what, and from whom, did Harry derive his inspiration? We cannot know when the stories about Wallace began to circulate.[40] The 'first' Wallace, the Wallace of the English and Scottish chronicles of the fourteenth century, still must rank as a historical figure.[41] It is possible that stories, as opposed to facts – of which the most certain were Stirling Bridge, Falkirk, and his execution – circulated over the period between his death in 1305 and the end of the century. If so, in their transmission to Harry some would become garbled, as in the way of oral tradition. Wallace would 'grow' with the years, from a man of great achievements to a man capable of impossible deeds, possible only if we are prepared to ignore time and distance. Interestingly, in his reflections on Harry, Major talks of his using 'deeds commonly ascribed to Wallace'; he makes no mention of their origin or of their antiquity.

From whom did Harry derive his inspiration? The accepted answer for many is John Blair, the Benedictine monk who was Wallace's personal chaplain. Blair's Latin life of Wallace is cited by Harry himself as his inspiration. Behind Blair, Harry tells us, was the bishop of Dunkeld, William Sinclair. The very existence of Blair's book on Wallace has been doubted but Sinclair is a historical figure and a prominent one. His courage in 1317 in repelling an English invasion of Fife earned him praise from Robert I, who referred to him as 'my bishop'.[42] Sinclair's fierce patriotism at this period as a supporter of Bruce has prompted one writer to postulate that 'commissioning a biography of Wallace would have been in character' for the bishop.[43] This argument is not without its flaws. John Blair is said to have been Wallace's friend since childhood, as well as his chaplain. He would be only too aware of Wallace's unbending commitment to the cause of Balliol. We must ask whether Sinclair would have commissioned a book from one such as Blair, so close for years to the quintessential Balliol defender, when he himself was a supporter of Bruce; Bruce, after all, was a usurper in 1306. Nor is it easy to believe that Sinclair would, as Harry tells us, forward to Rome a book lauding the very man, Wallace, who not many years before had been in Rome arguing with others for Balliol restoration.

Sinclair's own conversion, to the Balliol cause, evidenced by his part in the coronation of Edward Balliol at Scone in September 1332,[44] came too late to be relevant to the presumed commissioning of Blair.

Blair's work, if it ever existed, has disappeared and with its disappearance any realistic hope of ascertaining the degree to which Harry would be indebted to Blair. Would the missing life of Wallace have had any pretensions to historical accuracy? Would Blair's proximity to Wallace over a number of years have permitted of a 'warts and all' portrait of the hero? That same proximity, one might suppose, would be conducive to the kind of accuracy so absent in Harry; Blair, after all, would have been writing soon after Wallace's death, while memory had not yet gained the ability to deceive. If this is so, what, then, happened between Blair's supposed biography and Harry's day to explain the latter's version of Wallace's life? The obvious answer is the growth of oral tradition which was inevitable over the time between Wallace's death and Harry's day.

But it may not be the only answer. Harry may have had another source of inspiration, the audience for which he wrote and for which he performed across the south of Scotland. His was an audience composed of the more influential elements in society, among them men opposed to the policies of James III. As Major points out he earned his living from those of 'the highest rank'. We are not speaking here of the common people, usually seen as the repository of the oral tradition. It is of course indisputable that as he travelled across the country he would make contact with, and no doubt, absorb material from the common people. But to make a living, Harry, like any writer, had to understand his market. That was clearly the ruling class, the 'great and good', the 'image makers', in the terminology of today. We are accustomed to perceiving Harry as the educator, leading his audience to knowledge. Would it be incorrect to see the position as reversed? Harry would in this scenario be writing, less from conviction than to order, fed material and directed by men of 'the highest rank'. Blair's work on Wallace, if it had existed, would have been created near enough to the life of its subject to bear the burden of historical connection. Harry, by contrast, was remote from the hero's lifetime. He was thus free of the burden imposed on Blair but not free of the wishes of his audience. Was Harry persuaded to disregard Blair, and corrupted into producing a life of Wallace with little relation to reality?

We can trace the decline in the historical Wallace quite easily. There are three stages in perceptions of Wallace in the fourteenth and fifteenth centuries. The first we find in English accounts. Here the English are victorious over the Scots, and Wallace, the villainous, barbaric Wallace, meets the end he deserved. The second is the Scottish counter-charge. After much travail, Scotland has its own king – not a Balliol as Wallace would have hoped, but a Bruce, then a Stewart. The perception here of Wallace has, naturally, changed; his attributes are heroic, his physique splendid. He is a giant in Bower, as indeed he is in Harry. He is also a victim of the aristocracy in these accounts which precede Harry. This is a matter of interpretation, although widely believed, by Major, for one.[45]

Today, we are most familiar with the third stage in the various perceptions of Wallace, his third 'life' as we may term it. We derive it from Harry and its popularity, we may claim with confidence, is the result of *Braveheart*, which dates from 1995. Without the film, Harry would be as much neglected by the general public as, for example, Lanercost of the English accounts and Bower of the Scottish. Like them, Harry would have been the concern of the academic. But Harry was rescued from that fate by Hollywood. This was not the first occasion on which the poet had been rescued from virtual anonymity. By the beginning of the eighteenth century his language had become a barrier to the understanding of the text. In 1728, William Hamilton of Gilbertfield undertook the task of translating and abridging the text. A modern writer questions Hamilton's pre-eminence in the modernisation and accessibility of the work but does not deny its impact.[46] Hamilton's version ranked second in many Scottish households only to the Bible.

Most notably it affected Robert Burns. His letters reflect his emotions. In 1786 he wrote that the books he first read were biographies of Hannibal and William Wallace.[47] A year later, he was telling a correspondent how 'the story of Wallace poured a Scottish prejudice in my veins which will boil along there till the floodgates of life shut in eternal rest'.[48] He described himself as a pilgrim on a walk in search of Wallace: 'I explored every den and dell where I could suppose my heroic Countryman to have sheltered . . . my heart glowed with a wish to be able to make a song on him equal to his merits.' Burns' English contemporary, William Wordsworth, also took up Wallace. We come across Wallace in Book 1 of Wordsworth's autobiographical poem, 'The Prelude', published in 1799. Like Burns, Wordsworth reacted with enthusiasm to the ideals of the French Revolution and like Burns, he found inspiration in the Scot, as he found it in others. Wordsworth writes of 'how, in tyrannic times, some high-souled man . . . suffered in silence for Truth's sake', before moving on to Wallace, to relate:

> How Wallace fought for Scotland; left the name
> Of Wallace to be found, like a wild flower,

All over his dear Country; left the deeds
Of Wallace, like a family of Ghosts,
To people the steep rocks and river
Banks . . .[49]

Throughout the nineteenth century, Wallace continued to engage the attention, and the passions of many. We would not expect Sir Walter Scott to be immune to Wallace. Nor was he; the man who had spent years of his childhood immersing himself in the oral tradition of the south-east of Scotland, where Wallace harassed the English from the great Forest of Selkirk, found Wallace a worthy subject.[50] Wallace's renown was not limited to his own country. The Hungarian revolutionary, Lajos Kossuth, whose claim for independence for his country was thwarted by Russian intervention, admired him. Guiseppe Garibaldi and Guiseppe Mazzini, leading figures in the Italian Risorgimento, shared in that admiration. Indeed, their admiration for Wallace knew no bounds, if Mazzini is to be believed. He described Wallace as 'one of the high prophets of nationality to us all' and called upon people to 'honour him, worship his memory, teach his name and his deeds to your children'.[51] In an age when statues to Wallace were being raised throughout Scotland, the Europeans Kossuth, Garibaldi and Mazzini, who understood Wallace's love in independence for his country, all wrote letters in support of the proposed National Wallace Monument at Stirling. Neither the project nor its eventual manifestation met with universal approval in Scotland, but after much debate, discussion and argument, it was officially opened on 11 September 1869, the anniversary of the great victory over Warenne and Cressingham in 1297.

Both the site of the monument, Abbey Craig, and its scale are appropriate to perceptions of Wallace. Abbey Craig suggests itself as the place where he, with Andrew Murray at his side, watched the English deploy for battle. Here, perhaps, came the realisation that victory was possible over an enemy hitherto invincible. Here, too, we can envisage Wallace the soldier, always with an eye for the moment, restraining his eager troops until he judged that moment had arrived. Here is the Wallace of history. The size of the monument is fitting, and perhaps inevitable, in the case of one who, through the generations, has been portrayed as a giant of a man. The Scottish accounts are obsessed with this aspect of Wallace; in this regard, Bower and Major have an affinity with Harry. Bower stakes that Wallace was 'a tall man with the body of a giant . . . with lengthy flanks . . . broad in the hips, with strong arms and legs . . . with all his limbs very strong and firm'. Harry's Wallace reaches seven feet. None of this need necessarily be discounted; the Emperor Charlemagne was said to be seven feet tall. We have evidence to prove that Wallace's greatest enemy, Edward I, was six feet two inches tall.[52] There is no such certainty with Wallace. The English accounts, interestingly, are silent on this matter. If, however, Wallace was the massive figure we have grown accustomed to, would not these same accounts have seized on this as an opportunity for ridicule? Wallace, after all, is presented in Scottish versions not merely as tall but distinguished by exceptionally powerful limbs. It might be argued that such a Wallace suffered from giantism, if not acromegaly. If so, the English would have, surely, depicted him as a freak. They preferred to keep their ridicule for other aspects of Wallace.

The National Wallace Monument may thus be said to epitomise the dichotomy of perceptions of Wallace. On the one hand, Abbey Craig is where we are face to face with the historical Wallace. On the other, the scale of the memorial to him reflects the recurrent need to read into Wallace more than the man, more than the heroic and courageous patriot he was. For Wallace's achievements, great though they were and proof of surpassing ability and sublime spirit, have never been enough. Generation after generation has sought to define him outside the bounds of history and in some cases to exploit him.

We have seen this most recently in *Braveheart* and in the campaign to have him canonised. It is debatable which of the two is the more ludicrous or more damaging to the 'real Wallace', itself a phrase much in vogue. The success of *Braveheart*, with its bedaubed hooligans and a simple, one-dimensional Wallace, tells us more about its audience than of the nature of the patriot and his role. For the director and scriptwriter of the film, the concern was not liberty but the taking of liberties. Their Wallace was a noble savage, of the kind found in James Fenimore Cooper. The inaccuracies in the script are to be expected; Hollywood has in the past been free with the stories, among others, of Mary, Queen of Scots and Bonnie Prince Charlie. Our knowledge of Wallace, if derived solely from the facts available to us, is more than adequate to provide a film with all the elements Hollywood seeks. An opportunity to portray Wallace as he was and, at the same time, to bring his story, unadulterated, to the audience, was spurned.

The proposal that Wallace be canonised postulates a new Wallace – the saint. Those behind the proposal appear to be unable to distinguish between martyrdom and sainthood. Wallace died a martyr, but not for his religion. There is also, as Graham Greene reminds us, a need for a miracle if the candidate is to be accepted. It is fortunate that the Roman Catholic Church is rigorous in its requirements for a candidate for canonisation. Scotland already has its saints on both sides of the religious divide who, arguably, died for their religion. Wallace was neither a Patrick Hamilton nor a John Ogilvie. Wallace, by contrast, died *in* his religion, not *for* it. His religion, we may agree, was a comfort to him in his agonising, despairing, lonely last hours; it did not bring him to the scaffold.

We have no picture of William Wallace. Instead, to his detriment, we have many. He is a man for all times, constantly re-invented. But in a sense, we need no picture of him. He is to be found on the Abbey Craig, looking down on the English, whose attempt at a settlement he had dismissed in his own, memorable words, and in Westminster Hall, where, no less powerfully, he rejected the charge of treason against him. A leading authority on the period has averred that the tragedy of Wallace is in the anti-climax which his career became.[53] The tragedy of Wallace, however, is the inability of generations past and present to recognise that the essence of the man lies in his words and deeds. With Wallace, the words are the man, the deeds his assurance of immortality. The real Wallace is the Wallace of history.

NOTES

1. Above, chap. 8.
2. Ibid.
3. Barrow: *Robert Bruce*, 131; Barron, op. cit., 152ff; Young, op. cit., 196–97.
4. Above, chap. 7.

5. Ibid.

6. Young, op. cit., 168–69. The author provides evidence of continuing tension between Lamberton and the Comyns, 171.

7. Above, chap. 7.

8. Above, chap. 8.

9. Ibid.

10. Young, op. cit., passim, deals with this.

11. Prestwich: *Edward I,* chap. 2 and Powicke, op. cit., chap. V for the war and settlement.

12. Watson: *Under the Hammer*, 219.

13. Both again betrayed Edward in 1306 and were executed. On Boys' fate see Barrow: *Robert Bruce*, 357, n. 61.

14. As in the case of some Welsh rebels. For a summary of Edward's character, see Prestwich, 559ff.

15. And was not condemned in so doing by contemporaries, except by Ingram de'Umfraville in the case of David of Brechin.

16. Nicholson, op. cit., 326. The murder and its aftermath is dealt with in Brown: *James I*, 1994, chaps 8 and 9, and McGladdery: *James II*, 1990, chap. 1.

17. Brown, op. cit., 198.

18. Bellamy, op. cit., 39.

19. Lancaster himself was venerated as a saint: Office of St Thomas of Lancaster, Wright, op. cit., 268–72; Denholm-Young (ed.), *Vita Edwardi Secundi*, 1957, 125–27.

20. A scholar and a bibliophile, Tiptoft was much influenced in his interpretation of the law of treason by knowledge gained in Italy: Bellamy, op. cit., 160–62.

21. These trials are treated in Cameron: *James V*, 1998, chaps 9 and 8 respectively.

22. Book XII.

23. Opinions on Bower can be found, for example, in Morton: *William Wallace Man and Myth*, 2001, 22–24 and passim; Young, op. cit., chap. 1.

24. Young, ibid.

25. Reese, op. cit., 133: 'It was not long before his countrymen came to realise that, in fact, he had been different, that both his resolution and sense of patriotism exceeded that of others.' Wyn-

toun, whom Reese then quotes, wrote, of course, more than a century after Wallace's death.

26. As in Young, chap. 1.

27. Most recently in Morton, above. Not to be neglected are: McDiarmid: 'The Date of the Wallace', *SHR*, xxxiv (April 1955), 26–31, and Blind Harry, *Wallace*, 2 vols, 1968–69; McDougall: *James III A Political Study*, 1982, 117ff and chap. 12.

28. Morton, op. cit., 43–45, summarizes some conclusions.

29. See n. 27 above.

30. McDougall, op. cit., passim.

31. Ibid.

32. Magnusson: *Scotland: the Study of A Nation*, 2000, 267.

33. McDougall, op. cit., 118ff.

34. For his role in the lynching of James III's favourites at Lauder, 1582.

35. Magnusson, op. cit., 130 describes the work as 'violent, gory, nationalistic, and profoundly xenophobic – a sustained and bitter polemic against the English', words which might reasonably be applied to *Braveheart*.

36. If, as Harry says at one point, Wallace was forty-five at the time of his arrest, this would place his birth in 1260. Intriguingly, this appears to be the date on which Randall Wallace, author of the screenplay for *Braveheart*, relies.

37. Reese, op. cit., 111, finds an important role for Wallace at Roslin, although his presence there is no more a certainty than the existence of a battle at Biggar.

38. Above, p. ix.

39. Morton, op. cit., 144.

40. See n. 25, above.

41. That is, our limited knowledge can be checked against fact.

42. Barrow: *Robert Bruce*, 238, 246, etc; Barbour's *Bruce*: 608ff.

43. King: *Introducing William Wallace*, 1997, 17.

44. Nicholson: *Edward III and the Scots*, 1965, 94.

45. Major, op. cit., 199.

46. Morton, op. cit., 41.

47. Ibid.

48. Ibid.

49. Wordsworth: *Works*, 1994, 635.
50. *Tales of A Grandfather*, chap. VII.
51. Morton, op. cit., 107.
52. Prestwich: *Edward I*, 567.
53. Barrow: *Robert Bruce*, 138.

Select Bibliography

INTRODUCTORY NOTE

We lack any contemporary Scottish accounts of the life of William Wallace. By far the best-known life is that by Henry the Minstrel or Blind Harry which, however prejudiced and inaccurate, carries on that adulatory attitude towards the Guardian which first appears in John of Fordun, who died about 1385, eighty years after Wallace's execution. Fordun cannot wholly be discounted for he is the nearest source we have to Wallace's own time, and it is not unreasonable to assume, therefore, that he had recourse to material which has since disappeared. Fordun in turn was drawn on by the likes of Andrew of Wyntoun, the author of a chronicle of about 1420, and Walter Bower, whose *Scotichronicon* was written twenty years after Wyntoun. Both Wyntoun and Bower, whose work was, essentially, an amplification of Fordun, shared the latter's intention. They were concerned with politics and propaganda, with England the enemy as in Wallace's own day. Some thirty years after Bower, Blind Harry produced his account, fiercely anti-English and, as shown by Mr M. McDiarmid, unreliable for the serious student of history. The impact of the book on the popular imagination, particularly in the version in modern English by William Hamilton of Gilberton, cannot be ignored and lasts to this day, however. John Major or Mair, who died in 1550, while not entirely free of the tradition to which his predecessors subscribed, looked more to the future than they, and saw the virtue, which they would have scorned, of an eventual union between Scotland and England.

Bain, J. (ed.): *Calendar of Documents relating to Scotland, 1108–1509*. Edinburgh 1881–4

Barron, E.M.: *The Scottish War of Independence*. Inverness, 1934.

Barrow, G.W.S.: *The Kingdom of the Scots*. London, 1971. *Robert Bruce & the Community of the Realm of Scotland*. Edinburgh, 1976. 'Lothian in the First War of Independence, 1296–1328', *SHR*, LV, 2, no. 160, Oct. 1976, pp. 151–171. *The Anglo-Norman Era in Scottish History*. Oxford, 1980. *Kingship & Unity, Scotland 1100–1306*. London, 1981. *Scotland and its Neighbours in the Middle Ages*. London, 1992. *Feudal Britain*. London, 1956

Bellamy, J.G.: *The Law of Treason in England in the Later Middle Ages*. Cambridge, 1970

Bingham, C.: *Robert the Bruce*. London, 1998

Bower, Walter: *see* Goodall, W.

Broun, D., Finlay, R.J., Lynch, M. (eds): *Image and Identity: The Making and Remaking of Scotland*. Edinburgh, 1988

Brown, P.H.: *History of Scotland*. Cambridge, 1911

Brie, F.W.D. (ed.): *The Brut, or the Chronicles of England*. London, 1908

Calendar of the Close Rolls preserved in the Public Record Office

Calendar of the Close Rolls preserved in the Public Record Office

Calendar of Documents relating to Scotland, 1108–1509: *see* Bain, J.

Chronicles of the Reigns of Edward I and Edward II: see Stubbs, W

Clanchy, M.T.: *From Memory to Written Record: England 1066–1307*. London, 1979 von Clausewitz, C.: *On War* (ed. & trans. by M. Howard & P. Paret). Princeton, 1984

Cotton, Bartholomew: *see* Luard, H.R.

Cruden, S.: *The Scottish Castle*. Edinburgh, 1960

Davies, J.: *A History of Wales*. London, 1993

Denholm-Young, N. (ed.): *Vita Edwardi Secundi*. Edinburgh, 1957

Dickson, W.K.: 'The Scots Law of Treason', *Juridical Review* X, 1898, 243–256

Dickinson, W.C., Donaldson, G., Milne, I.A.: *A Source Book of Scottish History*, Vol. 1. London, 1952

Dictionary of National Biography

Documents Illustrative of the History of Scotland: *see* Stevenson, J.

Dodgshon, R.: *Land and Society in Early Scotland*. Oxford, 1981

Donaldson, G.: *Scottish Historical Documents*. Edinburgh, 1974

Duncan, A.A.M.: *The Nation of Scots*. London, 1970 (Historical Association Pamphlet) *English Historical Review* (EHR). *Scotland: The Making of the Kingdom*. Edinburgh, 1992. *John Barbour The Bruce*. Edinburgh, 1997

Ferguson, W.: *Scotland's Relations with England: a Survey to 1707*. Edinburgh, 1977

Fergusson, J.: *William Wallace, Guardian of Scotland*. London, 1938

Fisher, A.: 'Wallace and Bruce', *History Today*, February 1989, 18–23

Fordun, John of: *see* Skene, W.F.

Frame, R.: *The Political Development of the British Isles 1100–1500*. Oxford, 1995

Fraser, W.: *The Douglas Book, vol I*. Edinburgh, 1885

Goodall, W. (ed.): *Scotichronicron cum Continuatione Walteri Boweri*. Edinburgh, 1759

Grant, A.: *Independence and Nationhood: Scotland 1306–1469*. London, 1984

Grant, A. & Stringer, K.J. (ed.): *Medieval Scotland Crown Lordship and Community*. Edinburgh, 1998

Gray, D.J.: *William Wallace, the King's Enemy*. London, 1991

Gray, Sir Thomas: *see* Maxwell, H.

Guisborough, Walter of: *see* Rothwell, H.

Hamilton, W.: *The History of the Life and Adventures and Heroic Actions of the Renowned Sir William Wallace*. Edinburgh, 1816

Harry, Blind (Henry the Minstrel): *see* McDiarmid, M.P.

Hog, T. (ed.): *Nicholas Trivet: Annales*. London, 1845

Keen, M.H.: *The Laws of War in the Late Middle Ages*. London, 1965. *The Outlaws of Medieval Legend*. London, 1961. 'Treason Trials under the Law of Arms', *EHR*, 5th Series, xii, 1962

Kightly, C.: *Folk Heroes of Britain*. London, 1982

Laing, D. (ed.): *The Oryginale Cronykil of Scotland, by Andrew of Wyntoun*. Edinburgh, 1879

Lanercost, Chronicle of; *see* Maxwell, H.

Lang, A.: *History of Scotland*. 4 vols. Edinburgh, 1903–07

Langtoft, Peter of: *see* Wright, T.

Luard, H.R. (ed.): *Bartholomew Cotton, Historia Anglicana*. London, 1859

Lynch, M.: *Scotland: A New History*. Edinburgh, 1991

Magnusson, M: *Scotland: The Story of a Nation*. London, 2000. *Hakon the Old – Hakon Who?* The Hakon Hakonsson Lecture, 1981. Largs, 1982

Matthew of Westminster, *Flores Historiarum*, 3 vols. London, 1890

McDiarmid, M.P. (ed.): *Blind Harry: Wallace*. 2 vols. Edinburgh, 1968–69

McLynn, F.: *1066 The Year of the Three Battles*. London, 1998

MacDougall, N. (ed.): *Scotland and War AD 79–1918*. Edinburgh, 1991

Machiavelli, N.: *The Art of War*. Revised edition of the Ellis Farneworth translation. New York, 1965

MacKay, A.: *William Wallace; Brave Heart*. Edinburgh, 1995

MacKay, J.A.: *Robert Bruce, King of Scots*. London, 1974

Mackenzie, A.M.: *Robert Bruce, King of Scots*. Edinburgh, 1934

Mackie, J.D.: *A History of Scotland*. Edinburgh, 1964

MacNamee, C.: *The Wars of the Bruces: Scotland, England and Ireland 1306, 1328*. East Linton, 1997. *William Wallace's Invasion of Northern England in 1297*. Northern History, XXVI (1990), 40–58

Macpherson, D. (ed.): *Rotuli Scotiae, 1291–1516*. 2 vols. London, 1814 & 1819

Major, John: *Historia Majoris Britanniae*. Edinburgh, 1740

Maxwell H (ed. & trans.): *Chronicle of Lanercost*. Glasgow, 1913. *Sir Thomas Gray: Scalacronicon*. Glasgow, 1907

Morris, J.E.: *The Welsh Wars of Edward I*. Oxford, 1901. 'Mounted Infantry in Medieval Warfare', RHS 3rd Series, Vol. VIII, 1914

Morton, G.: *William Wallace Man & Myth*. Stroud, 2001

Murison, A.F.: *Sir William Wallace*. London, 1898

Nicholson, R.: *Scotland: the Later Middle Ages*. Edinburgh, 1974

Oman, C.W.C.: *The Art of War in the Middle Ages, 1378–1515*. New York, 1960

Palgrave, F. (ed.): *Parliamentary Writs and Writs of Summonds, Edward I and Edward II*. 2 vols. London, 1827–34

Palgrave, F. (ed.): *Documents and Records Illustrating the History of Scotland, 1237–1307*. London, 1837

Plucknett, T.F.T.: *Edward I and the Criminal Law*. Cambridge, 1960. *A Concise History of the Common Law*. London, 1956

Pluscardensis, Liber: see Skene, F.H.J.

Political Songs of England: see Wright, T.

Powicke, F.M.: *The Thirteenth Century, 1216–1307*. Oxford, 1953. *Henry III and the Lord Edward*. 2 vols. Oxford, 1947

Prestwich, M.: *Edward I*. London, 1988. *The Three Edwards, War and State in England, 1272–1377*. London, 1981. *Armies and Warfare in the Middle Ages*. Yale, 1996. *War, Politics and Finance under Edward I*. London, 1972

Ramsay, J.: *The Dawn of the Constitution, 1216–1307*. London, 1908

Reese, P.: *Wallace, a Biography*. Edinburgh, 1996

Reid, N.: *Scotland in the Reign of Alexander III 1249–1286*. Edinburgh, 1990. 'The Kingless Kingdom: the Scottish Guardianship of 1286–1306', *SHR*, LXI, 2, no. 172, 1982

Riley, H.T. (ed.): *William Rishanger: Chronica et Annales*. London, 1865

Rishanger: see Riley

Ritchie, R.L.G.: *The Normans in Scotland*. Edinburgh, 1953

Rothwell, H. (ed.): *Chronicle of Walter of Guisborough*. London, 1957. *English Historical Documents 1189–1327*. London, 1975

Rotuli Scotiae: see Macpherson, D.

Rymer, T. (ed.): *Foedera*. London, 1816–30

Salzman, F.: *Edward I*. London, 1968

Scalacronicon: *see* Maxwell, H.

Scotichronicon: *see* Skene, W.F.

Scottish Historical Review (*SHR*)

Skene, F.H.J. (ed.): *Liber Pluscardensis*. Edinburgh, 1880

Skene, W.F. (ed.): *John of Fordun: Scotichronicon* (trans F.S.H. Skene) 2 vols. Edinburgh, 1871–2

Stevenson, J. (ed.): *Documents Illustrative of the History of Scotland, 1286–1306*. Edinburgh, 1870. *Documents Illustrative of Sir William Wallace, his life and time*. Edinburgh, 1841

Stones, E.L.G. (ed.): *Anglo-Scottish Relations, 1174–1328. Some Selected Documents*. Edinburgh, 1964

Stones, E.L.G. and Simpson, G.G.: *Edward I and the Throne of Scotland, 1290–6*. 2 vols. Oxford, 1979

Stones, E.L.G.: *Edward I*. Oxford, 1968

Stringer, K.J. (ed.): *Essays on the Nobility of Medieval Scotland*. Edinburgh, 1985

Stubbs, W. (ed.): *Chronicles of the Reigns of Edward I and Edward II*, 2 vols. London, 1882–3

Tout, T.F.: *Chapters in the Administrative History of Medieval England*, 6 vols. Manchester, 1923–35

Traquair, P.: *Freedom's Sword: Scotland's Wars of Independence*. London, 1998

Trivet, Nicholas: *see* Hog, T.

Vickers, K.H.: *England in the later Middle Ages*. London, 1961

Warren, W.L.: *Henry II*. London, 1983

Watson, F.: *Under the Hammer: Edward I and Scotland 1286–1307*. East Linton, 1998

Westminster, Matthew of: *see* Luard, H.R.

Wilkinson, B: *Constitutional History of Medieval England*, 3 vols. London, 1948–1958

Wright, T. (ed.): *Peter of Langroft: Metrical Chronicle*. London, 1866. *Political Songs of England*. London, 1839

Wyntoun, Andrew of: *see* Laing, D.

Young, A: *Robert the Bruce's Rivals: The Comyns 1212–1314*. East Linton, 1997

Index

William, I 'the Lion, king of
Scots' (1143–1214), 9
William I 'the Conqueror',
king of England (1066–
1087), 136
William of Eaglesham,
Master, 190
Winchester, Thomas, 15
Wishart, Robert, bishop of
Glasgow
as Guardian of Scotland,
40
English hostility to, 65
and Wallace, 66, 75–76 80,
86
in rebellion against Edward
I, 65–66
at Irvine, 81–82, 87

Wallace raids palace at
Ancrum, 88
Edward I and, 209, 218–
219
Wordsworth, William, 267–277
Wyntoun, Andrew
and death of Alexander III,
36–37
and Wallace, 253

Yarmouth, 192
Yolande of Dreux, wife of
Alexander III, 32
York, Matthew of,
accused with William
Wallace, 21–22

Zouche, Alan la, 14